FAITH AND THE LIFE OF REASON

FAITH AND
THE LIFE OF REASON

by

JOHN KING-FARLOW
Professor of Philosophy, University of Alberta and University of Ottawa

and

WILLIAM NIELS CHRISTENSEN
Instructor in Philosophy, Douglas College

D. REIDEL PUBLISHING COMPANY/DORDRECHT-HOLLAND

Library of Congress Catalog Card Number 72–83376

ISBN 90 277 0275 6

Printed in The Netherlands by D. Reidel, Dordrecht

For Sylvia, Nick and Ann

For Ruby, Robin and Erik

and for all who pursue the riddles of religion
in a spirit of open-ness, brotherhood,
affection and desire for truth

PREFACE

This book brings together ideas and materials which we have discussed together over the years as friends and colleagues. We draw on four papers published by us both as co-authors and on several more papers published by King-Farlow alone. We wish to thank the editors and publishers of the following journals for permission to make use of matter or points which have appeared in their pages in the years indicated: *The Philosophical Quarterly* (1957, 1962, 1971); *The Thomist* (1958, 1971, 1972); *The International Philosophical Quarterly* (1962); *Theoria* (1963); *The Southern Journal of Philosophy* (1963); *Sophia* (1965, 1967, 1969, 1971); *Philosophical Studies of Eire* (1968, 1970, 1971); *Philosophy and Phenomenological Research* (1968); *Analysis* (1970); *Religious Studies* (Cambridge University Press, 1971; we acknowledge a debt to H. D. Lewis, Editor, on page 20).

This book is not, however, a collection of reprinted articles. It is a continuous work which deals with a vital cluster of problems in the philosophy of religion. In this work we attempt to utilize both our earlier thoughts, often considerably revised, and our very recent ones in order to argue for the good sense and rationality of making certain strong forms of commitment to some basic elements of primary wisdom in the Judaeo-Christian tradition.

While pursuing the investigations which have led to the writing of this book we have found ourselves becoming indebted to many individuals and institutions. We are indebted to many Catholics, Protestants and fellow-Anglicans for their tolerant stimulation, as well as to a number of strong religious sceptics for their even more tolerant willingness to argue with us as friends. We are deeply indebted to Sylvia Kostyk King-Farlow and Robina Ogilvy Christensen for their splendid personal, intellectual and religious encouragement. King-Farlow is much obliged to the benefactors of Christ Church, Oxford and of Duke and Stanford Universities who made possible his initial studies in philosophy – and to such inspiring teachers as Michael Foster, J. O. Urmson, Charles Baylis, Romane Clarke, N. L. Wilson, John Goheen and Patrick Suppes. He is no less

thankful for post-doctoral research awards from the A. W. Mellon
Foundation and the University of Pittsburgh (1960-61); from the Faculty
Summer Research Awards Committee of the University of California;
and from the Leverhulme Foundation and the University of Liverpool
(1966-68). Christensen is indebted to Derwin Owen and Eugene Fair-
weather of Trinity College, the University of Toronto for their encouragement and insights, and to Donald Kuspit of the University of Windsor.
Having served under him together, we are both indebted to the astute
administration and fine Cartesian scholarship of Professor P. A. Schouls,
Head in Philosophy at the University of Alberta, and also to another
friend in philosophy Señor Juan Espinaco-Virseda.

As philosophers, we are in the business of providing arguments and
criticism. It is part of the British and the historically associated Canadian
Parliamentary tradition wherein arguments and criticisms are desired to
be made vigorous and hard-hitting for the sake of the lively exercise and
protection of freedom, that one may speak out quite roughly in debate
against one's fellows without being taken not to esteem them and without
being taken to believe that one has a monopoly of wisdom on one's own
side. To debate politically or philosophically in that parliamentary
spirit, provided one first makes clear what one is about, seems to us
compatible with principles of Christian charity and democratic tolerance.
We ask then that we be read as criticizing others in that parliamentary
spirit, occasionally with a touch of tongue in cheek.

Faith and the Life of Reason begins with an account of 'hypothetical'
theism and of the crucial role of religious beliefs as offering Justifying
Explanations of human history. We believe that this account should
serve to banish the spectre of incompatibility between the best aims of
Science and Religion, of Empiricism and Faith. A family of criteria for
Rationality is similarly considered to show just how insubstantial that
spectre really is. Chapter II distinguishes two basic kinds of descriptions
accorded to God, kinds whose intellectual distinction and actual association seem crucial for understanding God's role as the Justifying
Explanation of history in a coherent Judaeo-Christian conceptual scheme.
We also attempt to vindicate the wisdom of Aquinas against Anselm
on the question of whether we can manipulate these descriptions to give
an *a priori* proof of the existence of God. In Chapter III we are centrally
concerned to expound a coherent concept of miracles that can serve our

later concerns with the objectivity of value judgments, the consequent possibility of tolerant but intellectually sound reasoning for the existence of God, and the relations between probability, utility, rationality, commitment and religious faith. Chapters IV and V are concerned with the nature of such reasonable inference of God's existence and with the related residual wisdom of both Aquinas and Anselm in believing that "God exists" is in some sense a *necessary truth.* Current shibboleths about rigid dichotomies between facts and values, between asserting existence and describing existents, etc., are weighed and found wanting: the shibboleths show the naïveté of philosophers, but show nothing inconsistent or incoherent about the Judaeo-Christian scheme. In Chapters VI and VII we examine the notions of *objective probability* and *maximizing expected utility* so as to argue that Aquinas' intellectualist tradition may properly be linked with William James' reasonable concern for man's passional nature in "The Will to Believe". Fresh light, we hope, is thereby shed on our contention that in certain ordinary settings clear, objectively reasonable arguments for God's existence and for commitment to a religious form of life can be given. In Chapter VIII we turn from the previous areas of relevance which the Judaeo-Christian tradition can have for reasonable people today, to show the great relevance of Thomist contributions to that tradition for modern concerns about war, punishment and human survival.

In the context of modern intellectuals' present avowals of admiration for fideism, relativism and scepticism it is not entirely paradoxical to say: We reach the *novel* conclusion that *traditional* intellectualist approaches to the reconciliation of Faith with the Life of Reason were basically very wise. The novel truth is that many much mocked forms of old-fashioned thought about religion and natural theology are far sounder than most of their modernist successors.

JOHN KING-FARLOW

WILLIAM NIELS CHRISTENSEN

TABLE OF CONTENTS

CHAPTER I

FAITH – AND FAITH IN HYPOTHESES

Where shall a sane man begin to look for criteria of reasonableness which will not immediately rule *any* commitment to live by religion, ideology or even systematic ideals right out of Reason's court? A substantial option is to begin with philosophy. And a good way to start in philosophy is by straightway challenging some current parrotisms of philosophical fashion.

Debate continues to rage among philosophers of religion over Anthony Flew's famous little paper 'Theology and Falsification' and the responses it provoked.[1] Flew issued the following challenge:

I therefore put ... the simple central questions, "What would have to occur or to have occurred to constitute for you a disproof of the love of, or of the existence of God?"

When it was first presented in 1948 R. M. Hare immediately replied on theism's behalf that, among other things:

The mistake of the position which Flew selects for attack is to regard this [religious] kind of talk as some sort of explanation, as scientists are accustomed to use the word. As such it would obviously be ludicrous. We no longer believe in God as an Atlas–*nous n'avons pas besoin de cette hypothèse.*

Now, twenty years later, we still find theists taking a similar tack. Recently H. E. Allison has commented in reply to Flew:

[Flew's explorer's] belief concerning the gardener ... is intended as an explanation of the observed phenomena. Viewed as such, Flew can easily demonstrate its inadequacy. But the real question concerns the tendency to view religious belief in terms of the model of a scientific hypothesis. Surely believing ... is radically different from entertaining an hypothesis ....[2]

J. Kellenberger still more recently has written:

Now let me try to say why Flew's challenge went wrong .... Flew and those with his concern have unduly concentrated on hypotheses and the logical model of the hypothesis. A hypothesis is, almost by definition, a tentative statement and it is explanatory of some phenomenon.[3]

In the same issue of the journal in which Kellenberger used this approach, J. F. Miller offered a different but importantly related tactic for answering Flew's demand that propositions like "God loves mankind" be subject to some kind of falsifiability conditions if they are genuine assertions. Miller replies that such propositions express *"religious first-order principles* of the Judaeo-Christian *Weltanschauung* and *as such* are not amenable to falsification". He continues:

These first-order religious principles bear resemblance to first-order scientific principles which ... are unfalsifiable since they are fundamental tenets of the contemporary scientific Weltanschauung.[4]

From his following remarks it becomes clear that Miller has in mind some kind of contrast between what he would consider decently falsifiable scientific hypotheses and what he takes to be unfalsifiable first-order principles of contemporary science such as

The principle of causality [described by Planck] according to which an event is causally determined only if it can be accurately foretold (p. 51).

He concludes:

To employ Flew's challenge is to exact too high a price for rejecting theological utterances; for it would entail rejecting science for the same reason (p. 68).[5]

Yet another contributor to the issue of the same journal is content obediently to quote Wittgenstein's first lecture on "Religious Belief". R. M. Bell cites the master:

With the concept of "religious belief" ... we don't talk about hypotheses ... (p. 11).

In what follows we will try to sketch what strikes us – and we suppose ourselves to be theists – as a much more rational strategy for modern believers of a liberal empiricist temper to adopt in response to the falsification challenge. *This will involve accepting analogies between theological statements and so-called hypotheses, insofar as the latter are propositions held and put forward in a somewhat tentative spirit with a view to explaining what we experience.* (We shall see that more than one type of *explaining* will be involved.) We will put forward a series of related claims which need to be seen as a coherent whole: only as such a whole can the claims be taken for a genuine alternative to the 'Much holier and much less hypothetical than thou' type of defence against Flew which is now so fashionable. And as our book evolves it may become clearer that this whole offers surprisingly helpful ways for bringing some of the kinds of committedness which one associates with "Faith" into worlds compossible with what ones better intuitions assure one would still be a *Life of Reason*.

I. FALSIFIABLE THEISM: SKETCH OF A POSITION

1. In urging a tentative-and-explanatory or 'hypothetical' approach to theological propositions like "God exists" or "God loves mankind" we are making no pretense of speaking as specially privileged amateur anthropologists, psychologists, sociologists, etc. On the contrary, it seems to us rather pretentious, if not downright hypocritical, for philosophers to talk about "the logic of faith" like men with privileged access. We doubt that armchair conceptual analysis or some approach in pure phenomenology can give philosophers heavily reliable – though largely *a priori* – DESCRIPTIVE powers to reveal how tentatively or non-tentatively actual religious believers do hold their various beliefs about God.[6] Rather, in urging a 'hypothetical' approach to Faith as the rational sort or as one very promisingly rational sort of approach, we are prescribing something like a liberal empiricist methodology. What justifies such a prescription? From a philosophical point of view one might look in answer to points made by such noted, and notedly diverse and often anti-religious champions of tentativeness as John Stuart Mill, Sir Karl Popper, W. V. Quine, William James, and W. W. Bartley. From a religious point of view one might suggest the saying "By their fruits ye shall know them": the actual and the likely fruits of closed societies and closed minds make plain enough the need to prescribe tentativeness and tolerance in our time.

2. Many theistic beliefs like those of Christianity, Judaism, and Islam can, perhaps, be consistently held in a mystical spirit of almost complete indifference to this world. But suppose a theist shares our premise that much of what is best in such religions demands from the believer considerable concern here and now for the welfare here and now of our fellow men. Such a theist should, we suggest, be moved to take a first pace in our direction by the following crude pragmatic argument. In a world where there is so much destructive power in the hands of ideologists (including religionists), man's best hopes of survival – short of a weapon-dissolving *deus ex machina* – lie in the possibility that ideological rivals can develop much greater mutual respect and far more ability to co-operate. This possibility would seem to turn on another – on the chance that all sides can become more empirical and pragmatic. This in turn seems linked with the possibility that rival ideologists can visibly move towards a really fundamental commitment to finding and teaching what is true and finding and doing what is good or right. Such a commitment, we believe, will have to be *visibly* prior to the rivals' allegiance to particular ontological and moral doctrines if there is to be much lasting hope of serious discussions and co-operation based on mutual respect. The closer men come to such a sense of identity of fundamental commitment the closer they can come to a sense of identity of values and even interest.

3. At first such a stand on fundamental commitment may seem to be just a garish piece of modern pragmatism. But actually it links well with the traditional stand of many theists against the Voluntarism of other believers. R. H. Popkin has aptly described the schism in question:

On the one hand, there are theistic theories which conceive the nature of God as co-eternal with certain eternal truths, such as the ultimate standards of value and truth which God accepts and employs in his relations with the world ... universal standards of value which even the Deity accepts and obeys. ... On the other hand, there are theories, sometimes called *Voluntaristic*, which assert that the power of the Deity is totally unlimited. ... Anything which God so wills is, by the very fact that God has willed it, necessarily right and just.[7]

It seems to be well within theism's anti-Voluntarist tradition for modern believers to suppose that God would wish any person's ideological commitments, theistic or otherwise, to spring from a still more fundamental commitment to what is true and to what is good or right. The extremely non-falsifiable position of R. M. Hare (who became in that paper of 1948 the inventor of *bliks* in reply to Flew's challenge), that the true believer necessarily counts nothing as telling against his creed and says he expects nothing from his religious beliefs remotely akin to scientific explanations, suggests the Voluntarist tradition. It suggests a blik for whose insistently uncritical subscribers a claim like "It is wise and right to have Faith because God wills that we should" is prior to or even excludes a claim like "God wills that we should and we should because – as critical reflection shows – it is wise and right". God's will creates the very criterion of goodness and wisdom. And when one remembers Hare's extremely 'prescriptivist', non-cognitive account of ethics in *The Language of Morals*, written soon after his piece on bliks, that suggestion can hardly seem coincidental.

4. We have already commented on the risk of confusion or hypocrisy involved in treating philosophy too seriously as a sort of *a priori* social science. We do not purport to be able to describe all the helpful and harmful functions which systems of belief called ideologies or religions discharge in human lives. But we do prescribe that one regard it as healthy function and a sound criterion of a satisfying religious ideology that it offer what we shall call a "justifying explanation" of the universe's existence and what men experience in it. A justifying explanation is in part a causal explanation: like a scientific causal explanation it must face the music of experience. It must be argued and arguable for on occasion against protests (such as those attacking theodicies) that the sort of effects we do experience cannot rationally be attributed to such a cause. Thus it must be held with at least some degree of tentativeness. It cannot purport to afford its supporters complete refuge from criticism in caves ringing with fideist slogans about bliks or about the philosophical enquirer's spade being ever turned on the bedrock of ways of life.[8] But a justifying explanation is not just any causal one. It must point to the sort of ultimate cause which would make one think it reasonable to expect that, if this is indeed the cause, then there is some saving sense and purpose and some lasting value in everything that happens.[9] "This is so and caused to be so by God because God is good and because ultimately it just is right" is such a justifying explanation. In short, something's being right justifies its being so: a justifying explanation locates an ultimate cause whose nature guarantees the intelligibility and value of its effects. Thus the ultimate cause in a justifying explanation is such that it gives one good reason for the effects being what they are and being valued for what they are. Providing such an explanation seems to us to have been an acknowledged function of many healthy forms of theism. It is, in effect, the function of enabling men to 'make sense' of their being in the world, so that their way of life can make every moment of existence something to treasure.

5. Thus we suspect that when religion is judged by such healthy standards Voluntarism fails as a *religious* account of reality. Such an account should give an ultimate justifying explanation of all we know. But the Voluntarist's causal explanation turns out not to be such an ultimate justifying explanation. His ultimate explanations ultimately fall back upon the sheer power of God to will this rather than that. He cannot give a justifying explanation of God's choices. For we can ask the Voluntarist more ultimately: "But why is God all-powerful and why does God so will it?" Though the Voluntarist might reply "Because God is good and it is good", this reply from him cannot be *meant* as an ultimate justifying explanation either. For if pressed to get to the bottom of things he would be committed to saying further *P*: "That is good because God as First Cause just does will it so and He just is all-powerful". And then one would ask (in response to *P*) "Why does He will it?", seeking an explanation which is a sense-giving reason and not just a brute fact. Sheer power alone, even if infinite, cannot provide a justifying explanation. Nor is an infinite regress, however infinite, any more promising a solution.[10] And, of course, the Voluntarist may reply: "So much the worse for justifying explanations as you understand them." Schisms are schisms. But we can at least try to indicate where we think some of the good sense may lie on the other side of the schism. It is not unreasonable to suspect that the Voluntarist in some cases thinks that *P* offers a justifying explanation because he tacitly believes, inconsistently with complete Voluntarism, that *P* entails *Q*: "Total, supreme might as first Cause *is* total, supreme right." Now *Q*, when the Voluntarist holds it inconsistently but comfortingly, trusting in his own interpretations of the Book of Job, means "Total might as First Cause is total right because *and only because* total might successfully WILLS its own total might and its arbitrary policies."

6. Another consideration indicates that justifying causal explanations in religion may be closer to scientific causal explanations than is at first believed. A philosopher of science like Stephen Toulmin would say that the philosophically exciting kind of scientific causal explanations are not just causal explanations of a sort that enable us to manipulate, predict and control events in our environment. Perhaps it was mainly such a 'technological' sort and only such a sort of explanation that Hare had in mind in the passage where we initially quoted him as denying that a religious claim is "some sort of explanation, as scientists are accustomed to use the word".[11] Toulmin would say that the philosophically exciting kind of scientific causal explanations are ones that delight the human mind by suggesting patterns, ones that delight the human mind with the relief of newly found understanding and intelligibility. If Toulmin is right, or even close to being right, then justifying explanations in religion are still less to be thought of as totally different from all scientific causal explanations.

7. One paradigm of reasonableness in religious beliefs worth considering is their resemblance to the paradigm W. V. Quine puts forward for reasonableness in scientific beliefs. Consider some famous sentences from "Two Dogmas of Empiricism":

... our statements about the external world face the tribunal of sense experience not individually but only as a corporate body .... A conflict with experience at the periphery [generally] occasions readjustments in the interior field. Truth values have to be redistributed over some of our statements .... [But] any statement can be held true come what may, if we make drastic enough adjustments elsewhere in the system. Even a statement very close to the periphery can be left true in the face of recalcitrant experience by pleading hallucination or by amending certain statements of the kind called. logical laws. Conversely, by the same token, no statement is immune to revision. Revision even of the logical law of the excluded middle has been proposed as a means of simplifying quantum mechanics; and what difference is there in principle between such a shift and the shift whereby Kepler superseded Ptolemy, or Einstein Newton, or Darwin Aristotle? ... Each man is given a scientific heritage plus a continuing barrage of sensory stimulation; and the considerations which guide him in warping his scientific heritage *to fit his continuing sensory promptings* are, where rational, pragmatic.[12]

As metaphysicians of a more traditional sort, theists can take the idea of the "continuing barrage" of *experience* into areas of feeling, insight and moral reaction well beyond what Quine would count as *sensory* stimulation or promptings. And theistic pragmatism, as we prescribe it, is the policy of seeking to wrest ever anew the discovery of what is now most clearly true and good from the continuing barrage or bombardment of experience and to bring about as much good as possible by learning from experience.[13] Such a theistic pragmatism can usefully be guided quite a way by Quine's scientific holism. Some so-called *central* beliefs of the rational theist's, like those about God's existence and nature, are to be held much less tentatively than other more peripheral ones, like those about monogamy, tithing, responsibility to the civil power. But all must face the music of experience together, even the most central ones. To treat "God exists" as quite unfalsifiable, come what may, is not to be committed primarily to truth – let alone to rationality.

8. We earlier quoted J. F. Miller as offering religious believers a different paradigm of scientific rationality. In effect, he invites the believer to resort to saying: "It is just as rational to believe in God's existence as in a 'first order principle' of science." Miller tries to leave himself a certain amount of room for a post-Kantian manoeuvre by writing:

Whether more or less permanent, 'first order principle' refers to what at this stage in our conceptualizing is fixed and being used logically in a way such that nothing could falsify it. Perhaps this will change, but if it does it will not affect our analysis of either religion or science at the present time.[14]

But even with this kind of qualification Miller's position is still unduly rigid and seriously confused. If descriptive analysis be meant, such talk about "analysis of either religion or science at the present time" is likely to fall foul of empirical evidence that not all scientists now practicing do presuppose universal determinism to be true. Contrasting the writings of philosophers with modern scientific training like Ernest Nagel and the late Friedrich Waismann one can conclude empirically that some do presuppose the Ism's truth and some don't and some treat the Ism more as a useful imperative than as a statement of truth. Among current religionists it appears that Hare and Miller do hold "God exists" as something quite unfalsifiable while we and Kellenberger do not, and while some like Basil Mitchell try to straddle the fence by saying that experience of only a finite amount of evil counts against God's existence, though never decisively or conclusively. But it is likely that Miller is also using the term 'analysis' to bring in a prescription about how scientists and religionists should think. And we suggest that our somewhat Quinean prescriptions for both a scientific and a religious paradigm of rationality, holding no central beliefs as immune from criticism now in the light of changing experience and reflection, are preferable at least because they involve a great deal less danger of dogmatism and of blindness to new truth. Is there not perhaps an unadmitted concession to Voluntarism in Miller's solution for "the falsification challenge of Flew and others" – a concession which will make it seem less than rational to the anti-Voluntarist? Flew's challenge, it would appear, is largely met by the assertion: "Well we as a community do by our deeds just CHOOSE to follow 'first order principles' unquestioningly in *both* science and religion. That's what science and religion must be like." But the important question here is "*Why* must they be followed so unquestioningly, so non-tentatively?"

9. We have been emphasizing the paradigm of openness to experience, willingness to think again in response to the barrage of experience. A connected paradigm of rational belief is openness and toleration in rela-

tion to criticism and to people who think differently. Consider the following questions. Is the man who holds the view willing to discuss it seriously?
Is he willing to try and clarify it for himself and for others? Is he willing
to accept the serious possibility of having made an error? Is he willing to
listen to criticism, to give objections to his view a fair hearing? Is he willing to give the critics of his view what he himself considers good reasons
or grounds for retaining his view and for rejecting the arguments and
proposals of those critics? Does he show tolerance and respect for others?
Is he willing to entertain the possibility that he can learn from the beliefs
of others? Is he well-disposed to those who disagree with him – at least as
long as they try hard in turn to be open and tolerant with him? The criteria
of rational belief must be complex, but the sorts of paradigms which we
endorse indicate that the rationality of a belief may lie far more in its
manner of entertainment than in its content.

10. It may be objected that our suggested paradigms could be suitable for
tentative rational belief in hypotheses, but that no beliefs held in this way
may be held in matters of Faith as matters of Faith. For, we may be told,
Faith requires a kind of serious commitment which excludes contemplation of any possible revision as a form of unfaithfulness or "backsliding".
We answer that the relevant criteria of genuine faithfulness, seriousness,
committedness, etc., in matters of Faith should be matters like willingness
to make sacrifices for one's belief, to risk one's comforts, affections, and
even one's life, or willingness to re-examine and criticize oneself often in
the light of Faith's demands and sometimes to try forcing oneself to change
a great deal to meet those demands. But meeting relevant criteria such as
these need not and should not entail meeting such criteria as a total unwillingness to change one's mind when experience profoundly suggests
that the seeker of truth and good should change it.[15] At this stage it might
help to let the Ghost out of the Machine, to let the little Knight of Faith
inside us come out and deliver an analytical homily on the Dog Latin for
"Reason in a Relevant Sense". It may clarify, along with the previous
remarks of this paragraph, the *two-fold fatuity* of so many in philosophy
of religion: one must, they say, explicate the criteria of "faith" in ways
that exclude the criteria of "Reason", and *vice versa*. The exclusionary
policies turn out to be fatuous indeed, unfaithful to Reason and unreasonable about "faith".

Apologia pro Vita Fidelium Rationis Amantium

"Consider a distinction between two types of attempt to justify a creed. Once religious or anti-religious passion has prompted in us the self-absorption natural to discussion of innermost convictions, the ways of self-justification tend to obscure, or even be confounded with, the ways we would naturally try to justify other people's beliefs. This tendency may make a religious view of the world sound less worthy of being called reasonable than it really is. The tendency can blind us to what is here the most relevant paradigm of rationality.

"It is one thing for me to justify my own creed as being true. It is a very different thing for me to justify someone else's religious tenets as being reasonable. To justify someone else's beliefs as reasonable, in the sense of 'reasonable' which really concerns us most, is not to show that there are reasons I find very plausible, let alone conclusive, for accepting them as true. To assert that Alius's beliefs deserve the title of 'reasonable' need here imply no value judgment on their plausibility for me. Rather, the assertion implies that the views are entertained by Alius in a manner I value as proper to the thinking habits of reasonable men. Someone who shares my own beliefs may be regarded by me as holding unreasonable views, in this admittedly transferred sense of 'unreasonable'. For his views may seem true enough to me, yet I cannot but grade very poorly his manner of entertaining them.

"Concentrating on the reasonableness one expects from others suggests that at least *prima facie* faith cannot be the sort of province from which reason is altogether excluded. For we seem to know, when we are not theorising, what we mean by 'reasonable religious belief'. And our clarity arises from the easy and natural way we distinguish cases of unreasonable belief. As Locke asked us to stop enquiring whether Will be free and see instead whether men are, so our natural distinctions suggest that we cease worrying whether Religious Belief be reasonable and ask instead whether believers are. Well, let us take a cue from Austin and ask what sort of person 'reasonable believer' would be happily used to exclude. Here one is not held back by lack of ideas but simply by the fear of sounding so banal in a tolerant but intellectually curious age. For the antonyms that wear the trousers and animate the idea of a reasonable religious believer are ones like 'bigoted', 'stupid', 'ignorant', 'undiscerning', 'intolerant' and 'unreflecting'. To be a reasonable believer one must both believe and not qualify for such antonyms. The reasonable believer must be able to conceive seriously of the possibility that he is mistaken and of alternative world views which might be more appropriate if he were mistaken. He is not deterred from considering this possibility honestly by fear of Jove's sudden bolt or Jehovah's eternal wrath: any deity worth worshipping by a reasonable man would want him to use and follow unreservedly reason in these matters. He cannot be ignorant of objections to religious belief, or unready to discuss them and admit their force. He may not lack a supply of what he sincerely considers to be good reasons for faith; he must not be unacquainted with the standards of logic and clarity his contemporaries favour. He should acknowledge the likelihood that some equally honest enquirers will conclude that the best reasons support very different views.

"To assert, as I do, that the Paradigm Case Argument from what we would naturally say and mean is not decisive nor everywhere of equal weight, and yet to maintain that this paradigm of reasonable religious belief discredits any apriorist's shotgun divorce of faith and reason, is really a flagrant piece of self-commitment. It is to endorse, not indubitably to demonstrate, the wisdom of a particular commonsense idiom. But the commitment and endorsement themselves seem flagrantly reasonable if we but ask: 'What more could reasonably be asked of a man in this kind of world? What more could be asked in the name of rationality for his manner of entertaining a Weltanschauung? What more, that is, except more of this same sort of thing?' It may be objected that this paradigm only yields what is 'reasonable' for a believer, for what is really irrational but least distressingly so. The objection fails because we would demand the same sort of standards of a reasonable agnostic or a reasonable atheist. There are those sceptics, of course, who define irreligion into the requirements of reason. Likewise, some theists would refuse to allow that anyone who met my paradigm was really religious. Such a believer is free to *say* that anyone whose love of good reasons and of an intellectual life which leaves no question completely closed makes these requirements too fundamental to be compatible with a truly religious view. But then 'religious' will simply be denied a priori to myself and other admirers of faith *and* the Life of Reason. Such believers would say that they do believe strongly in a benevolent Creator to Whom men owe affection and obedience, but

they remain deliberately open to, and indeed welcome, arguments that
they are mistaken. If these are to be denied the title of 'religious', in defiance of what seems to be common sense and common usage, the firm
believer's argument looks like becoming a mere exercise in fideist lexico-
graphy and homage to Kierkegaard's ghost.

"Attention to the case of justifying others' belief by this sort of transferred reasonableness suggests that most fears are baseless when we turn
to self-justification concerning the truth of our own beliefs. To be reasonable by these standards of self-justification we must have good reasons to
consider our creed correct. Exclusive concentration on such self-justification may well spur us on to ask too much of ourselves, to forget what kind
of good reasons are really good enough in the context. Either, says self-
mistrust, we must have the Cartesian certainty of self-evidence. Or we
must despair of rational justification and take the Leap of Faith without
any reservations for intellectual honesty. But the dilemma's horns prove
spectral once we turn back to the paradigm of justifying others' beliefs by
their reasonableness of manner entertained. We do not normally require
ideal Cartesian feats of others to count them reasonable in their beliefs;
nor do we consider that their appropriate good reasons must resemble
deductive chains based on indubitable axioms. 'Reasonable' excludes 'Unreasonable' in a much clearer sense: we ask that the reasonable believer
eschew certain forms of ignorance, stupidity and intolerance. If the religious man tries to meet the natural paradigm of reasonableness he would
set both for other, diverse believers and for 'sensible', 'open-minded' unbelievers, he will soon be justified in considering his beliefs correct. Or at
least he will have his beliefs justified as far as anyone who reasonably seeks
or rejects such all-embracing truths can ever hope to find justification."

11. One further paradigm of rational faith, again closely related to a
paradigm already prescribed, is what one might call "the Network-by-
Degrees paradigm". To revert to previous sorts of examples, by our view
there are centrally held religious beliefs, like "God exists" and "God loves
all mankind" and "all persons are unique and precious in the eyes of God".
These seem to the holder either to entail, or at least to warrant in conjunction with other relatively central religious and moral beliefs, various more
peripherally held beliefs about what is right (and so about what God
judges right) in matters like organising a ministry, like evaluating military

service, euthanasia, birth control, abortion, and so on. Thus, speaking loosely, there is a 'logical priority' which some religious beliefs enjoy compared with many others. Degrees of 'logical priority' radiate from the highest degree at the centre to the lowest near those at the periphery. This philosophical property of degree of 'logical priority' – compare very roughly the difference between axioms and theorems in a formally axiomatized theory for a physical or social science – goes for our rational believer with psychological degrees of relatively more tentativeness about peripheral matters and relatively less willingness to change on central matters. He is content with such psychological distinctions, though *all* his beliefs are held by him to be falsifiable and to face the tests of experience as a corporate whole. Some religious groups have sometimes seemed scarcely less passionately committed to "One should go to Church every Sunday" or "One should not accept blood transfusions" or "Every sentence in the Bible is literally true" than they are to "A loving God exists" or "Each person has dignity and value". The absence of clear-cut psychological and 'logical' priorities in matters of belief suggests lack of rationality in the believer. For it suggests lack of judgment and sense of proportion, lack of plausible systematic structure in thought, lack of openness on the boundaries of experience, and so on. Thus the 'Network' paradigm which we prescribe forbids that all religious propositions be held as equally safe (or equally unsafe) from questioning.

12. It will still sound to unbalanced philosophers and theologians as if our belief in God is less than serious if we count that belief as conceivably worthy of revision in the light of fresh experience and reflection on it. Norman Malcolm, for example, appears to be making this point when he suggests at a passage dear to Wittgensteinian fideists that if one truly believes in God, then there is no such question for one as "Does God exist?".[16] Malcolm intimates that if one believes *in* God one has an affective attitude quite incompatible with any detached consideration of the so-called 'belief' *that* God exists. But part of the appropriate measure of seriousness in Faith is clarified by our remarks about willingness to act and suffer for Faith. Another possible part of that appropriate measure is this: speaking for ourselves we would both say that "God exists" is nearly as central among our beliefs as are other crucial metaphysical beliefs like "I exist"[17], "Matter exists", "Other minds exist", "Most of my apparent memories are trustworthy", "Someone will still be alive after this argument is completed", etc. If one gives or tries to give such a central place to God's existence in one's system of fundamental beliefs then it is hard to see why it should be held that, because one counts all these beliefs to be falsifiable in principle, therefore one still fails to make a real commitment to take Faith in God seriously. And we fail to see why one's believing *in* something very seriously should stop one believing dispassionately (or passionately!) *that* it exists. Next one should ask: Does a man fail to take himself and his personal identity seriously because he grants that conceivably the having of certain alleged mystical experiences would lead him to say that only a Spinoza's Deus-Sive-Natura or another philosopher's 'World Soul' or a Hindu's Brahman is the one real individual that exists? Does a man not love his wife wholeheartedly if he conceives that given certain highly unexpected experiences he would take himself to have been fooled by a robot-like human female? For "love wholeheartedly" one might read "have proper affective attitudes towards" to court the company of Malcolm.

13. We accept Quine's view that unexpected results at the periphery do not [*ipso-facto-modo-tollendo*] compel rational people to reject as falsified the much more central beliefs which generated quite other expectations. Falsification is by no means always the straightforward sort of thing perhaps once envisioned by some Positivists whereby the First Party says: "$(x)(Px \supset Qx)$" and the Second Party can just reply "Quite false! For $(\exists x)(Px \cdot \mathord{\rceil} Qx)$". Truth values can be adjusted pragmatically and distributed so as either to save the appearances or to save preferred tenets. Thus preferred tenets like "God exists" or "I, a distinct person, exist" can as a matter of logical possibility be spared indefinitely. But beyond a certain point it may well become quite irrational even for flexible pragmatists to preserve such tenets in the face of recalcitrant experience. For the rational theist the falsification of "God exists" and "I exist" is possible, *but not simple*.

14. Thus we do not wish to claim that a truth about a human's experience need logically entail the falsity of "God exists". But certain batteries of experiences might eventually afford a reflective believer very good reasons for rejecting "God exists" as false and for rational purposes falsified. For example, what if communication between humans and more intelligent life on other planets in other galaxies revealed apparently excellent reasons to conclude that Judaeo-Christian beliefs had been inculcated on Earth and similar planets by fantastically powerful, brilliantly imaginative hoaxters from Alpha Centauri? What if after what seemed to be experiences of our own funerals we very protractedly seemed to be having experiences of a life after death much more consonant with Homer's suggestions than with those of the Book of Revelation? Could not items like these *conceivably* give us good reasons for rejecting as falsified belief in the Judaeo-Christian God? If they could, then in relevant and important ways "God exists" might possibly be falsified. And rational Faith in God must come to terms with *genuine possibilities*.[18]

Thus, from our anti-Voluntarist but admittedly prescriptive standpoint, philosophers like Flew, Hare, Mitchell, Miller, Allison, Kellenberger, Bell and others are wrong to say that the believer's approach cannot be tentative or hypothetical in matters of Faith. Of course by this time we have prescribed rather a lot. And what we prescribe may strike some other theists as bitterly and bittily Empiricist bitter medicine. But at least we have sketched an alternative approach to scarcely concealed dogmatism. And that, in the current impasse, may well be what is now most needed.

II. HYPOTHETICAL FAITH: CRITERIA OF RATIONALITY

We hope that this sketch of a theist position will now illuminate much of what we tentatively take to be the central cluster of criteria for rationality in religious belief. In the course of this book we shall take detailed looks at several members of the cluster. We hope in turn that this listing of these overlapping criteria will reveal a cluster worth completion by others for themselves, a cluster with an integrating power and beauty which will capture many of man's 'intuitions' about rationality and which will strengthen our claims for the good sense of the position sketched. Most of these criteria will only be mentioned briefly at this point.

(A) The demand that a system of religious doctrines supply what we call a *justifying explanation* for everything that happens: otherwise the tenets of the system are irrelevant to religious aspirations.

(B) The demand for a person NOT to conclude (1) that there must be such a 'justifying explanation' for all events and (2) that it is clearly best supplied by *this* system EXCEPT after a good deal of experience and a great deal of reflection on it.

(C) The demand for the believer to admit that he may, after all, still be quite mistaken about his conclusions on both these counts; that he should accordingly respect both socially and intellectually those who also seek truth and wisdom seriously and tolerantly but continue to disagree with him.

(D) The demand for primacy of commitment to what is true, rational and good – a primacy asserted over dread of Power *qua* Power, over dread of dependence *qua* dependence and the like, over terrors which too often characterize too much of religious life and reflection guided by extreme Voluntarism. (In turn, we endorse William James' attacks in *The Will to Believe* on those sceptics who so sanctify dread of being possibly mistaken as to make serious consideration of any religious – or substantive metaphysical and Humanistically ideological – claims impossible.)

(E) A belief in a 'natural light' of human reason which, however limited, enables man to work slowly towards objective truth: man is not limited to truths dictated by what fideists now speak of as "bliks" or (ultimately unjustifiable) "forms of life".

(F) The openness to actual and possible criticisms from others, so emphasized by Sir Karl Popper in dealing with rationality, and willingness to have one's views changed or 'tabled' by criticisms one cannot meet.

(G) A sympathy for the sort of 'holist' approach (to interaction between changing experience, conceptual truths and basic beliefs) espoused by Quine when dealing with rationality in "Two Dogmas of Empiricism" and *The Web of Belief*. Such holism allows both for their interaction and for one's ability to alter any part of one's system of concepts and beliefs in order to do the greatest possible justice to experience's suggestions *without hopelessly dislocating* systematic thought about experience.

(H) Concern for the meaningfulness and justifiability of apparently sound beliefs, so long as such concern does not become hysterical and set logically impossible demands for meaningfulness and justification.

(I) The sense of proportion which enables one to distinguish between centrally important and peripheral matters in one's system of religious and moral beliefs.

(J) Attention to the 'Game-Theoretical' notion of maximising expected utility when one commits oneself to a crucial new belief or sub-system of beliefs about religion. (Here again we sympathize with the William James of *The Will to Believe*. James in effect points, like the Game-Theorist, to the necessity for considering *not only* the evidence for or probability of a possible belief's truth. One must also be concerned with evaluating the consequences of accepting it as a true belief and acting on it in the event that it is correct and *in the event that it is not*. Note that James' evaluations, unlike Pascal's in his famous Wager, are based on a desire to live wisely and in harmony *now* with 'eternal things' as they truly are – Pascal seems concerned far more to evaluate the possible (posthumous) pains and pleasures of successful blind obedience or unsuccessful disobedience in a way that smacks strongly of Voluntarism.)[19]

(K) Interest in the 'dialectical' approach to philosophically opposed positions urged by John Wisdom in *Philosophy and Psychoanalysis* – (Oxford 1953). Such interest need not lead one to go so far with Wisdom as to divide the opposed pairs into platitudes and illuminating falsehoods. But one might profitably believe, for example, that, although God is a *substance* or *individual* and not a *process*, the process model of some theologians might throw valuable light on what sort of substance or individual God is.[20] One might derive similar profit from trying to see how much religious sense and insight there is in the conceptual models of both sides when people champion an Atemporal God against a Temporal God, Monism against Pluralism, 'Immanence' against 'Transcendence', *Analogia Entis* against almost complete Mysticism and Ineffability, God as Necessary Being against God as Contingently Existent by Hume's criteria of contingency, and finally, for all we have said, Voluntarism against Intellectualism. Doubtless there is much wisdom in many Voluntarist writers, notably the author or authors of the last chapter of *Job*. Doubtless for many sorts of person the fear of God is the *beginning* of wisdom. But perhaps one has to be basically more of an Intellectualist to see the real limitations of that position and one's own.

Even at this stage of the exploration someone might still retort: "These criteria indicate about how close to rationality a believer can get. But this is never close enough! Faith is never rational, only scepticism or atheism can be rational since only they can make intelligible and warranted claims." Several of our criteria of rationality incline us to say that possibly he may be right and we may be wrong. On the other hand, we suggest that all or all but the first of the criteria reflect 'intuitions' about rationality that one would wisely apply to almost any systematic thinker, whether he be theist, sceptic, or atheist. Very probably those of us who want to do philosophy in a reasonable way are all in the same logical boat. By trying to rock that boat hard in order to expel one another we are most likely to serve only the forces of unreason against which we should be taking a common stand.[21]

NOTES

[1] See the articles on 'Theology and Falsification' in *New Essays in Philosophical Theology* (edited by A. G. N. Flew and A. C. MacIntyre), London 1955 – especially Flew and Hare on pp. 99-103.

[2] *Review of Metaphysics* **22** (1969) 501.

[3] *Religious Studies* **5** (1969) 75.

[4] *Religious Studies* **5** (1969) 50.

[5] There are other passages in Miller's paper which may indicate sympathy for something like a more flexibly Quinean, pragmatic approach. But if these really do indicate this, they would seem inconsistent with his main answer to the falsification challenge.

[6] A similar protest about tentativeness among believers seems to be raised by T. M. McPherson against Kellenberger at *Religious Studies* **5** (1969) 82, para. 3. But McPherson immediately follows the protest up not by prescribing a wiser form of empiricism, only by commending the 'internal' approach of Peter Winch, D. Z. Phillips and others to religious evidence. Dubious armchair generalizations seem to underlie Miller's talk of "the majority of believers" and "the logical use of terms" at *loc. cit.*, p. 52.

[7] R. H. Popkin, *Philosophy Made Simple*, New York 1956, p. 114. There is a profound attempt to clarify and criticize Voluntarism in Plato's *Euthyphro* where we discover Socrates asking Euthyphro whether pious deeds are pious because they please the gods or please the gods because they are pious (10a). P. Vignaux, *Philosophy in the Middle Ages*, London 1959, quotes Duns Scotus, "*Omne aliud a Deo est bonum quia a Deo volitum*" (p. 206), and Ockham, "*Eo ipso quod ipse vult, bene et juste factum est*" (p. 207). Cf. Vernon J. Bourke, *Will in Western Thought*, New York 1964, pp. 80–100. For an example of modern writing which often reflects this tradition see Peter Geach, 'The Moral Law and the Law of God' in his *God and the Soul*, London 1969. Note his attack in a Voluntarist strain on the argument in Plato's *Euthyphro* at pp. 177ff, and his later comments on the worship of supreme power (comments to be discussed again in another chapter): "I shall be told by such philosophers that since I am saying not: It is your supreme moral duty to obey God, but simply: It is insane to set about defying an Almighty God, my attitude is plain power-worship. So it is: but it is worship of the Supreme power, and as such is wholly different from, and does not carry with it, a cringing attitude towards earthly powers. ... 'I will show you whom you shall fear', said Jesus Christ to his disciples" (p. 127).

No less striking examples of Voluntaristic views are to be found in Peter Damian and Descartes. Whether a perceptive philosopher can remain totally and consistently Voluntaristic in his approach is doubtful. For example, Geach also writes in this essay: (a) "obviously a revelation from a deity whose 'goodness' did not include any objection to lying would be worthless"; (b) "I agree, indeed, with Hobbes that gratitude for God's benefits would not be a sufficient ground for *unreserved* obedience if it were severed from fear of God's irresistible power." It seems that (b) is a watering down of Voluntarism. (God is to be obeyed as supremely good because He is supremely powerful *as well as* because He has shown Himself extremely good to us?) Accepting (a) appears to be taking a very long step in the direction of rejecting Voluntarism altogether. For a valuable survey of some other very recent arguments involving Voluntarism see J. P. Reeder, 'Patterson Brown on God's Will as the Criterion of Morality', *Religious Studies* 5 (1969) 243–49. (We shall say more on Geach in Chapter II, Section I.2.)

[8] Cf. Kai Nielsen's useful attack on 'Wittgensteinian Fideism' in *Philosophy* 43 (1967) 191ff. The family of positions he criticizes would include those of writers on philosophy of religion like Peter Winch, D. Z. Phillips and Norman Malcolm. It strikes us as an evasion of worthwhile 'intuitive' demands on rationality for Kellenberger to suggest in a later paper (by analogy with a person impulsively convinced of a relative's innocence) that a man of true faith must hold his views non-tentatively even though he may grant to the empiricist that evidence could count seriously against his views. See *Religious Studies* 5 (1969) 246–47.

[9] For the introduction of this term "justifying explanations" and for discussion of the concept's possible application to attempted proofs like the Five Ways, see John King-Farlow, *Reason and Religion*, London 1969, especially Chapters VI and VII. We deviate somewhat from this account in order to make it clearer that justifying explanations are partly *causal*.

[10] We suspect that the Voluntarist's explanation is not satisfactory for still another reason. In its attempt to prove satisfactory it gives rise to what some would call a super-ultimate "why". In accounting for the rightness or wrongness of a thing in terms of God's willing it to be so it gives rise to the more ultimate question "Why does God will it to be so?" It has been argued, however, that such a super-ultimate "why" is meaningless [Paul Edwards, *Encyclopedia of Philosophy*, New York and London 1967, Vol. VIII, pp. 299–302], since it introduces questions that are devoid of sense. Nothing can count as an answer to it. Our notion of *justifying explanation* avoids this problem – it gives one good reason for the effects being what they are and being valued for what they are. "This is so because ultimately it just is right and is caused for that reason."

[11] See our note 1. Compare Toulmin's comments on the nature of scientific progress in *The Philosophy of Science*, London 1953, *passim* and in *Foresight and Understanding*, New York 1963, *passim*.

[12] W. V. Quine, *From a Logical Point of View*, Boston 1953, pp. 42–46. See Quine's recent work for the layman *The Web of Belief* (co-authored with J. S. Ullian), New York, 1971, *passim*.

[13] Goodness may be co-eternal *ontologically* with God, but, even if one believes rationally in God, one's epistemological grasp of what is good fluctuates with the flux of experience and the variations in one's ability to act and understand that flux.

[14] *Op. cit.*, p. 52.

[15] Thus Faith can and should be tentative, with even the passionate believer able to admit that he *may be mistaken*. If this still sounds paradoxical, a confusion may be the main cause. One may confuse (a) *backing down on a partly uncertain belief P in the face of inconveniences which do not raise serious questions about P's truth value* with (b) *backing down on a partly uncertain belief P, which it IS convenient to believe, in the face of experiences that call P's truth seriously into question.* Backing-down of type (a) is *unfaithfulness* according to the sort of religious view we advocate, but backing-down of type (b) is not. Intermediate cases between (a) – unfaithfulness and (b) – 'unfaithfulness' may be much easier to confuse but still worth the pains of trying to distinguish.

[16] Cf. Malcolm's contribution to John Hick's *Faith and the Philosophers*, New York 1966, pp. 103ff. See Chapter II, Section I. 2 for further discussion of Malcolm on belief in God.

[17] For reflections on intelligibility of doubts about one's own existence see John King-Farlow, 'Myths of the Given and the "COGITO" Proof', *Philosophical Studies* (U.S.) **12** (1961) 49–53; J. King-Farlow and J. M. Rothstein, 'Dialogue Concerning Natural Metaphysics', *Southern Journal of Philosophy* **6** (1968) 24–30; J. King-Farlow, 'Quantification Theory and Ontological Monism', *Zeitschrift für Allgemeine Wissenschafts-theorie* **3** (1972) 1–12.

[18] Someone might here try to resurrect Basil Mitchell's old attempt to salvage Faith-with-a-pinch-of falsifiability. (See his contribution on 'Theology and Falsification' in *New Essays in Philosophical Theory* – cf. note 1.) Thus he would object to us that our possible reasons here for rejecting theism could not *conclusively or decisively* falsify theism. But from our quasi-Quinean view of truths as an adjustable system or network Mitchell's idea of conclusive or decisive falsification is either incoherent or at least a non-starter. (Cf. Quine on the second dogma in 'Two Dogmas of Empiricism'.)

[19] It will be evident that we disagree considerably with D. H. Mellor's attack on the idea of using 'subjective probabilities' *ever* to support the rationality of religious commitments. See his 'God and Probability', *Religious Studies* **6** (1969), especially pp. 228–30. Until he clarifies his position in relation to James' pragmatism about belief's value in this life, as opposed to opportunism about posthumous pay-offs, it will not be clear where a reply should begin.

[20] Compare – up to a point – I. T. Ramsey's frequent advocacy of one's scanning various 'maps' and 'models' for disclosures of religious insight. See his *Religious Language*, London 1957; *Prospect for Metaphysics*, London 1961, etc. P. K. Feyerabend has valuably emphasised the importance of cultivating interest in different conceptual schemes in order to be rational about *science*.

[21] We are indebted for encouragement (through agreement and *dis*agreement) to Professor H. D. Lewis who has written to us concerning the questions of this first chapter: "I think what you say is most important in the present study of religion and religious controversy... I entirely agree with the main point made by you... I am sure that it is quite wrong to suppose that our only choice is to accept or reject things in some total way. It seems clearly possible to have good reasons for holding some things more tentatively... some things as more firmly established than others. The only point where I would personally not go along with you is the *existence* of God ...everything *else* we know about God depends upon *some* kind of evidence..." Compare Lewis' *Our Experience of God*, London 1959, pp. 30–31, 36, 41, 44, 47, 59–60, 65, 80–81, 102, etc.

TWO SIDES TO A THEIST'S COIN

The concepts of a personal God that prevail among many committed Judaeo-Christians who are not (or are not primarily) Voluntarists can usefully be linked with concepts of Reason through the mediating teleological notion of *reasonable persons as persons naturally and wisely prone to seek for Justifying Explanations*. Reasonable persons do not necessarily conclude *in the end* that their existence has a theistic Justifying Explanation, nor even that their existence must have some Justifying Explanation or other. But for reasonable persons the justification-seeking "Why?" sort of question arises naturally. It is a question that appears to them for a long time to demand thoughtful answering. And, if for many reasonable persons it appears eventually unprofitable to reflect on further, then often some form of philosophical reflection also appears required for its removal by agnosticism, by scepticism or by sheer mysticism.

Numerous lunatics may also be haunted by justifying "Why?" questions, but that does not make reasonable persons lunatics. The point seems obvious. Yet when we first presented some of the material in this chapter at a philosophical conference an irate man, who actually *hated* religion as a form of 'poisonous madness', began shouting like a Fire and Brimstone Preacher that mental asylums are full of people seeking Point, Purpose, Value, etc. in Life – that there is and *could be* no tie between reasonableness and an interest in Justifying Explanations. Not too surprisingly, the protester was a hyper-dissolutionist type of 'Ordinary Language' devotee, harshly bent on dismantling traditional questions of Metaphysics as abuses of common speech, fiercely opposed to associating Philosophy with Logic, frantically seeking to have Philosophy of Science and Logic both expelled from the curriculum of his unfortunate Philosophy Department! At any rate, when Socrates declared at his trial that (for him as a person with Reason) "the unexamined life is not worth living", he did not mean that some reasonable persons *qua* reasonable persons do ask fundamental philosophical questions often and seriously and some do not. Socrates meant that all reasonable persons have a natural bent, which is part of their real though limited potentiality for wisdom, to ask just such questions; that, moreover, it would be degrading for a man as a reasonable person not to raise them often and seriously.

One can deny that a reasonable person *as such* is going to be seriously interested in man's perennial search for Justifying Explanations during a good part of his existence. One can deny that any attempt to formalise any part of Logic or Linguistics could ever shed any light on what it is to be a reasonable person. One can deny that there is ever anything worth calling a necessary *connection* between being a reasonable person and *not* taking (or SEEKING *not* to take) pleasure in the unhappiness of others. One can deny that *reasonable* persons are essentially more than Pentagon Paperman Parodies, than Problem-Solving Animals with enough sense not to query the point or value of their main goals. One can deny such things very profitably – because, if one is a reasonable person, the increasingly obvious disparity between the accumulated denials on the one hand and truth or wisdom on the other tends increasingly to illuminate the complex framework of what it is to be a reasonable person. One looks away in denial, then one looks again AND ONE SEES MORE *or* SEES BETTER. We shall have more to say about the reasonableness of such old-fashioned Intuitionist talk about *Seeing* in the next two chapters. Here we try to show further how a theistic concept of God as no less basically good than powerful lends itself well to embedding Faith within a Life of Reason, how distortions of such a concept lead to unnecessary attacks on theism and undesirable (often sadly authoritarian) defenses of it. After undertaking these tasks in Section I ("The Two Sides Distinguished"), we shall turn in Section II ("The Two Sides and the PROSLOGION") to reaffirming with Aquinas against St. Anselm that *speaking intelligently* of the concept of *God* as the concept of somthing perfectly good and greatest in respect of goodness, etc., need not involve implicitly *knowing with certainty* that an actual and all powerful being falls under the concept. Thus our first two chapters will minister in Chapter III to new versions of the Five Ways, to restatements of 'Cosmological' and 'Teleological' arguments. But here in Section II we shall be at pains to endorse Aquinas' rejection in the *Summa Contra Gentiles* and the *Summa Theologica* of what we take to be Anselm's most interesting form of 'Ontological' argument.

I. THE TWO SIDES DISTINGUISHED

According to many believers there is no end to the enlightening things that may be truly said about God.[1] Perhaps there is no end for them either to the useful ways of dividing these things up into illuminating classes. But as fairly traditional theists we suggest a need to stress two basic classes as two indispensable sides to a traditional (mono-) theist's coin. We suggest that neglect or rejection of either side can debase the currency under philosophical investigation, can lead a philosopher – or at least his puzzled readers – into costly muddles about the analysis or evaluation of religious discourse and claims.

These all too familiar classes are:

[A] Expo-Statements about God's Existence and Power (which make no reference to His Goodness, to His moral attributes as a Person).

[B] Gooper-Statements about God's Goodness as a Person (which presuppose His Existence but not His Supreme Power).

We shall try to show briefly how such very different philosophers as Sartre, Malcolm and Geach are led to say confused – or at least very confusing – things about God by failure in context to stress one class as much as the other. But first consider a particularly pious pair of such statements:

Expo-Statement: "It really is the case that a Being whom I call 'God' (an all-powerful, eternal, utterly non-dependent cause of the world's coming-into-being *ex nihilo*, and an ever-active cause of the world's now remaining-in-being) does indeed exist."

Gooper-Statement: "God is a person-like Being, but unlike us He is utterly loving and good – so perfectly, and infallibly good that He offers men eternal happiness with the complete and unending fulfilment of all human needs, emotions and talents; that He gives meaning and point to anything that happens in history; that He and He alone makes all moments of human existence forever precious and worthwhile."

I.1. *Sartre*

There are certain years of Sartre's writing which historians of ideas may find it helpful to call his high period of 'radical individualism' and 'atheistic Existentialism'. The most prominent works expressing his 'atheistic Existentialism' are his three books *Being and Nothingness* (1943), *Ex-*

istentialism is a Humanism (1946), and *What is Literature?* (1948), also
his play *The Flies* (1943).[2]

In *Being and Nothingness* he contends that the idea of God is contradictory in itself and traceable to man's wishful thinking (pp. 79–90).
Sartre's optimism in making this claim is largely based upon three
arguments: about the intrinsic contradiction in the notion of God
(pp. 79–81), about the impossibility of creation (p. 84), and about the
genetic explanation of the idea of God (pp. 89–90). In each case the
problem of God discloses itself as the problem of Human nature as well.
Sartre treats the concept of God as that of an absurdity which our
inevitable anguish about lack of stable identity and lack of objective
values continually misleads us to pursue. It is, he argues, the absurd and
incoherent idea, found at the core of almost all human aspirations, of
coincidence between an unchangeable ideal object and the ever-changing
flow of a real personal consciousness.

The being toward which human reality surpasses itself is not only this reality as a
totality. ... When this totality of being and absolute absence is hypostatized as transcendence beyond the world, by a further movement of meditation, it receives the name
of God (pp. 89–90). But the idea of God is absurd and we lose ourselves in vain. Man is
a futile passion (p. 615).

In *Existentialism is a Humanism* and *The Flies* we seem to get a very
different position. Belief in God is almost certainly a barbarous superstition, but even if a God does exist He is quite irrelevant to human aspirations. At least, however, the existence of some sort of God seems to
be a possibility that can be seriously spoken of in order to make important philosophical points.

Existentialism is not atheist in the sense that it would exhaust itself in demonstrations
of the non-existence of God. It declares, rather, that even if God existed that would make
no difference from its point of view. Not that we believe that God exists, but we think
that the real problem is not that of His existence; what man needs is to find himself
again and to understand that nothing can save him from himself, not even a valid proof
of the existence of God. (*Existentialism is a Humanism*, p. 56.)

Sartre clarifies this conviction in his play *The Flies* through a dialogue
between Zeus and Orestes which runs:

ORESTES: You are the king of Gods, king of stones and stars, king of the waves of the
sea. But you are not the king of man.
ZEUS: Impudent spawn! So I am not your king? Who, then, made you?

ORESTES: You. But you blundered; you should not have made me free.
ZEUS: I gave you freedom so that you might serve me.
ORESTES: Perhaps. But now it has turned against its giver. And neither you nor I can undo what has been done.
ZEUS: Ah, at last! So this is your excuse?
ORESTES: I am not excusing myself.
ZEUS: No? Let me tell you it sounds much like an excuse, this freedom whose slave you claim to be.
ORESTES: Neither slave nor master. I am my freedom. No sooner had you created me than I ceased to be yours. (Act III.)

By relating these strands in Sartre's 'Existentialism' to our dichotomy between types of God-statements one can get a coherent and illuminating interpretation.

To avoid the charge of inconsistency, Sartre could be understood as saying that when the theist makes only Expo-statements he need not contradict himself. But then, Sartre would add, the theist only offers us a being which, however powerful, cannot fulfil our aspirations. This God is at best 'necessary' *qua* being non-dependent on anything else for its survival as an object; it remains 'contingent' *qua* being yet another gratitous object in need of justification, however many other objects it brings into existence. Thus if such a God exists and is an individual with an identity, an 'en-soi' as well as a personal consciousness, then He is a contingent person and as such He too faces anguish. "In a word, God, if he exists, is contingent" (*BN*, p. 81). Such a God lacks the sort of necessity and the ideality which human aspirations demand (*BN*, p. 93). For a simple believer, let alone a philosopher to confound necessary value with mere power or force that is itself *de trop* is to compound Bad Faith. On the other hand, when the theist makes Gooper-statements offering men something personal but non-human as an 'objective foundation' for human values and an 'objective point' to all human history, then the theist really does offer men something relevant to their aspirations. But such relevance is bought at the price of contradiction. And to cling to the contradiction as a possible truth is again to be in Bad Faith (*BN*, pp. 76, 93–94, 566).

We suggest that such a distinction between what might be called Sartre's attitude to Expo-Statements and his attitude to Gooper-Statements does make fairly consistent sense of his moves as an Existential atheist. But we also suggest that had Sartre tried more seriously to take Expohood and Gooperdom as two sides of the same coin, he might have been able to formulate and even consider with some sympathy a Sartrean type of hypothetical theism. *Suppose* that there is, as Pico della Mirandola claimed in his Renaissance classic, *The Oration on the Dignity of Man*, a loving God Who freely created man somewhat according to Sartre's 'Existentialist' image. Suppose that a Piconian Deity maintains the sort of Creative Life-Style in relation to Man that is suggested by these words near the start of *The Oration*:

> ... there was not among His archetypes that from which he could fashion a new offspring, nor was there in His treasure-houses anything which He might bestow on His new son as an inheritance, nor was there in the seats of all the world a place where the latter might sit to contemplate the universe. All was now complete; all things had been assigned to the highest, the middle and the lowest orders. But in its final creation it was not the part of the Father's power to fail as though exhausted. It was not the part of His wisdom to waver in a needful matter through poverty of counsel. It was not the part of His kindly love that he who was to praise God's divine generosity in regard to others should be compelled to condemn it in regard to himself. ... He therefore took man as a creature of indeterminate nature ... (paragraphs 2 and 3). [And He said:] "The nature of all other beings is limited and constrained within the bounds of laws prescribed by Us. Thou, constrained by no limits, in accordance with thine own free will, in whose hands We have placed thee, shalt ordain for thyself the limits of thy nature" (paragraph 3).[3]

Accordingly, *suppose* that man is unique in creation because he has no fixed essence – because (as Pico held) God gives each man the entirely free choice of becoming 'angelic' through a life of creativity and benevolence, of being 'bestial' through cruelty and sloth, etc. *Suppose* that the existence of conscious free beings, including God's own existence, always depends on the continuing exercise of God's power. *Suppose* that God intervenes very little in the lives of humans from concern lest He abuse their freedom, yet He does intermittently aid those who act most clear-headedly in the cause of increasing human tolerance, benevolence and free co-operation. Finally, to accommodate Sartre's rejection of dualism, let us *suppose* (like Hobbes) that God is a material being.[4]

Given such suppositions of Expohood and Gooperdom functioning in tandem, what follows about such an hypothetical God's relevance to human aspirations? In so far as Sartre in his high Existentialist period thought of values as irrational, or non-rational-and-arbitrary human cravings, then this deity would be valuable to some when they so craved and valueless to others when they did not (cf. *BN*, p. 94). In so far as Sartre then thought of values as incoherently imagined Platonic *objects* wished for by self-deceivers as a means of avoiding personal responsibility, the supposed deity would be valueless (cf. *BN*, pp. 39, 90). But it also seems that in this period Sartre could easily slip into thinking of some personal qualities as intrinsically and absolutely valuable.[5] These included honesty, charity, affection, co-operation, tolerance, anti-nationalism, anti-racism, and even concern for all conscious beings' freedom on the ground that they constitute a Kantian Kingdom of Ends. Thus if such a hypothetical God existed, He *would* be relevant to rational human aspirations for realizing and contemplating such values. From the standpoint of Expohood His existence and power would be the First Cause of all that is intrinsically good. From the standpoint of Gooperdom He would be the supreme example of intrinsic goodness, which is always for the high Existential Sartre personal goodness. Sartre, in so far as he takes the third view of values, might much more consistently argue that we have no evidence of such a God's existence, and that what evidence we do have points to His non-existence. But he could not, however, argue at all consistently that, had we such evidence, His existence would remain totally irrelevant to our aspirations for values.

I.2. *Norman Malcolm and Peter Geach*

Consider two passages from Malcolm's writings on God, which may seem to form a puzzling combination when juxtaposed:

[A] What is the relation of Anselm's ontological argument to religious belief? ... I can imagine an atheist going through the argument, becoming convinced of its validity, acutely defending it against objections, yet remaining an atheist. .... It is hardly to be expected that a demonstration should, in addition, produce in him a living faith – 'Anselm's Ontological Arguments' in Malcolm's *Knowledge and Certainty*, Englewood Cliffs. N. J. (1963), pp. 161–63. (The paper is reprinted from *Philosophical Review* **69** (1960) 41–61.)

[B] The assumption is that there is a particular belief that God exists, and with this belief as with any other we must make a distinction between causes of the belief and grounds or evidence for its truth. What is unrealistic about this assumption? I must confess that the supposed *belief that God exists* strikes me as a problematic concept, whereas *belief in God* is not problematic ... the inclination we are discussing is to hold that you could believe *that* God exists without believing *in* God. As I understand it, we are supposed to think that one could believe that God exists but at the same time have no affective attitude towards God. ... The belief that he exists would not logically imply any affective attitude toward him, but an affective attitude toward him would logically imply the belief that he exists. If we are assuming a Jewish or Christian conception of God I do not see how we can make the above separation. If one conceived of God as the almighty creator of the world and judge of mankind how could one believe that he exists but not be touched *at all* by awe or dismay or fear? – 'Is it a Religious Belief that 'God exists'?', in *Faith and the Philosophers* (ed. by J. Hick), New York 1966, pp. 106–07.

Well, what if the man who at least formerly was an atheist in [A] is convinced of the 'validity' – we take it Malcolm means *soundness*, not just *formal* validity – of Anselm's ontological argument in *Proslogion* III as Malcolm expounds it? How can he be spoken of as convinced and yet still an atheist? We suggest that the most intelligible interpretation or reinterpretation is that quite conceivably some reasonable, if rather gullible atheist could be convinced by Malcom's Anselm of the soundness of an argument yielding reliable Expo-conclusions about God, but only Expo-conclusions; that as with Sartre such Expo-conclusions seem irrelevant to him in following a way of life, and hence fail to produce 'living faith' or 'affective attitudes' in him.

Malcolm's Anselm may lead this man who certainly *was* an atheist, Mr. A?, to allow the *a priori* truth of God's necessary existence, necessary omnipotence and certain other necessary 'perfections'. But for Mr. A? such 'perfections' remain irrelevant to his human needs; the 'perfections' may lead him to say "God is necessarily good, and supremely good", but only in what philosophers following R.M. Hare would call an *ossified* sense of *good*. The 'perfections' are too much like forms of mere power and he declines to idolize power. Hence the attitudinally unaffected Mr. A? is rational here. On the other hand, if he believed that Malcolm's Ontological Argument could also deliver very strong Gooper-conclusions like our original example, then Mr. A? would be irrational not to take the argument's soundness as a matter for deep concern, as producing a conclusion that 'makes a difference'. For a man to be unconcerned about the question of what gives his own life its point, of what he and other humans need for happiness and fulfilment, etc. (*if* an answer really does seem rationally given), would indeed be irrational. Because of these and related reasons a worthwhile argument for theism must 'make a difference' to a rational person who seeks what is good for man. It must yield a *justifying explanation*[6] for his own plight and for all human history. Thus a worthwhile argument must provide requisitely strong Gooper-conclusions to make the Expo-conclusions 'make a difference'.

It might be argued that no formal argument for the existence of a

Supreme Being (or, for that matter, the existence of anything else) can give rise to affective attitudes. A person who argued in this way might go on to claim that this is exactly the point which Malcolm is making in [A]. Such a move would tend to conflate two distinct psychological questions. These are (a) whether non-monotheists are very often convinced – *mainly convinced* – of God's existence by rather rigorous, abstract, technical types of deductive proof. To which question the answer is probably "No" – few even understand such proofs. Question (b) is whether former non-believers, once convinced by plain theist arguments (however sloppy and/or unsound), are likely to exhibit affective attitudes. Here surely there are *many* psychological possibilities. We need to ask about *rational* ones. So once again suppose that someone who *was* an atheist, a Mr. A??, becomes strongly convinced that Malcolm's argument is formally valid *and* based on true premises. Then a number of alternatives, as *rational reactions*, would be open to him, once truly convinced.

(i) Mr. A?? can conclude that mere power is an unworthy idol. Hence for him there are no appropriate affective attitudes towards God as the argument yields only Expo-conclusions. (ii) He can conclude that only Expo-conclusions follow, but that affective attitudes like fear, dread, eagerness to be obedient, etc., are appropriate towards this proven deity from a prudential point of view. Here prudent self-love may well elicit these affective attitudes in Mr. A?? (Cupboard love can really warm the heart in time.) (iii) He can conclude that the argument yields Expo-conclusions and only *ossified* Gooper-conclusions. Then he can be moved in either of the first two directions with respect to affective attitudes. (iv) He can conclude that Malcolm's argument about a Being *quo maius cogitari nequit* yields Expo-conclusions explicitly and strong Gooper-con-clusions explicitly or at least implicitly. Then, given that he is rational enough to have been seeking eagerly for an answer to human needs, his affective attitudes can easily become for sound conceptual reasons, as well as contingent psychological reasons, those of the fully-rounded theist. Such attitudes will include fear and *great joy*, awe and *great love*, etc.

Perhaps the most charitable reinterpretation of Malcolm's [B] is that within a fully committed Jewish or Christian way of life one has such strong affective attitudes connected with one's Gooper-beliefs that ab-stract Expo-questions cannot be posed with complete emotional and intellectual detachment, with an effortlessly or painlessly complete objectivity. Such a reinterpretation, we suggest, makes [B] illuminatingly compatible with [A], once [A] is construed as the thesis that if an 'atheist' takes Malcolm's Anselm to offer only Expo-conclusions, he may very understandably remain unmoved. Moreover each of these reconstructions may well seem independently true as well as compatible. But we wish to register three protests against [B] as Malcolm words it.

(Protest I) "Almighty God exists" can be used to make a pure Expo-statement of Judaeo-Christian belief. The relatively 'intellectual' Expo-belief *that* God exists or *in* God's existence occurs on one side of a theist's coin, where it is or should be balanced by the relatively 'affective' Gooper-belief *in* God's goodness or the relatively 'affective' Gooper-belief *that* God is supremely important for man on the other. Either sort of belief, we would stress, is referentially pregnant – is belief that such-and-such exists. Malcolm's way of drawing the *belief that*/*belief in* distinction tends to confuse at least as much as it may clarify. For roughly speaking, from the standpoint of Russell's 'On Denoting', that one has consistent, clearheaded belief in God as our Saviour and in the truth of "God is our Saviour" entails that one believes that God exists and we do, that there is just one x such that x is divine and x is our Saviour, and the like. Roughly speaking from the standpoint of Strawson's 'On Referring', that one has felicitous, clearheaded belief in God as our Saviour and so in the truth of "God is our Saviour" presupposes one's belief that God exists. If Malcolm really has some theory of reference utterly different from Russell's or Strawson's, he must explain rather a lot. Malcolm's sloppiness about the *referential implications* of using key Noun-Phrases[7] in common-garden 'God-Talk' is philosophically so unfortunate and unfortunately so infectious in differing ways that it is worth pausing to note a much more recent but interestingly related attempt to beg questions about intendable Sense by ignoring questions about coherently intended Reference. (Also it is important to eliminate such confusions before appealing to Decision-Theoretic hypotheses about existence in later chapters.) R. S. Heimbeck in *Theology and Meaning* (London 1969) tries centrally to show three things. These things tend to run counter to what Malcolm wants to say about the cognitive status of "God Exists". Nevertheless Heimbeck tends to renew and reinforce Malcolm's venture in irresponsibility about reference while arguing for the three.

The first is that a broad Judaeo-Christain tradition employs what he calls G$_2$-statements, like *God is one but yet three, God exists necessarily* – statements that are cognitively meaningful although they do not have any "empirical entailments, incompatibles" (p. 172). The second is that the tradition employs G$_1$-statements like God *raised Jesus of Nazareth from the dead near Jerusalem at t_2* which (a) are cognitively meaningful anyway, but also (b) have logical relations with checkable empirical statements and further, (c) have "only empirical evidence as their primary data" (p. 172). Third, he wants to show how to "reverse" what he considers a prevailing, wrong-headed tendency of philosophers to concentrate on "the super-structure" of G$_2$-statements, when G$_1$-statements both *are* empirically checkable, and are *"the foundation"* (p. 175) of this traditional theism.

If the crucial reasoning of Heimbeck's pp. 177-84 were cogent, the author would perhaps be in fair shape to further all three aims – but he seems here just to beg too many questions. Let us try to speak in Heimbeck's dialect of Strawsonese and employ some of the assumptions which go with adopting such jargon. Despite Heimbeck's occasional absentmindedness, the assumptions dictate that to know whether the sentence "God raised Jesus, etc." can be consistently used by the traditional theist to make statements with empirical entailments and incompatibles involves *inter alia* knowing whether the traditional theist consistently means anything cognitively significant in using the allegedly intelligible sentence "God exists". If not, he cannot genuinely presuppose with full cognitive decency either *that God exists* or the truth of *"God exists"*. But to understand whether this allegedly intelligible sentence and genuine presupposition really are intelligible and genuine, when interpreted as part of much traditional theism, is to understand already the semantic status of a 'core' of much used declarative God-sentences. (In more Russellian terms, to know whether a theist's use of "God-RAISED-Jesus" makes sense requires knowing whether the theist's essential Divine-property-predications, supposedly revealing the meaning of "God" in "$(\exists x)(D_1x...D_nx\&x$-RAISED-Jesus)", really make sense.) Now this body of sentences seems essentially for Heimbeck – to judge by his wholesome citings of Creeds and Scriptures – to include many G$_2$-sentences like "God is one, yet three". If we already allow that all or most of these do make sense, then we may, may, be able to allow too that the sentence "God raised Jesus, etc." can be used to make a G_1-statement that has empirical entailments and incompatibles. We may, may, likewise be able to say with Heimbeck that "God" can be immediately prefaced before "raised Jesus, etc." to form an intelligible sentence for use in making a genuine (cognitively meaningful) English statement whereas "Downward" and "the round-square cupola" cannot be prefaced to that end (p. 180). But Heimbeck in pages 177-84 tends simply to insist over and over that "God", unlike "Downward", etc., is an expression of the right 'category' or the right ('logical') 'type'. On this showing, at least, it seems that Flew and others attacked would turn out to be especially wise to emphasize G_2-statements, if we accept Heimbeck's own quasi-Strawsonian standpoint and clarify some of what it involves. Heimbeck might reply that he had earlier shown (pp. 69–76) that *in principle* G_2-sentences CAN be used to make cognitively significant G_2-statements since the latter "have entailments and incompatibles, reflecting their truth-and-falsity conditions" (p. 76). But despite his disclaimers of desire to utilize mere syntax, his cavalier confidence in theism's G_1-cognitivity suggests there that he is bewitched by the facts like this: from the 'surface-grammatical' sentence (possibly unknown as to meaning or even meaningfulness) "Godot exists" we can syntactically construct the contradictory-looking sentence "Godot does not exist", the entailed-looking 'Godot exists or Churchill exists'. (Compare J. Kellenberger on the pitfalls of attacking people like Flew with purely "*syntactical denials*": *Religious Studies* 5 (1969) 70–71.) Both Heimbeck and Malcolm need to take a fresh look at Frege and even Carnap: too often it is philosophically fruitless as well as a trifle unseemly to rob Herr Bedeutung to pay Frau Sinn and vice versa, to overdo devotion to Syntax or Pragmatics in sinning against Semantics.

(PROTEST II) In passage [B] Malcolm weakens the Judaeo-Christian case for the appropriateness of men's having agapeïstic affective attitudes towards God and His creatures by stressing exclusively His properties *qua* powerful being as almighty Creator and Judge, not His properties *qua* lovable being who is good for man. (It is one thing to be a judge, quite another thing to be a righteous and understanding judge. Again it is one thing to have the *power* to *relieve* men of a sense of infinite guilt. It is quite another thing to have the *right* and *moral authority* to *forgive* them for their sins.) God's Expo-relevance to man becomes too much like Big Brother's relevance to Winston Smith.[8] As we saw with Sartre, a man's acceptance of certain Judaeo-Christian beliefs about God, which only attribute to Him existence and power, is quite compatible with his showing a rational indifference and an understandable lack of affective attitudes towards God. As we saw with [A], "Anselm's Ontological Arguments" seems most felicitously construed as endorsing the same conclusion.

(PROTEST III) Malcolm apparently fails to see believers' relatively detached work in natural theology concerning God's existence as the natural outcome of a theist's way of life when surrounded by unbelievers or by rival theists (like Medieval Muslims) who threaten his particular theistic way of life. For some excellent remarks by a passionate theist on misunderstandings of natural theology, on its possibility and use-fulness for theists, we commend Peter Geach's "On Worshipping the Right God" in his recent book *God and the Soul* (London 1969), especially his words at pp. 113–14.

But Geach himself seems to wobble confusingly in the most exciting chapter of this book, "The Moral Law and the Word of God". He first writes very plausibly:

For obviously a revelation from a deity whose 'goodness' did not include any objection to lying would be worthless; and indeed so far from getting our knowledge that lying is bad from revelation, we may use this knowledge to test alleged revelations (pp.119–20).

This passage, in effect, asserts our ability to have sound moral beliefs without Revelation and our ability to judge on moral grounds whether any being, however powerful, should be revered as God. And this entails that Expo-statements without Gooper-statements cannot add up to expressions of a worthwhile theism. But Geach goes on to write:

I shall be told by [some modern] philosophers that since I am saying not: It is your supreme moral duty to obey God, but simply: It is insane to set about defying an Almighty God, my attitude is plain power-worship. So it is: but it is worship of the Supreme Power, and a such is wholly different from ... a cringing attitude to [limited, dependent] earthly powers (p. 127).

The latter passage reads like the expression of a Voluntaristic form of attitudes to God and values, strongly attacked by many theists as heretical and – more important for philosophical purposes – ably criticized by some sceptics as incoherent.[9] To avoid the charge of incoherence Geach need only return to his earlier point and remember to stress all along *both* sides of a theist's coin. Accordingly he might say something like this: "Suppose someone seeks happiness and cares for human fulfilment, as a rational person does. Suppose he believes that a God exists Who is all-powerful *and* Who satisfies our moral intuitions, including those concerning perfection in a person and a Creator. Then he would indeed be insane, given his beliefs, to set about systematically defying an Almighty God!"

II. THE TWO SIDES AND THE PROSLOGION

'Ontological' arguments for God's existence tend to be used to infer the Extension of 'Expo'-predicates from the Intension of 'Gooper'-predicates. In recent years much interest has been aroused by the idea of reading or rereading some passages early in St. Anselm's *Proslogion* as constituting steps for some valid modal argument or modal arguments to the conclusion that God necessarily exists. Shortly after Malcolm's popularization of this idea first appeared in 1960 Gareth Matthews offered important textual evidence that Malcolm's distinction between *Proslogion* II's and *Proslogion* III's 'arguments' was based on very dubious Latin scholarship. Recently and very forcefully Craig R. Harrison has argued that, if one judges modal 'proofs' like those of Malcolm, F. B. Fitch and Charles Hartshorne on their own logical merits (in the light of modern Possible Worlds Semantics), one finds striking causes for doubting the worth of pursuing such 'proofs'. Among them one may mention the likelihood that Lesniewski's criteria for acceptable definitions (non-creativity and eliminability) are indeed rational criteria – yet they seem to *need* to be violated by such 'proofs'; the likelihood that a definition of "God" which allows one to derive the theorem "God exists" from previously unyielding axioms is a definition which violates a rational criterion for a non-creativity criterion; also the likelihood that somewhere behind the symbolic maze there seem to be interpreters bent on confusing epistemic and ontological senses of "possibility", "necessity", etc. To these doubts we add that of Quine which Harrison like Hartshorne and Fitch (and Malcolm perhaps by implication), rejects. The doubt presents the question: What real and clearly intelligible domains can the honest interpreter yet feel sure in saying that 'consistent' and 'complete' modal calculi are reliably *true OF?*

But lack of trust in modal logic, at least as derived from the tradition of C. I. Lewis, need not forbid one to treat existence as a predicate. One can

so treat it in a way that enables one to use Quantification Theory as a tool
for assessing Aquinas' attack on Anselm's most obvious move from
'Gooper'-Sinn to 'Expo'-Bedeutung. Indeed we do not need more than
First Order Predicate Calculus with Identity to reinforce Aquinas' insights. [For those who wish still to rake over the modern modal approaches
we can especially commend as *optimists'* contributions: Norman Malcolm, 'Anselm's Ontological Arguments', *The Philosophical Review* **69**
(1960), 41–61; Charles Hartshorne, *The Logic of Perfection*, La Salle, Ill.
1962, *passim* – especially p. 51; Frederick B. Fitch, 'The Perfection of
Perfection', *The Monist* **47** (1963), 466–71. Useful pessimistic contributions include the numerous replies to Malcolm, to which the January issue
of *The Philosophical Review* **70** (1961), 1ff. is devoted – see especially G. B.
Matthews, 'On Conceivability in Anselm and Matthews'; M. J. Kitely,
'Existence and the Ontological Argument', *Philosophy and Phenomenological Research* **19** (1958), 533–35; Alvin Plantinga, *God and Other
Minds*, Ithaca, N. Y. 1967, pp. 26–94; Craig R. Harrison, 'The Ontological Argument in Modal Logic', *The Monist* **54** (1970), 302–13. For an
admirable account of Lesniewski's contribution to illuminating the concept of rationality by clarifying the criteria of a proper definition see
Patrick Suppes, *Introduction to Logic*, New Jersey, 1957, pp. 155–56.]

Hans Reichenbach in his *Elements of Symbolic Logic* (New York 1947,
pp. 333–34) declared that treating existence as a predicate showed why
the Ontological Argument was fallacious. Existence can be made part of
the definition of any individual whether it be a deity or a sea-serpent. But
the *biconditional* form of all correctly proposed definitions prevents any
unmediated inference from the definition of an individual to its existence,
whatever properties are postulated by the definition. More recently this
view has been revived by G. Nahnikian and W. C. Salmon with special
reference to Anselm, yet their formulation scarcely seems to do justice to
the subtle implications of Anselm's Latin text – let alone to offer an adequate refutation. In the interests of fairness not fantasy, we would like to
suppose that Anselm and Aquinas, doubtless from the realms of the Bless-
ed, have acquired some basic resources of modern formal logic. How
would they set out their original differences with such resources? Consider
a Celestial Dialogue.

ANSELM: Hither, Tom, for the machinations of modern logicians amuse
me much, albeit they treat me ill. Look yonder where two of those Amer-

icani claim to show that existence *is* a predicate, a *tautological* predicate, for all their mischievious friends have said from Kant to Ayer.[10] And, what is more, they hold that by introducing existence as a predicate into their symbolism they may best disprove my Ontological Argument whereby Faith seeking Understanding is uplifted to contemplate the Divine.[11] Admitting the formula "*Ex*" as a legitimate predication of existence they write of my argument:

To say that the concept of the greatest possible being involves "exists" means that having the property of being the greatest possible being implies having the property of existing – this would seem to be a reasonable rendering of the thesis that God's essence implies His existence. But we had no need of the Ontological Argument to prove this point. This is merely an instance of the analytic formula "If anything is a greatest possible being it exists". Letting "*Gx*" mean "*x* is a god", we may formulate the conclusion to this form of the argument as follows:

(i) $(x)(Gx \supset Ex)$.

But the fool who says in his heart "there is no God" is not involved in a contradiction for he does not assert:

(ii) $-(x)(Gx \supset Ex)$.

Rather he holds:

(iii) $(x)(Gx \supset -Ex)$.

Formulas (i) and (iii) are not contradictories....The treatment of "exists" as a predicate does not therefore render the Ontological Argument valid. If anything it helps to clarify the invalidity of the argument.

AQUINAS: This seems at least to be an excellent answer to the form of proof given in Descartes' *Fifth Meditation* and in the *Ethics* of the most heretical Spinoza. For the (i) and (iii) above are but contraries, which only lead to thy desired contradiction and *reductio* if it be already established that the subject class is non-empty. The direct appeal to 'real definitions' in those two Rationalists seems well covered by the symbolism proposed.

ANSELM: Yet, thus these Americani reduce the necessity of God's existence, which is apparent to us (as I demonstrate in my *Proslogion*, Chapters II to IV), from the very concept we have of Him, to a mere "for all *x*, *x* is God implies *x* exists." That is, to a mere admission that God, by

definition, must exist if He does exist. Yet although they mention me by
name they would seem, both from the brevity and haste of their symbolic
argument and from their use of a single "E" symbol to denote existence as
a predicate, more fairly to be tilting with some *infima species* of neo-
Spinozist who failed to elaborate my argument properly. I hold that if the
modern logician will but allow me to introduce, besides the concept of a
"maximum cogitabile" or greatest thinkable entity, *separate* predicates of
existence in reality (*esse in re*), and of existence in the mind (*esse in intellectu*), into their *Principia* notation, then the argument of my chapters can
be seen to withstand both their attacks and thy charge that I make an
unfair transition from thought to fact.[12]

Let me proceed to the proof using symbols that fairly reflect the significance and complexity of my original Latin argument, seemingly ignored
by these *Americani*. "Let Cx" mean "*x cogitari potest*", "*x* can be conceived"; "*Px*" mean "*x est homo*", "*x* is a man"; "*Kxy*" mean "*x cogitare
y potest*", "*x* can conceive *y*"; "*Gxy*" mean "*x est maior quam y*", "*x* is
greater than *y*"; "*Rx*" mean "*x est in re*", "*x* exists in reality"; "*Ix*" mean
"*x est in intellectu*", "*x* exists in the mind". Now my first three premises
are obvious enough once we stipulate that the use of the existential opera-
tor does not by itself commit us to "*esse in re*":

I $(\exists x)[Cx.(y)((Py.Ry) \supset Kyx) \cdot (z)((Cz.z \neq x) \supset Gxz)]$.   *Potest
aliquid cogitari ab omnibus quo maius cogitari non potest.* All
men can conceive something greater than which nothing can
be conceived. (Compare my *Proslogion*, Chapter II, lines 6–9.
[13])

II $(x)[(Px.Rx) \supset (\exists y)(Kxy.Ry)]$. *Omnes possunt cogitare aliquid
quod est in re.* All men can conceive something which exists
in reality. (Enthymematically omitted in my text.)

III $(x)(y)[((Cx.Ix.Rx).(Cy.Iy. - Ry)) \supset Gxy]$. *Si quid potest cogitari
quod est in re et in intellectu, maius est quam quod est in solo
intellectu.* Whatever can be conceived that is both in the mind
and in reality is greater than what is only in the mind. (Compare
my Ch. II, lines 18–23.)

Now from premises II and III we may derive:

IV $(x)[(Cx.(y)(Cy.y \neq x) \supset Gxy)) \supset (Ix.Rx.)]$. *Si quid est quo maius cogitari non potest, dein est non solum in intellectu verum etiam in re.* If there is anything than which nothing greater can be conceived, then it must exist both in the intellect and in reality. (See Ch. II, lines 23–25.)

From IV and I we may further derive:

V $(\exists x)\,[Cx.(y)((Py.Ry) \supset Kxy).(z)((Cz.z \neq x)) \supset Gxz).Rx]$.   *Est aliquid quod ab omnibus cogitari potest et quo maius cogitari non potest et hoc est in re.* There is something all can conceive greater than all else conceivable, and that does exist in reality. (See Ch. II, lines 23–25.)

Since at Chapter IV, line 16, I point to the obvious definition of God as the greatest conceivable being we must of needs conclude from Step V that there really is a God. I shall be interested to hear if thou findest at any stage that my arguments do not follow: surely the concession of these *Americani* that existence is a predicate, *if reinterpreted in two existence symbols*, is all that I need to make my argument clear and conclusive.

AQUINAS: Before I proceed to the refutation let me preface a valid derivation of the Ontological Argument in a sibling of the notation which thou hast cunningly proposed. For thy five steps constitute but a spectre of a tolerable proof. Five premises will be needed which are as follows. (By no means all of them are made explicit in thy Proslogion, but I shall try to indicate where thou appearest to subscribe to them.) First there are people (see thy Ch. II, lines 8–9).) Second, if there are people, they can conceive something greater than which they can conceive nothing else (Ch. II, lines 8–9). Third, if there are people something can be conceived by them which exists both in the intellect and in reality (Ch. II, lines 13–15, 23–25). Fourth, if the greatest thing which can be conceived by people did not exist both in the intellect and in reality then (forsooth *per impossible*!) nothing which can be conceived by people would exist in reality as well as in the intellect (Ch. II, lines 18–20). Fifth, there exists a God in reality if and only if there exists in reality something greater than which nothing can be conceived (Ch. IV, lines 1–16). *AMEN.* Now let us use again "*Rx*" to mean "*x* exists in reality" and "*Ix*" to mean "*x* exists in the intellect". Also let us use "*Px*" to mean "*x* is a person"; "*Cx*" to mean "*x* can be conceived by people"; "*Sx*" to mean "*x* is the greatest possible entity conceivable by people". Now there is a clear and formally rigorous proof of the argument from the syntactical standpoint of deductive validity.

From our first premise we have:

(1) $(\exists x)(Px.Rx)$, *i. e., there exists in reality at least one person.*

By our second premise:

(2) $(\exists x)(Px.Rx) \supset (\exists y)(Cy.Sy)$, *i. e., if there exists at least one person in reality, then there is (at least in thought) a greatest possible entity conceivable by people.*

But (1) and (2) yield by *modus ponens*:

(3) $(\exists y)(Cy.Sy)$, *i. e.,* the apodosis above.

Now take the third premise:

(4) $(\exists x)(Px.Rx) \supset (\exists y)(Cy.Ry.Iy)$, *i. e., if there is at least one person, then there is at least one individual conceivable by a person which exists both in mind and reality.*

But (1) and (4) yield by *modus ponens* the apodosis of this proposition:

(5) $(\exists y)(Cy.Ry.Iy)$.

Now take our fourth premise:

(6) $(\exists x)(Cx.Sx. - Rx) \supset -(\exists y)(Cy.Ry.Iy)$, *i. e., if there is an individual such that it is the greatest conceivable by people yet does not exist in reality, then it is not the case that there is an individual conceivable by people which exists both in mind and reality.*

But (5) and (6) yield by *modus tollens*:

(7) $-(\exists x)(Cx.Sx. - Rx)$, *i.e.,* the denial of the protasis in (6).

This is equivalent to:

(8) $(y) - (Cy.Sy. - Ry)$.

This again is equivalent to:

(9) $(y)((Cy.Sy.) \supset Ry)$: whatever is a greatest conceivable individual exists in reality.

Now by *Universal Instantiation* we have in the temporary libertinage of an Open Sentence:

(10) $(Cy.Sy) \supset Ry$.

And similarly by *Existential Instantiation* on (3) we have.

(11) $Cy.Sy$.

But (10) and (11) yield by *modus ponens*:

(12) Ry.

Hence we have by conjunction of (11) and (12):

(13) $Cy.Sy.Ry$.

From there we derive by *Existential Generalization*:

(14) $(\exists x)(Cx.Sx.Rx)$: *there exists in reality that individual than which none greater can be conceived.*

Quod erat demonstrandum! For by our fifth premise such an individual would be God.

Before I proceed to the refutation let me preface two further remarks.

ANSELM: "Proceed to the refutation"? But, good friend, it seemed from thy truly angelic proof that thou had received the Divine Illumination.

AQUINAS: Await these remarks, for illumination is indeed to be ours in this matter. In prime, because many commentators concentrate on the versions in Spinoza and Descartes (or in Kant's critique thereof) they often overlook the great ingenuity and complexity of the Ontological Argument as variously framed in thy *Proslogion*, Chapter II to IV. And second, it is more idle to dispute whether existence is a predicate in the abstract than to calculate the number of angels on a pin – we must relate the query to the role of "existence' in a specific corpus of metaphysical belief instead of prejudging metaphysical beliefs about existence by some imposing but nonsensically abstract, ('absolute'?, 'meta-philosophical'?) answer to the query. If one accepts Plato's Divided Line or my doctrine of *Analogia Entis*, then it does not seem to me helpful to call such hierarchically *categorized* existence no true predicate or even a merely tautological predicate ... in fact the strict analytic-synthetic distinction often presupposed by the use of "tautological" seems out of place in such metaphysical language games, (as it often is at a more mundane level).

The trouble with symbolizing arguments of any complexity, especially if their validity turns on the meaning of possibly ambiguous words or phrases, is that either side is likely to feel in the event of defeat that the symbolism could not have been fair. Wherefore I often favour, tactically speaking, the followers of THE Philosopher, Aristotle, and of The Second Philosophers, Wittgenstein and Austin, more than those of symbolic reduction. However, I shall use the tactics of both, dear friend, in order to show thee the philosophical, (though not the devotional) unserviceability of the *Proslogion* II type of argument. Thy chief aim seems to be to involve in a contradiction those who deny that God exists. Why I mistrust thy symbolism is because thou seemst in thy chapters to equivocate with quite alternative *criteria* for one thing being graded as *maius* or greater than another. Thou sayest at Chapter II, line 18ff: "*et certe id quo maius cogitari nequit non potest esse in intellectu solo. Si enim vel in solo intellectu est, potest cogitari esse et in re: quod maius est*". Or, *lingua Americana loqui*: "and assuredly that than which nought greater can be conceived cannot be in the intellect alone. For if it is in the intellect alone it can be conceived to exist also in reality which is greater." But there is in sentences about others' beliefs and in the Oratio Obliqua of Golden Latin concerning someone else's thoughts a considerable difference between "*Petrus cogitat aliquid esse in re*" ("Peter thinks that something exists in reality"), and "*Petrus cogitat aliquid quod est in re*" ("Peter thinks [of] something that exists in reality"). Such locomotion of this Anglo-Saxon "that" must be noted well on pain of promiscuity. Yet the needed distinction thou hidest from thyself (despite thy precaution about painters' images in Chapter II), by virtue of the possible *performative* functions of "*cogito*", "I conceive", "I think" in thy First Person present indicative. For in the use of the sentence "*Cogito aliquid esse in re*" the Oratio Obliqua infinitive clause plus the main verb often serves not just to 'avow' mental operations but to *vouch for* the Oratio Recta sentence "*x* est in re". Since in this context "*Cogito*" unlike the Third Person "*Cogitat*" involves expression of *prima facie* commitment to the verb's object as existent, it usually makes scant sense for me to say "*Cogito aliquid esse in re et non est*", "I think there's an *x* and there ain't"), but very good sense for me to say "*Petrus cogitat aliquid esse in re et non est*". Sometimes you seem to imply that once the Fool allows that he too (among *all men*) can conceive of a greatest conceivable being and that such a being must contain the property of existence in its conception then he is forced into a "*cogito*" judgment which admits God's existence – but this would only serve to foist on the Fool a spurious entailment relation between "*Cogito*"-uses of disparate logical types ("*Cogito*"-uses as performatory and "*Cogito*"-uses for mental description.) However, the trouble goes relatedly deeper than that. Thy criterion of greatness in the passage I quoted at II, 18 is beguilingly ambiguous: thy words suggest both the sense of "great" whereby thy premise III is true in the proof you sketched and the very different sense of "great" whereby thy premise I is true. There is quite a locomotion *in intellectu* between "*x* is thought of and *x* exists" as thy criterion is elsewhere and the less presumptuous "*x* is thought of and *x* is thought to exist". The implicit confusion of Oratio Recta and Oratio Obliqua serves to hide this further equivocation in the chapters.

To make this clear let us take a universe of discourse consisting of one green field, one tree, one man and one winged giant – a being of far greater size than the field and of far greater beauty, wisdom and moral excellence than the man. Now by thy varying sets of criteria for "greatness" the man should agree the greatest thing he can conceive is: (1) the giant, because of his superlative qualities and because he can be conceived and because he exists; or (2) the giant again because of his qualities and because he can be conceived, and because unlike round squares he can be conceived to exist and because he exists; or (3) God (an omniscient, omnipotent, morally perfect, unbounded being), because the qualities involved in His conception transcend all other conceivable qualities, because He can be conceived and because (although actually He does not exist) He can be conceived to exist.

Now let us take thy first premise:

I $(\exists x)[Cx.(y)((Py.Ry) \supset Kyx).(z)((Cz.z \neq x) \supset Gxz)]$. "All men can conceive something greater than which nothing can be conceived."

In this universe of discourse if "greatest conceivable thing" is referred to criteria sets (1) or (2) then the relevant *x* is the giant. If (3) is the desiderated set then *x* is God although God exists not at all. (Unless we want to say over theologians' protesting cadavers that by definition the giant is what is meant by "God", since the giant is unsurpassed in our universe.) However if there were TWO giants of equal size, worth and so on in our universe (two distinct *maxima cogitabilia*), your first premise by reference to sets (1) and (2) will not hold as it posits *uniqueness*. In any universe of discourse the concept of God is *maximum* by (3) but it is not *maximum* by (1) and (2) unless it happens to be a universe of discourse which includes God. And it is precisely the nature and content of our universe which must be determined before we can expect the Fool, let alone a follower of Solomon or the Stagirite, to accept thy first premise and thy third premise (that "being greatest" implies "existence"), when they are so conjoined. Hence the valid derivation I wrought for you rests likewise on a *petitio principii*, the conjunction of my second and fourth premises.

I therefore conclude with you, good Anselm, that the Americani were in error to suppose that one existential predicate is adequate to represent, and so to refute thy *Proslogion* proof. But I hope to have reinforced their point that treating existence as a predicate and even as a perfection helps us best to discover where thou didst stumble. As thou knowest now so well from thy posthumous perusal of my *Summa Theologica* I, Q. I, Art. I, many a proposition like "God exists"[14] or "There is an x such that $P_1 x$, $P_2 x \ldots P_n x$" may be Self-Evident-in-Itself (i. e., indubitably known for the perfectly unclouded mind). Yet what is *PER SE NOTUM SECUNDUM SE*, Self-Evident-in-Itself, need not be *PER SE NOTUM QUOAD NOS*, Self-Evident-for-US, when the extension of "NOS" in a use happens to a group of earth-bound minds, an *US* which is very cloudy indeed about what counts most in the end. Come, dear friend, for those who still see through a glass darkly there are more things in Heaven and Earth than can be derived from any new-fangled notation.

NOTES

[1] For examples of faith in the endless variety of such enlightening things, see John 21:25; Pseudo-Dionysius, *The Divine Names*, Chapters 2, 4 and 13, and *Mystical Theology*, Chapters 2 and 3; John Scotus Eriugena, *De Divisione Naturae*, Book I, pp. 11–15 and 69–72.

[2] The above are the dates of the original French publications. The translations we shall refer to by page numbers are: *Being and Nothingness* (trans. Hazel E. Barnes), New York 1956, hereafter *BN*; *Existentialism is a Humanism* (trans. Philip Mairet), London 1948; *What is Literature?* (trans. Bernard Frechtman), New York 1949; *The Flies* (trans. Stuart Gilbert), London 1946.

[3] John Pico, 'Oration on the Dignity of Man', in *The Renaissance Philosophy of Man* (ed. by E. Cassirer, P. O. Kristeller, and J. M. Randall Jr.), Chicago 1948.

[4] If God is a material being, then He is not a pure *pour-soi*, and thus Sartre's argument

against the impossibility of creation collapses. Cf. *BN*, pp. 79, 620, 623; and Gabriel Marcel, *Homo Viator*, New York 1962, pp. 180–81.

[5] For example, *Existentialism is a Humanism*, pp. 33, 40, 51–52, on co-operation, p. 36 on a Kantian Kingdom of Ends; *What is Literature?*, pp. 52, 117, 196 on honesty, pp. 41, 46, 50–51, 105 for Sartre's anti-racism and anti-nationalism and tolerance. Cf. Gabriel Marcel, *The Philosophy of Existentialism*, New York 1963, pp. 86–87; Robert G. Olson, *An Introduction to Existentialism*, New York 1962, pp. 17–19, 25–27 and 170; Mary Warnock, *The Philosophy of Sartre*, London 1965, pp. 131, 177–81.

[6] See our Chapter I 'Faith – and Faith in Hypotheses'. Cf. R. C. Coburn, 'A Neglected Use of Theological Language', in D. M. High (ed.) *New Essays in Religious Language*, Oxford and New York 1969, pp. 215–35.

[7] Cf. Zeno Vendler, *Linguistics in Philosophy*, Ithaca, N. Y. 1967, expecially Ch. III, 'Singular Terms', pp. 33–69; P. F. Strawson, 'On Referring', *Mind*, New Series **70** (1950), 320–44; B. A. W. Russell, 'On Denoting', *Mind*, New Series **14** (1905), 479–93.

[8] Taking up the distinction which Martin Buber and others have drawn between an 'I/Thou' relationship and an 'I/It' relationship, we suggest that the theist for whom God is truly a 'Thou' must have both Expo-beliefs *and* Gooper-beliefs. Pure Expo-beliefs with respect to a cosmically powerful It (or impersonal force) make affective attitudes of fear and awe very understandable. So do pure Expo-beliefs about a cosmically powerful Him (a Him of Deism of Voluntarism). Only Expo-beliefs that are crucially linked with Gooper-beliefs make the full range of affective attitudes involved in Buber's 'I/Thou' relationship appropriate. It would appear that without Gooper-beliefs a purported 'I/Thou' relationship would be too much like love of 'the almighty leader' (idolatry). The description elsewhere of Wittgenstein's sad thoughts of God as a dreadful judge suggests a gross imbalance of Expo-thoughts over Gooper-thoughts in Wittgenstein's philosophical and religious diet – G. H. Von Wright, 'Biographical Sketch', p. 20: "The thought of God, he [Wittgenstein] said, was above all for him the thought of the fearful judge. ... His outlook was typically one of gloom. ... His idea of the helplessness of human beings was not unlike certain doctrines of predestination" – Reproduced in Malcolm's *L. Wittgenstein, A Memoir*, Oxford, London and New York 1962. On the matter of relieving men's sense of infinite guilt see Malcolm's closing paragraphs of 'Anselm's Ontological Arguments'.

[9] Cf. C. B. Martin's 'The Perfect Good' in A. G. N. Flew and Alasdair MacIntyre (eds.), *New Essays in Philosophical Theology*, London 1955; also numerous replies in the literature to T. P. Brown's 'Religious Morality' *Mind*, New Series **77** (1963).

[10] See G. Nahnikian and W. C. Salmon, '"Exists" as Predicate', *Philosophical Review* **66** (1957), especially pp. 540–42. We quote from those pages.

[11] Cf. *Proslogion* I.

[12] See Aquinas, *Summa Theologica* I, Q. II, Art. I, Reply to Second Objection: "Nor can it be argued that this exists in reality, unless it be granted that there does exist in reality something than which nothing greater can be thought: those who deny that God exists do not grant that."

[13] Line references are given as in Haas' Tübingen Latin text of *Opuscula Anselmi*, I.

[14] See *Summa Contra Gentiles* I, Chapters 10 and 11 for the point that "God" is not even *thought* to mean by everyone what Anselm claims everyone must take "God" to mean – "God" may be taken by some as a flattering synonym for "The universe".

CHAPTER III

MIRACLES: NOWELL-SMITH'S ANALYSIS AND TILLICH'S PHENOMENOLOGY

I. THE MATTER BRISKLY INTRODUCED

The concept of a *justifying explanation* may be usefully employed in pointing towards at least two salutary explications for the still vexed notion of a *Miracle*. In at least two ways, a person can take something to be miraculous, and can reasonably take it to be so. Either he can if he reasonably takes it to be a sign that there *is* some (perhaps still hidden, but real) justifying explanation of the world and human history. Or he can if he reasonably takes it to be a sign that some *particular* religious, metaphysical or broadly ideological position supplies the wisest form of justifying explanation for a limited and fallible, but rational mind like his own. What does "reasonably takes" signify? If he takes it to be a miracle *reasonably* then he must meet most of the criteria for reasonableness that were discussed in Chapter I.

To say that one reasonably (*qua* someone just interested in the truth of the matter) takes the overhanging presence of black clouds to be a good reason for believing that it will soon rain is not quite to say: One reasonably (*qua* truth-seeker) takes their presence to be going to be followed by rain because one is aware that very, very frequently such black clouds have been followed by rain and few, if any, counter-instances are known. The notion of a truth-seeker *qua* truth-seeker's reasonably taking P to be a good reason for believing that Q is, one might crudely say, to be construed *generically*, not *specifically* and *gerundively*, not *psychologically*: there are, one might crudely say, inductive sorts of cases of good reasons for being justified in drawing a conclusion, deductive sorts of cases, *and other sorts*. And there seems to be very good reason – in the light of well-known work by John Wisdom, H. L. A. Hart, N. R. Hanson, F. Waismann, Stephen Toulmin and others, AND in the light of Wittgenstein's work on Family Resemblances, AND in the light of *some* exposedly futilitarian Naturalistic Fallacies about "GOOD", etc., etc. – to suppose that one can *not* spell out any specific number of clearcut classes into which all the good reasons of a reasonable truth-seeker *qua* reasonable truth-seeker for believing something must always fall. Let us say then that for such a truth-seeker the set of sorts of reasonable believings (or of reasonable warrants for holding) that *P* is a good reason for concluding that *Q* (or that very likely *Q*) is open-ended. It is as open-ended a set as is the set of sorts of reasonable *'becauses'* for concluding that *A* is (or very likely is) a good work of Art, or for concluding that such-and-such is in violation of a complicated piece of criminal law with many relevant precedents, or that so-and-so had good intentions, or that this unfailing assumption of previous scientists for centuries concerning the earth's core is now properly ripe for serious doubt, is now more wisely to be questioned than the alleged data that allegedly do not fit the assumption. We cited W. V. Quine in Chapter I as endorsing *pragmatic* adjustments of the latter sort in the name of rationality and we have, not surprisingly, heard Quine say in person that his life's purpose has been to get at *truth*: we say thus that the sorts of reasons for finally committing oneself in science to such pragmatic adjustments for getting at the truth can be called both *truth-seeker's* reasons and *pragmatic* reasons, at least if it is allowed that they form an *open-ended* family. "Good [truth-seeking] reasons" is a term that can be usefully treated as univocal in Sense and heterogeneous in Reference.

In this chapter we shall turn back to some noted discussions of the concept of *Miracles* by Patrick Nowell-Smith and Paul Tillich, relating them to positions in Hume and Aquinas. These discussions appeared about twenty years ago and we do not wish to seem to slight such later writers as R. F. Holland (see note 34), Alastair McKinnon, Richard Swinburne and others who have toiled interestingly enough at the subject of this concept. Indeed we commend the interested reader to Swinburne's own Bibliography at p. 75 of his recent work *The Concept of Miracle* (London and New York 1970). But we still believe that the discussions by Nowell-Smith and Tillich can be best used to take us to the heart of the matter. And it is a matter on which we find ourselves, by contrast with the previous discussions, in considerable *dis*agreement with Aquinas. Saint Thomas as a wise man and a realist wished to come to terms with what seemed the most plausible approach to science in his own time: the approach of Aristotelian Physics. Indeed Aquinas, who chose to join what was then an unfashionable Teaching Order, risked being banned from teaching altogether by insisting that the newly available writings of the pagan genius Aristotle be considered and judged on their own merits. Like many *sensible* and *courageous* religious believers (including John Locke and Immanuel Kant) who have wished to be honest about the claims on Reason of Physical Science, Aquinas tended to confuse the importance of Physics as such with the validity of a particular systematic account of Physics which would later be outdated. We suppose that in criticising the influence of Aristotle and Aquinas here on modern debates about the concepts of *Miracles* and *The Supernatural* we are working in the Angelic Doctor's own pioneering spirit.

II. THE MATTER REINTRODUCED

What makes arguments about the *miraculous* so elusive is that the meaning of the term is elusive. Giving him a Moorean twist, we can imagine the plain religious man as saying: "Of course I believe in miracles, but I am at a loss to give a satisfactory analysis of my belief." For a well-rounded education leaves us familiar with reports like these: a Galilean carpenter brought the almost putrid corpse of a man called Lazarus back to life and soundness of limb; thirty hired assassins fell dead on catching sight of the Buddha; there was an unprecedented rise in monstrous births before Julius Caesar's death; a sufferer pronounced incurable returned in perfect health from Mecca (Lourdes, Benares); prostitutes who talked briefly to Mr. Gladstone often changed their lives to meet Victorian society's strictest demands. The question "Is this one likely to be true?" might draw for these cases an ascending number of affirmatives. Now there is also the question: "If this one were true, would you call it the report of a miracle?" That question might call forth in each case a proportionately diminishing assent. But to ask "Why?" and "What exactly would it mean to call it a miracle?" might be to court a ghastly silence.

There is indeed an attractive account of miracles, which gained considerable support in the Middle Ages and remains influential. But against this medieval view Patrick Nowell-Smith has so sharpened the objections of Hume that we must probably look elsewhere for an account, or abandon miracles altogether. Nowell-Smith's analysis might lead one to answer to our second question: "Unlike Hume on the possibility of Queen Bess's resurrection, I am quite prepared to believe all five reports – if, that is, a fair number of reliable-sounding witnesses confirmed them. But no hypothetical event, however surprising and however well-confirmed, would I call a miracle. The very notion is self-defeating. In no possible worlds could there be Nothings to noth or miracles to miraculate."

Yet, if Nowell-Smith's analysis of the long favoured account seems all but devastating, it may also be an inadequate analysis – *of miracles*! Nor does it license the immediate conclusion that no satisfactory concept can be found, for theologians Catholic and Protestant may in some cases turn out to have gone profitably beyond the medieval tradition. We begin by reviewing Hume and Nowell-Smith in Parts 1 and 2 of the next section; in Part 3 we examine some possible criteria for a satisfactory account of the miraculous. In Part 4 we try to relate these criteria to a striking account of miracles by Paul Tillich, an account based on what he calls a phenomenological approach to the problem of meanings in theology. Finally we attempt to go beyond Tillich's contribution and show that the theist's belief in miracles should be, in at least one important way, acceptable to all reasonable men.

II.1. *Hume's Critique*

Hume's main objections to what was the current conception of the miraculous were partly logical and partly an empirical blend of the psychological and the historical.[1] If one can penetrate Hume's irony they seem to include these: (1) The basis of rational inference from experience is belief in natural laws or regularities. But a miracle must, by definition, *violate* and not merely expand our understanding of natural laws. The occurrence of miracles is therefore contrary to all rational inference. (2) The principle behind (1) can be reformulated even more damagingly. The probability that numerous and careful witnesses could be wrong may sometimes be very low; whereas the probability of what is by definition totally improbable is always nil. Therefore it is always rational to reject an account of the miraculous, whoever the witnesses. (For all non-negative n, $[n \neq 0] \supset [n > 0]$.) (3) Moreover the probability of the witnesses' being untrustworthy is here quite overwhelmingly high anyway. For it is almost always ignorant and savage people who do claim *direct* knowledge of miracles. (4) If, *per impossible*, the world's store of miracle tales were acceptable to reason and each report bore the construction its reporter intended, this would be as grave an embarrassment to Christianity as to other competing religions.

It may be at least partly as a result of Hume's criticisms and ironical conclusion, that miracles were a glorious province for unaided Faith, that radical changes took place in many Christian circles. A Protestant historian, discussing Hume at the turn of our century, comments:

Few who now affirm miracles view them as the Eighteenth Century did, as the prime proofs of Christianity. Rather the revelation is regarded as carrying faith in the miracles far more than their lending support to it.[2]

Father J. Hardon, in an essay on the development of Roman Catholic thinking on miracles, suggests that ever since the pronouncements of Benedict XIV in the 1760's serious questions have arisen among sensitive Catholics concerning the range of 'natural laws' and the criteria for establishing a miraculous transcendence of such laws. Benedict's stress on "*the religious purpose of miracles*" was, according to Hardon, followed by an increasing return of apologists to "the full concept of miracle as a divine sign, so frequently stressed in the Scriptures and used by the Fathers, but obscured in the Middle Ages".[3] It was, as we shall soon see, partly disguised versions of the medieval or Neo-Aristotelian view of miracles, held by so many Protestants and Catholics in the 18th century, which drew Hume's and Nowell-Smith's fire.

There are certain weaknesses in Hume's argument which deserve to be noted.[4] In fact, noting these will serve to bring out the importance and far greater adequacy of Nowell-Smith's attacks on a not too untypically 'modern' exponent of the medieval view.

(a) It must be recognized that physics, the queen of the natural sciences, has undergone a considerable transformation since Newton inspired a good deal of the thought in Locke, Hume, and Kant. When modern physics was just born and diverted philosophers from other paradigms of Reason; when noble principles led one to dream that the physicist's data always seemed to present unfailing regularities of the form "Whenever A, B, C ...N, then always Z" at both macroscopic and microscopic levels, it was indeed natural for a philosopher to make inference from careful observations *on the assumption of infallibly repeated patterns* the paradigm or standard case of rational inductive inference. Even so, it would be reasonable a while after the miraculous birth to ask whether the most frequent pattern of inductive inference in physics should be considered the paradigm for *all* non-deductive reasoning fit to be called rational. Moreover, with the development of certain branches of modern physics in terms of statistical probabilities it is no longer the case that "Whenever A, B, C ...N, then always Z" is quite such a revered paradigm for physicists. Curiously enough, this development both weakens Hume's first and second objections *and* also undermines the beliefs about miracles of his and Nowell-Smith's most obvious opponents.[5]

(b) Hume gives no satisfactory criterion of what would expand and what would actually violate our understanding of regularity and natural laws. Too liberal a criterion in favour of expansion could easily lead to 'superstition' and utter irrationality. But too rigid a criterion against expansion – and it is extreme rigour which Hume's stand against the possibility of the first Queen Elizabeth's resurrection seems to endorse – might have forced scientists to reject the evidence of some of those startling experiments which transformed physics and psychology in the last hundred years.

(c) Hume does not make clear how large a sample would be needed to establish that a given occurrence or sequence is regular or irregular. Hence Mary Boole, wife of the great British contributor to modern logic, replied to Hume that an irregularity relative to the limited sample of our experiences might really be a regularity relative to a vastly larger sample. Thus events 'miraculous' to us would be part of an unthinkably large and complex creation. Mrs. Boole's criticism would be fairly congenial to Moses Maimonides, the medieval Jewish philosopher, who like Aquinas was greatly influenced by Aristotle but who remained more of a traditionalist about miracles. In his *Guide for the Perplexed* (II, xxix), Maimonides holds that miracles do not deviate from the natural structure of the cosmos but were built into that structure when God created it. Unlike Aquinas at his most Neo-Aristotelian, but like many ancient and modern theologians, he was careful to stress that their usual significance *qua* miracles lay in their *sign* character in conjunction with prophecy and faith. Mrs. Boole's criticism of Hume is also an interesting ancestor of Nelson Goodman's Neo-Humean 'New Riddle of Induction' with which he has aroused British and American philosophers. Mrs. Boole was much influenced by a pioneer in computing science, Charles Babbage, who offered a fascinating mathematical attack on Hume in *The Ninth Bridgewater Treatise* (London 1837, Chapter X and XI).

We do not wish to suggest that these three points remove the full sting from Hume's attack on miracles. For the very weaknesses they expose in

Hume expose correlative weaknesses in the Neo-Aristotelian medieval concept itself and show that he was partly on the right track. At any rate Hume was attacking a concept greatly strengthened in medieval Christendom by the success of Aristotelian Physics and cosmology on the one hand and of Aquinas' closely related metaphysics and theology on the other. In an early work Aquinas gave the following account of miracles:

There are three characteristics of a miracle; first, that it is above the power of natural forces; second, that it is beyond the natural disposition of the subject; third, that it is beside the normal course of events.[6]

He gives a more developed account in *Summa Contra Gentiles* (II, 101):

[1] Things that are at times divinely accomplished, apart from the generally established order in things, are customarily called *miracles*; for we *admire* with some astonishment a certain event when we observe the effect but we do not know its cause. And since one and the same cause is at times known to some people and unknown to others, the result is that, of several who see an effect at the same time, some are moved to admiring astonishment, while others are not. For instance the astronomer is not astonished when he sees an eclipse of the sun, for he knows the cause, but the person who is ignorant of this science must be amazed, for he does not know it. And so, a certain event is wondrous to one person, but not so to another. Now absolutely speaking the cause hidden from every man is God. In fact we proved before that no man in the present state of life can grasp his essence intellectually. Therefore, those things must be called miraculous which are done by the divine power apart from the order generally followed in things.

[2] Now there are various degrees and orders of these miracles. Indeed the highest rank among miracles is held by those events in which something is done by God which nature could never do. For example, that two bodies should be coincident; that the sun reverse its course or stand still; that the sea open up and provide a way through which people may pass. And even among these an order may be observed. For the greater the things that God does are, and the more they are removed from the capacity of nature, the greater the miracle. Thus, it is more miraculous for the sun to reverse its course than for the sea to be divided.

[3] Then the second degree among miracles is held by those events in which God does something which nature can do, but not in this order. It is a work of nature for an animal to see, live and walk; but for it to live after death, to see after becoming blind, to walk after paralysis of the limbs, this nature cannot effect. But God at times does such works miraculously. ...

[4] Now the third degree of miracles occurs when God does what is usually done by the working of nature, but without the operation of the principles of nature. For example, a person could be cured of a fever by divine power although it could be cured naturally. Likewise it may rain independently of the working of nature's principles.

We quote this chapter in full because its opening remarks contain the seeds of what we shall later call the *psychological* and the *gerundive* criteria for an acceptable concept of miracles. It would appear that Aquinas was

and must answer in the negative the momentous question "whether all phenomena recorded and witnessed by man are due to purely natural causes, such as the actions of the human will or physical causes". Moreover, it is on the authority of the scientists themselves "that we declare that a particular phenomenon is inexplicable as the effect of natural agents and must therefore be ascribed to supernatural agents".[12]

Nowell-Smith begins by mildly touching on Hume's objection (4), that too many miracles spoil the dogmatist's broth. He follows this with a comment on the conjunction of Lunn's (a) and (d), that miracle is so *defined* in (a) that (d) is not a compatible assertion. For if miracles are by definition what defy scientific explanation, then the scientist *qua* scientist has no hypothesis about them to offer. Nowell-Smith next waives most of Hume's main objections and supposes "that extraordinary phenomena occur". However, to accept the evidence for extraordinary phenomena is not to accept a claim for miracles. Lunn has simply defined his theological principle of explanation right into the description of extraordinary events. He challenges his opponents to be empirically open-minded about the evidence for extraordinary events while demanding by definition that they should not be open-minded about rival explanations of the extraordinary.

Nowell-Smith then develops at length a near *coup de grace* to the whole Thomistic tradition on this point. Scientific explanation is not contradicted by extraordinary events because science is not rigidly tied to unchanging laws and concepts. Scientific hypotheses are frequently falsified and thus restricted, revised, or discarded. But if this is so, then no such falsification can *per se* lead to the conclusion that the realm of the Natural is clearly shattered and here we know the supernatural to be at work. Nowell-Smith tacks on two more questionable assertions: that the very meaning of "supernatural" in such an alleged explanation is unfathomable; that, whereas Lunn uses "supernatural" in a verbally vacuous way, genuine explanations must have serious predictive fertility. The latter point is open to the answer, from a philosopher of science like Stephen Toulmin, that it is by no means self-evident that all scientific theories have to be predictively fertile to be scientific, some may simply *explain*. *Explanation* is perhaps a notion not reducible to that of *prediction* (and *retrodiction*) – perhaps not even in physical science, let alone in history.

More misleading is Nowell-Smith's suggestion that Lunn's way of explaining is incomprehensible. Lunn's supernaturalist way is quite comprehensible within the framework of certain presuppositions, all historically famous but all of which may be highly contestable today. Unless we elucidate these presuppositions to make "supernatural explanation" intelligible we shall miss seeing the real basis of the conception of miracles held by people like Lunn, and miss grasping just how out of date and question-begging such a conception is. These presuppositions belong partly to Aristotelian Physics and partly to a dogmatic brand of monotheism. Aristotle provided, and the medievals possibly debased, the notion that the cosmos, which is limited and geocentric, consists of certain substances; that the scientist after a period of acquaintance with various types of things comes to know by ἐπαγωγή (a combined induction – *cum* – intuition of essence) the laws of their *essential behaviour*. Compare (Neo-Aristotelian) medieval talk of abstracting from the *sensible species*. In the superlunary realm of ἀεὶ ἐνεργοῦντα ("absolute regularities") this essential behavior is perfectly regular. In the sublunary realm of τὰ ὡς ἐπὶ τὸ πολύ ("the for the most part things") there may be slight fluctuations and the choices of human agents are not determined. But even here fire nearly always burns, stones nearly always fall in air, men are mortal and once buried always remain dead. Science will yield some knowledge of essential laws throughout almost every corner of nature. A scientific programme would prescribe a certain amount of observation and ἐπαγωγή to fix the laws of some realms once and for all; then the really substantial part of science could begin, i. e., massive deduction. Such deductive programmes were envisioned for science long after My Lord Bacon.[13]

Now tack on to such a picture of the material world an unquestioning belief in a particular set of non-material individuals, interested in the world. Waiving a distinction sometimes drawn between supernatural and preternatural, let us set out certain presuppositions:

(1) There exist the following non-material individuals: God (Supreme Being and maker of all), benevolent angels and malevolent devils, human souls (attached to sensible bodies); all these are hidden from man's senses.

(2) There exist material things open to the senses which almost always function in fixed ways according to essence unless non-material beings intervene.

(3) Man can grasp the essences of material things through science, but not the essences of non-material things; for science (in the sense of physical science) rests on epagogic abstraction from sense experience.

(4) The behaviour of material things can always be explained *naturally* by (E^1), known laws pertaining to their known essences or by (E^2), reference

to the free wills of incarnate human souls; or *supernaturally* by (E^3), reference to the wills of non-material beings not attached to any corporal bodies.

(5) The laws of (E^1) are fixed and known, the limits of human will power are fairly well determined for settling the scope of (E^2). Therefore whenever an event defies explanation by (E^1) and (E^2), which is sometimes patently clear, we must invoke (E^3).

(6) Depending on the seriousness and desirability of cases only explicable under (E^3), we should refer them, first, directly to God in His love or wrath; second, to God through the mediation of angels; third, to the mischief of devils.

(7) To a limited extent Revelation gives us knowledge of God, angels, and devils.

Here we have a fairly full list of the presuppositions or kinds of presuppositions which make Lunn's Neo-Thomist and not uncommon view intelligible. The supernatural is the realm of essentially unobservable non-material beings, which epagogic science by definition cannot study; miracles are those events in the material world which science cannot explain by reference to the known range of essential behavior or to the known range of essential powers of freely choosing human agents; miracles are therefore those events which the scientist must admit to belong outside his sphere as due to supernatural intervention; since we know by Revelation who the supernatural beings are, we know Whom to bless and Whom (or whom) to fear when miracles occur; 'miracle'-explanations have a sort of conditional predictive fertility: if we can know about supernatural beings to some extent by Revelation, then we can make some correct predictions both about events in the material world that will follow the occurrence of miracles and as to where miracles may be expected to occur again. Moreover, we have paradigm cases of explanations, as explanations are in many contexts more normally understood, in that supernatural explanations refer to the *intentions* of personal agents in saying "why" something happened.

In the context of all these presuppositions Nowell-Smith might be judged unfair in his concluding remarks. He holds that, if Lunn's 'supernatural' yields any sort of genuine explanation,

[it] will be nothing but a new field for scientific inquiry, a field as different from physics as physics is from psychology, but not differing in principle or requiring any nonscientific method. The supernatural is either so different from the natural that we are

unable to investigate it at all or it is not. If it is not, then it can hardly have the momentous significance that Mr. Lunn claims for it; and if it is it cannot be invoked as an explanation of the unusual.[14]

These words are misleading because in this context the dogmatic religious believer, relying on Revelation, understandably feels that he can usefully fashion at least some sorts of predictive hypotheses on the basis of 'miraculous' explanations. "If such and such a miracle occurs, I / will prosper if I continue in my present form of behaviour, / will find peace of mind if I follow this man who heals the sick, / will come to greater grief unless I have the priest perform an exorcism, / and so on." Moreover, the dogmatic believer likewise can believe that although the Supernatural explanation has predictive fertility, this does not entail therefore that the supernatural can itself be an object of scientific enquiry. For scientific enquiry is bound to premises derived from sense experience as explained in the presupposition.

None of this vindicates Lunn, however. For of all the presuppositions only (2) is the slightest bit in accord with the *modern* scientific methods which Lunn specifically claims and admits he needs as a support. Even (2) refers to a long outdated essentialism in science and to a view of concept formation (*nihil in intellectu nisi prius in sensu*), severely put to question by Wittgenstein, Frege, Geach (see Geach's *Mental Acts*, London 1957), and many others. Moreover the non-scientific, or *supernatural*, tenets are by no means held by all people normally called religious, nor even by all religious people who believe that in some sense there are miracles. One is reminded here of Santayana's point against the pragmatic argument for Christian theism (sometimes called *Pascal's Wager*). It is not as if fantastic events, were we convinced they do occur, would confront us with a clear choice between The Faith and denying true religion. There are so many religions whose claims could be related to the event by their supporters. Lunn can only relate them to the intervention of a personal and all-powerful God interested in the world because he *already* accepts a particular Revelation that espouses one. Within a framework of beliefs fantastic events may psychologically strengthen Faith. But that is very different from logically strengthening the claims of the framework. This indicates that if "miracle" is to be given an acceptable meaning, we must move away from the interpretation that treats them as *proofs* of a system for someone outside the system.

II.3. *Possible Criteria for Miracles*

Modern science acknowledges no fixed, unrevisable laws of nature, for
the 'miraculous' to contradict. Even if there were such laws, why would
the occurrence of alleged 'miracles' prove the truth of any one religion
rather than another? Granting the wrongheadedness here of the Thomistic
tradition, we may proceed to ask whether a more promising account can
be found. Well, promising *for what*? The account we need is one that will
allow the speaker to speak in a way he feels appropriate to certain events
his faith or ideology proclaims, but without his being thereby committed
to misinterpretations of science, or to faulty logic and insufferable
dogmatism.

This leads to a question which such a person can only ask himself:
"Would a psychological interpretation be appropriate?" Call this question *P*. Suppose the answer to *P* for the speaker is "Yes", that is, in the
strong sense that purely psychological terms are both necessary and sufficient for explicating miracles. (In future we shall say that a "Yes" to *P*
means only that psychological descriptions are necessary for explicating
the miraculous.) Then he could be taken as saying something like this:
"The events which I call 'miracles' are those the observation, or memory,
or hearing of which evokes in me feelings of deep wonder, awe, and
reverence. Compare *miraculum* from *mirari*, 'to wonder'. A good criterion
of a man's particular religious outlook or ideology would be the
supposed events, if any, toward which he has these 'miracle'-feelings.
Quite possibly a man of a certain religious desposition could have such
feelings about practically everything in his experience. I do not wish to go
beyond the psychological and claim that because I have a 'miracle'-feeling
about *X*, therefore *X* has some objective significance which any rational
being should recognize."

An affirmative answer to *P* yields a sense of "miracle" with which
Hume and Nowell-Smith do not quarrel. Aristotle speaks of philosophy
as beginning in wonder: whatever their views of the Homeric pantheon,
some Milesian philosopher-scientists seem to have been religious in
having such miracle-feelings about the very existence of the world.

Another very different question, which we shall call *G*, may be raised
about the appropriateness for a religious person of any miracle concept.
And here again he must answer for himself. *G*: "Must the 'miraculous' be

explained largely in *gerundive* terms?" Those who answer "Yes" to *G*
might comment somewhat like this: "An event may be miraculous whether
I have eyes to see and ears to hear or not. It is only miraculous if it *ought*
to inspire in me the deep feelings of awe and wonder mentioned in the
psychological account. Again an event which inspires such feelings in me
need not be miraculous at all – I may be deceived by a charlatan, by
drugged senses, by mass hysteria, by a false report, by superstition, and so
on. It is this gerundive sort of point that Aquinas was getting at when he
said that the astronomers will not wonder at eclipses as will the ignoramus.
The very meaning of *religion* and *ideals* is debased by turning a basic
religious and ideological concept into one of purely psychological description."

Compare some words of Rudolf Otto on a not unrelated concept:

The "holy" will then be recognized as that which *commands* our respect, as that whose
real value is to be *acknowledged inwardly*. ... *"Tu solus sanctus"* ... recognises and
extols a value, precious beyond all conceiving.[15]

Now consider the following gerundive terms, most of which occur in
Otto and in the Greek and Latin versions of the Bible: *mirandum,
mysterium, tremendum, sanctum, augustum*, σεμνόν, θαυμαστόν,
σεβαστόν. *Miraculum* and θαῦμα (wonder) look like words of the gerundive family; just so *mirari* and θαυμάζειν (to wonder) seem usually to be
quite different words of psychological description and, in some first
person present uses, psychological expression.

Others may be satisfied with a compromise "Yes" to both *P* and *G*;
a miracle is then to be construed as that which is worthy of awe and which
believers do often find a source of excitement to wonder and reverence.
This compromise does not rule out the possibility that some miraculous
events sometimes fail to excite the wonder due or that sometimes one has
'miracle'-feelings which are not appropriate. But the compromise does
entail that when the believer says "That was a miracle" he is at most
times both evaluating the wonder-worthiness of the event and bespeaking
his own feelings of awe.

Two other questions or complexes of criterion-questions should next be
raised concerning the appropriateness of a miracle concept for our
speaker, at least if he believes in or has some degree of curiosity about a
personal deity or deities.[16] And in answering "Yes" to these two the
believer may expose himself to controversy of the kind which Nowell-

Smith indicates. Whether he *must* so expose himself is a main issue to settle. As our P stood for "psychological" and our G for "gerundive", so let E stand for "extraordinary" and S for "sign." We can note in advance that "extraordinary" and "sign" may themselves turn out to be terms open to psychological and gerundive as well as other less obvious interpretations. E: "Is it not necessary that 'miraculous' be an *extraordinary* description? That is, must not the events we call 'miraculous' be comparatively few and rare?" One who says "Yes" to E might justify his verdict like this: "I agree with those who find it worthy of wonder that anything should exist or happen at all. Everything is miraculous, [wonderworthy] if you like to use the word that way. But we seem to need it to describe events which inspire in us and are worthy of a very special degree of wonder and awe. We need it, that is, if we do believe that there are such events. Just so, it may be that everything in existence is beautiful – worthy of, and capable of eliciting, aesthetic enjoyment and praise. But, even if we admit this, we need to have 'beautiful' or some other word in reserve to describe a superlative sunset, the best work of Bach and Dylan Thomas, and so on."

The Extraordinary Criterion can be combined with the Psychological and Gerundive Criteria to create a concept of the miraculous acceptable for a wide range of religious and ideological attitudes – though not as wide as was served by the pairing of the latter two alone. Thus the Extraordinary Criterion will still suit many anti-theological creeds. 'Humanists,' 'Naturalists,' and other untitled devotees of physical science and despisers of 'supernatural' explanations for anything, may all subscribe to the miraculousness, or special aweworthiness, of a restricted class of extraordinary events without violating their principles.[17] Alongside "miraculous" it is worth placing two similarly gerundive and selective terms: "heroic" and "saintly". Any creed may have its saints and heroes: John Stuart Mill, for example, has been hailed by some secular liberals as a 'saint of atheism'; Bernard Mayo's *Ethics and the Modern Life* gives a secular moralist's views of saints and heroes; Camus' *The Plague* has been thought to portray two types of sanctity, that of the irreligious being every bit as wonderworthy as that of the religious; hordes of dedicated dialectical materialists file past Lenin's tomb in Moscow every year to pay their *homage*, and not a few bring the wreaths of *rededication* and *reverence* to Marx's grave in London. The saints and heroes of a creed are those whose occasional deeds, or whose very lives, are *miraculous* in our present sense by the standards of the creed. If it is objected that the terms "miraculous" and "saintly" must be given 'supernatural' associations, we reply that no such *must* is called for, at least at this stage of the conceptual game. On the contrary, it is worth suggesting for purposes of conceptual analysis that supporters and opponents of the 'supernatural' may often share various evaluative and reverential attitudes much more closely than either side cares to admit. That they direct these attitudes to different sorts of presumed 'objects' is here beside the point.

S: "Is it not necessary that a fully fledged candidate for the title of 'miracle' be not merely a special and wondrous event but also deserve to be taken as some sort of *sign*?" There are at least three types of affirmative answer to this criterial question which deserve our consideration. We leave a host of analogous possibilities to the reader to imagine for himself."

Answer S[1]: "Yes, to be a miracle an event must be worth labelling '*Sign!*', but in a limited sense out of those possible for this rather ambiguous word. It must, to be a miracle, meet what one may call the Indefinite Sign Criterion. It must offer a *good reason*, an extraordinarily good reason, for undertaking a radical examination and possibly a reorganization of one's whole world view and conceptual scheme. To be a miracle an event need not offer a good reason for accepting any definite creed. But it must present a remarkable challenge to that sloth and complacency into which the preoccupied human mind ever tends to lapse."

Answer S[2]: "Yes, to be a miracle an event must be a sign. And it must be one in a stronger sense than is required by the Indefinite Sign Criterion. Someone who held to this 'Indefinite' requirement could say that the circumstances of the lives of Buddha, Christ, and Mahomet, the art of Cézanne, the deliverance of the Jews from Egypt, the success of the Russian Revolution, and the historical vision of Marx are all miraculous. In his eyes all deserve to challenge the adequacy of our conceptual scheme very deeply, but none need point to any definite set of beliefs able to resolve the strains of the challenge. I say that a full-blown miracle must offer a shockingly good reason either for adopting some definite creed to which we are already to some extent inclined, or for retaining more passionately a creed we already hold. Whether that creed be Scientific Humanism, Fundamentalism, Marxism, Buddhism, or what you will, is not important. At least it must be something definite. Let me call this the Definite Sign Criterion."

Answer S[3]: "Yes, to be a miracle an event must be a sign. And to be a miracle in the fullest sense it must be a sign in a stronger sense even than is required by the Definite Sign Criterion. A miracle must offer a good reason for believing in the love, wrath, or malevolence of a definite, personal individual or individuals, not occupying space corporeally or doomed to die, capable of making or blighting our whole universe. Unless there are events which offer good reasons for believing in these, at least to those disposed to believe in them, there are no miracles. A good reason is not a logically necessary demonstration, but that does not prevent its being a good reason. As a Christian, for example, I feel entitled to believe in miracles. For it seems to me very probable that at least some of the reports in the New Testament are true. It is also probable in my view that enough of those reports *are* true, whose truth would offer good reasons for my believing in the *divinity* of Jesus. In the New Testament Greek a frequent word for the type of event sometimes described in English as 'miracle' was σημεῖον (*sign*). Jesus told those who pestered him for miracles that it was a wicked generation that demanded a sign. It was not, I like to think as a Christian, that He objected to a man's asking for reasons for taking his words seriously. He was exasperated rather by the sort of things which they considered would be good reasons for taking His words seriously. They were much more interested to find reasons in His playing the magician or the fairy godmother, than in His personality, in the wonderful intensity, ethical and aesthetic, of His utterances, or even in the possibility that His claims might prove on closer inspection to be consonant with the prophecies of the Scriptures they professed to honor.

"Even if it were granted that none of the astonishing physical feats ascribed to Jesus ever took place, one could still believe His life to have been charged with signs and miracles – charged, that, is with good reasons for accepting His claims to divinity. But if thoughtful Christians can believe this, equally thoughtful and intelligent Jews can and do reply that, alleged physical feats apart, they find nothing so special, new or wonder-worthy about Jesus' life and message – hence no good reason for questioning Judaism in favor of Christianity. For treating signs in terms of apparent good reasons, instead of indubitable *proofs*, puts a premium on tolerance and humility among holders of conflicting beliefs; it rules out claims to absolute certainty, however great the miracles we hail for our own faith. But only certainty and indubitable proofs could begin to justify a theist's very human desire to restrict or persecute those who speak for other religious or antireligious creeds. The abandonment of indubitable proofs for a more personalistic approach to religion, which relies tentatively on what appear to be good reasons to *me* in my present context as a man, deprives me as a Christian believer in miracles of any presumed right to ignore possible good reasons for rejecting Jesus' divinity later on. Nor may one ignore reasons for querying the authority of any group, Church, or Party claiming a unique position as interpreter of the miraculous. I am forced to recognize that what appear as good grounds to myself need not appear so to others of equal sincerity and intelligence, *and that the others may quite possibly be right.* At any rate I personally do believe that there are special events offering good reasons for belief in the agency of God and other unimaginably powerful non-material beings. You might call this a personalistic belief that there are events which meet a *Definite-Theological* Sign Criterion."

The difference between answers S^1, S^2, S^3 indicates a considerable ambiguity involved in the assertion that a miracle must be a sign. To call a miracle a sign is, then, not to say anything very clear until more is specified. "Good reason", like "worthy of wonder" and "extraordinary", is of course well worth calling an *evaluative* term here. This explains why someone who asserts that an event is a miracle is so likely to court opposition in a world where men differ profoundly in their values, and why the ensuing argument will be so hard to settle. Certain crucial value judgments, which a tolerant society leaves to the individual's discretion, are here at stake. Our search for necessary criteria has led us to some of the evaluative uses of language. This may foil any aspiration to prove to everyone that there really are miracles and that they include events A, B, and C. But at least it makes the *meaning* of the controversial terms a good deal clearer. Clarifying questions of meaning is a prime task of any philosophy worth the name. This is not, however, an excuse for resting on tin semantic laurels and stopping here. We must go on to put some meat on these conceptual bones. To do this we shall consider the account of miracles given by Paul Tillich in his *Systematic Theology*. This is an account which, as our earlier quotations indicated, is not so far out of sympathy with much Catholic and Jewish, as well as Protestant thinking on the question: Tillich tries to put into an 'existentialist' idiom the pre-medieval interpretation of miracles as signs.

In order to ease the transition to Tillich let us consider one further question. *D*: "Must not the term 'miracle' be restricted to those especially awe-inspiring events which are signs of the *divine* activity being revealed without the intermediation of any lesser spiritual agents?" Some of those theists who say "yes" to *D* might be expected to say: "Certain awe-inspiring events are the work of angels and devils. All these creatures depend for their agency, good or evil, on the ultimate agency of God. Certainly their acts are worthy of awe and even dread, but they cannot merit the wonder due to God's unmediated gestures to men. Perhaps the term 'miracles' should be reserved for such Divine activity, the term 'sorcery' given to the work of devils, and the term 'marvels' to the unusual ministrations of angels." Such an answer, hard as its specifications might be to work out in practice, would be fairly similar to Aquinas' suggestion that some miracles should be called *relative* and attributed partly to the intermediation of *preternatural* agents. It would also favour Benedict XIV's distinction between *major* and *minor* miracles.[18]

II.4. *Tillich's Phenomenology of Miracles*

Tillich works up to his account of miracles, first, with some remarks on the phenomenological approach to meanings in theology and then with some prior definitions. Speaking of Husserl's method in the *Ideas*, he says that the aim is

... to describe "meanings", disregarding, for the time being, the question of the reality to which they refer. The significance of this methodological approach lies in its demand that the meaning of a notion must be clarified and circumscribed before its validity can be determined. ... Theology must apply the phenomenological approach to all its basic concepts, forcing its critics first of all to see what the criticized concepts mean. ... The test of a phenomenological description is that the picture given by it is convincing ... that the description illuminates other related ideas and that it makes the reality which these ideas are meant to reflect understandable.[19]

Whether or not one agrees with Husserl on the nature of meanings, one can commend the phenomenological approach of Tillich's initial propositions: that before asking whether there are miracles we must be quite clear what we are asking; that in formulating our definition we must be sure it is serviceable to the type of theology we have in mind. In the sense indicated by these propositions it is essentially to begin treating miracles by invoking a Husserlian *epoché*. For Tillich, a serviceable account of *"miracle"* will involve reference to three other technical concepts, those of "revelation", "mystery", and "ecstasy". The form in which these three are expounded may seem somewhat dark and baffling after his campaign promises of rigorous explication. Indeed it shows why critics question his right to call himself a Christian theologian at all. (Should he not declare himself, they ask, the creator of a much less marketable Spinozistic pantheism with a strong twist of Heidegger and a dash of Christian symbols?)

A revelation is a special and extraordinary manifestation which removes the veil from something which is hidden in a special and extraordinary way. This hiddenness is often called *mystery*, a word which has a wider and a narrower sense. ... In the narrower sense ... it points to something which is essentially a mystery, something which could lose its very nature if it lost its mysterious character. ... Mystery characterizes a dimension which "precedes" the subject-object relationship. ... Whatever is essentially mysterious cannot lose its mysteriousness even when it is revealed.[20]

These assertions are clarified slightly, but still inadequately, by the following words:

Revelation is the manifestation of what concerns us ultimately. The mystery which is revealed is of ultimate concern to us because it is the ground of our Being. Revelation ... is invariably revelation for someone in a concrete situation of concern.[21]

Mystery and *ecstasy* are both terms which refer us to the grasp of reason's "ground and abyss", to the fact *preceding* reason that there is something and not nothing. Contrary to the view of the Reformation Enthusiasts, Tillich maintains that

Ecstasy is not a negation of reason; it is the state of mind in which reason is beyond itself, that is beyond its subject-object structure. ... "Ecstatic reason" remains reason; it does not receive anything irrational or antirational – which it could not do without selfdestruction – but it transcends the basic condition of finite rationality, the subject-object structure.[22]

Ecstasy is cognitive, not a merely subjective state of religious overexcitement: "Something happens objectively as well as subjectively in every genuine manifestation of the mystery." There is however an objectively based overexcitement which is not ecstasy. "Demonic possession destroys the ethical and logical principles of reason; divine ecstasy affirms them."[23]

Since miracles are going to be defined through these three terms, it becomes evident that Tillich's account will be very different from Lunn's. Tillich begins his section 'Revelation and Miracle' by rejecting the "ordinary definition" which refers to events contradicting the laws of nature. Rationalism, he complains, treated the negation of natural laws as the point of miracle stories. This gave rise to an anti-rationalistic rationalism "in which the degree of absurdity in a miracle story becomes the measure of its religious value". The more impossible, the more revelatory! [24]

A phenomenologically serviceable account of miracles, on the other hand, must not make the mystery of Being manifest in such a way as to "destroy the structure of Being in which it becomes manifest"; it must not offer man an ecstasy through the miraculous which would destroy the receiving mind's rational structure. Events which do exalt the irrational are "demonic" and to make God *interfere* with the rationality of natural processes would be to make him a self-defeating "sorcerer". Tillich therefore turns for illumination to the word σημεῖον (*sign*), frequently found in the New Testament Greek. To understand the religious meaning of miracles we should think of them as *sign-events*. "The original meaning of miracle, 'that which produces astonishment', is quite adequate for describing the 'giving side' of a revelatory experience." [25] Unfortunately the meaning became corrupted with talk of supernatural interference and this "bad connotation is avoided in the word 'sign' and the phrase 'sign-event'." [26]

After all these preliminaries we are now in a better position to make sense of Tillich's crowning account of the miraculous. We do not pretend to find it entirely clear, but we do find Tillich's phenomenological approach already more promising than that of Lunn and Aquinas. Let us quote the central passage:

A genuine miracle is first of all an event which is astonishing, unusual, shaking, without contradicting the rational structure of reality. In the second place, it is an event which points to the mystery of being, expressing its relation to us in a definite way. In the third place, it is an occurrence which is received as a sign-event in an ecstatic experience. Only if these three conditions are fulfilled can one speak of a genuine miracle. That which does not shake one by its astonishing character has no revelatory power. That which shakes one without pointing to the mystery of Being is not miracle but sorcery. That which is not received in ecstasy is a report about the belief in a miracle, not an actual miracle. This is emphasized in the synoptic records of the miracles of Jesus. Miracles are given only to those for whom they are sign-events, to those who receive them in faith. Jesus refuses to perform "objective" miracles. They are a contradiction in terms.[27]

Tillich concludes his section on 'Revelation and Miracle' with the claim that one can accept both revelation through miracles *and* scientific methods without qualms of conscience. Science is a useful ally to religion

against superstitious and demonic interpretations of revelation. These
spring from supranaturalistic distortions of the miraculous.

Scientific explanation and historical criticism protect revelation; they cannot dissolve
it, for revelation belongs to a dimension of reality for which scientific and historical
analysis are inadequate.[28]

II.5. *Comments on Tillich's Account*

Whether or not Tillich's work is to be construed as suitable for Judaeo-
Christian theology, he seems to be answering "Yes" to at least four of
the five questions posed in the last section. To say that X is a miracle is to
say something about one's own *psychological* states (P). "Miraculous"
must be restricted to a limited subset of events and not applied to all –
miracles must be special or *extraordinary* events (E). Miracles are *Sign*-
Events pointing to a momentous reality usually less manifest to us (S^3).
"Miracle" is a term properly applied only to a Sign-Event manifesting
the *Divine* activity (D). In important ways, too, Tillich has all but said
"Yes" to our question as to whether "miracle" is a gerundive term (G).
If miracles are said to have an "objective" as well as a "subjective"
aspect, if they are called manifestations of a hidden Ground of Being
which elevate our rationality, this is very much like saying that they are
worthy of praise, gratitude, awe, and so on. But if this gerundive conclusion is in keeping with what Tillich says here, it does not follow that
he is greatly clearer about the *evaluative* force of so much miracle-language
than were Aquinas, Lunn, and Nowell-Smith. Certainly Otto shows fuller
conceptual awareness than any of them in the remarks that we quoted
from *The Idea of the Holy*. Again, if the words *sign* and *extraordinary*
are themselves evaluative, then some further analysis is needed immediately, before we explain "miracle" in terms of them.[29]

   Another trouble with Tillich's account is that even a fairly sympathetic
reader is driven by the imprecisely defined but momentous-sounding ter-
minology to ask questions like these: "What is a miracle a sign of? Of
the personal, transcendent God of the Bible and the Koran? Of an impersonal, imminent One like the Hindu Brahman or like Spinoza's *Deus sive
Natura*?" Vague talk about the Ground of Being, about going beyond
the subject-object structure, about the objective element in ecstasy, and
such-like seem to bespeak an impersonal, immanentist sort of 'theology':
how are we to construe this as restating the substance of the Christian

message?[30] Is there any criterion of an apparently 'ecstatic' experience being genuine, i.e., being informed by an objective element? And how does this reference to an objective element fit talk of going beyond the subject-object structure? Again a sympathetic reader might wonder whether Tillich's talk of a rational structure of reality, which miracles do not defy, does not still involve some degree of confusion between the Aristotelian and the modern scientist's approach to laws (or a confusion of what Schlick distinguished as descriptive and prescriptive laws). It might be added that Tillich cannot really silence scientific naturalism simply by retracting theology's claim to contradict scientific expectations. That theological claims need not contradict scientific ones is no reason why theology should not be judged superfluous and no reason why the scientist should acknowledge another 'dimension of reality'.

Raising these complaints against Tillich's account of miracles should not preclude our paying tribute to his valuable advance on the answers of the Neo-Aristotelian tradition regarding the main problems. A conception of the miraculous begins to emerge from his words which may yet prove philosophically respectable.

II.6. *Towards a Philosophically Respectable Belief in Miracles*

We considered under *Answer S*[3] the view that miracles are signs of a *Divine* Agent. What, indeed, would a philosophically respectable belief in such miracles be like? It is natural to reply: *respectable* in *which* philosophical circles, do you mean? There is a type of liberal mind to be found among those who are avowedly 'religious' in views, yet slow to brandish 'proofs' or to make many theological assertions; or again among those who assert many theological doctrines to be true, yet confess themselves, like G. E. Moore on common sense's truisms, to be unsure what would be the correct analysis of these doctrines; or, still yet again, among those who incline to a Naturalistic view of the world, yet would not disvalue a fellow human being *a priori* as irrational simply because he believed in some Supreme Being or Beings, or even in souls and in survival after death. It is before the tribunal of people like these that we would plead the respectability of a "Good Reasons"-minded construction of the miraculous.

In her famous paper 'Natural Rights' Margaret MacDonald gave an empiricist's defence of statements like "all men are born free and equal".[31]

Such statements about human equality and dignity, she pointed out, might seem to flout the scientific temper of the age. For they are not universally acceptable definitions of "being a man"; nor do they look very promising as verifiable hypotheses to be subsumed under one of the special sciences. However, as value judgments about how all men *ought* to be looked upon and treated, they are perfectly intelligible. The political and legal value judgments of democracies cannot be *proven true* by pointing to facts, but they can be supported and defended. In political and aesthetic matters it is absurd to seek arguments of the scientific type, but quite rational to make moves of the jurisprudential and critical sort.

Miss MacDonald concludes with these words:

There are no certainties in the field of values. For there are no true and false beliefs about values, but only better or worse decisions and choices. And to encourage the better decisions and choices we need to employ devices which are artistic rather than scientific. ... The result of a confusion of logical types is to leave the field of nonscientific persuasion and conviction to propagandists of the type of the late Dr. Goebbels.[32]

Here we are at a loss: how can *no* statement of value be true when there can be truly said to be better choices and worse? She seems to be saying, in effect, that although value statements about the world are neither true nor false, value statements about value statements about the world do have truth values. Unless at some stage we allow cognitive, ontological content to value assertions, then Miss MacDonald's talk of "better choices" and her jurisprudential approach, expanded by Toulmin and others into a vast "field-dependent" programme of advocating relevant "good reasons", will lack the necessary basis of *authority* to give it point.[33] If we really mean that there *are* good, though non-deductive, moves to be made in their favor, then we must be committed to something more than psychological statements and emotive moves concerning the Good – or we have no business to be talking in this way. Nor have we any business, on any basis, to be talking as if the fact that we *do* use certain types of persuasion and not others in various areas of dispute entails that the kinds used are good ones, unless "good" merely signifies here "*good* according to current ways of talking." (See Chapters IV and V.) Possibly Miss MacDonald was influenced by what may be called a *Self-Defeating-Liberal Fallacy* about ethical cognitivism – cf. "cognoscere": "to KNOW". Ethical cognitivism is merely the position that many moral judgements are true and many false, thus are *in principle* know-ABLE to be such. The S-D-L (modal) Fallacist thinks that Liberals ought to reject dogmatic claims that we do know exactly what's wrong and right – hence one ought, knows one absolutely ought, to reject ethical cognitivism!

The realm of religion is very much the realm of Miss MacDonald's two favoured terms for politics and art criticism. We mean "*values*" and "*decisions*". Like politics or aesthetics, it is also a realm where we are forcibly reminded of the point that scientific and purely deductive reasons are not always the relevant kind. There is a *case for* abolishing the remnants of slavery, for emphasizing the good intentions of Richard III, for respecting Cubist painting, for introducing a more graduated income tax and for accepting the Gospel story of the Resurrection with all its religious implications. But no such case, of course, could be usefully expounded only in terms of rigorous deductive arguments, laboratory checks, and statistical probabilities. There may be a better *case against* one or more of these. But this too would have to be put to some extent in a non-deductive, non-statistical way! Nor would the *pro* and *con* be settled simply by adducing fresh 'observation statements'. At least, however, to say that there is a better case *pro* or *con* is to say that there are better reasons for deciding one way or the other. And talk of better reasons is gerundive talk. For our liberal tribunal, the evaluation of good and bad reasons is, within certain limits, a rational man's own business. Provided his preliminary thinking meets certain qualifications, then his evaluation of where the best reasons are is to be accepted as rational – even if his 'best reasons' favour a theology that most of the tribunal would reject.

To say of an event that it is *extra-ordinary* could be given a fairly descriptive meaning. To be *extra ordinem* is to be outside, beyond, or contrary to the previously observed pattern; with an Aristotelian view of natural laws, still more prevalent than one might suppose, it is easy to move further and say: the extraordinary is that which is *indubitably contrary to Nature*. Yet it is easy to avoid this trap and say gerundively: the extraordinary is that which merits our very special attention and awe in a way which the vast majority of events do not – in *this* sense it is *extra ordinem*, 'outside' the regularly observed pattern of wonderworthiness in the world. Here it might be objected that to call something extraordinary in this sense is also to call it *indubitably contrary to Nature*, since this idea of indubitable and Naturalistically intractable Nature-defiance would be the only ground for such special awe. Here it may be replied that many people have appeared to find events extraordinary although they had no such idea of indubitable Nature-defiance. (See our quotations from Strong in Part 1.)

To say of an event that it is a *sign-event* can be construed descriptively as meaning that the event is not in keeping with known essential regularities of nature; that its occurrence can be taken, in conjunction with other presuppositions, to demonstrate the intervention of specific supernatural powers. Or worse, and more typically, it can be construed this way without the half-saving clause "in conjunction with other presuppositions". But this sense, "event which definitively proves", is neither in keeping with the use of "sign" in English, nor of σημεῖον in *Koiné* Greek, nor of the three other main New Testament terms: τέρατα (*wonders*), δυνάμεις (*powers*), and ἔργα (*works*). Indeed, in the earlier technical, but influential, Greek of Aristotle σημεῖον is chosen with εἰκός (*the likely*), to be the technical opposite of a τεκμήριον or ἀπόδειξις (*rigorous deductive proof*). It seems much more reasonable then, to construe "sign-event" gerundively as "that which affords good reason for practising a way of life and religious behaviour in which one is already inclined to believe", or as "that which offers good reason to a truth seeker to opt for a particular Justifying Explanation".

Hume might reply, of course, that there could be no such good reasons since all rational inference is from like to like. The *necessity* of this judgment eludes us: in such cases it seems much safer to say that what are and are not good reasons is a matter for the individual to try to discover. (At least it is for him to try if he is reasonable by the criteria discussed in Chapter I.) "Miracle," we are suggesting, is usually to be explicated gerundively in terms of *being an extraordinary sign-event*. And gerundive decisions about miracles can be rational yet favourable to Justifying Explanations.

Let us try out this approach on examples and see if it appears plausible in such a test. The heroine in Graham Greene's novel *The End of the Affair* may be taken as claiming that the return of her lover from death was a miracle. In the context of a theology more flexible than Greene's, one could case her claim with pedantic clarity like this:

I had every good reason to believe that my lover was dead. Yet after I had prayed to

God and promised to give him up, if restored to life, I found him alive and well as you see him now. I regard this sequence of events as the best ground I know for acting on my belief that there is a God Who wishes me to go back to my husband and be faithful to him until I die.

A tribunal of the liberal minds that we have described would feel entitled to raise all sorts of questions. Is she sure she had good reason to believe the man dead? (Was she not too hysterical to tell?) Why is she so sure that there is good reason to link his surprising recovery with her prayer to God? (Perhaps he had already recovered before she prayed.) Even if her prayer was in some sense *answered*, does this signify that God wants her to give her lover up? Would God wish to restore him only to make them both desperately unhappy in separation? (If there is a God, must we assume that He forbids remarriage and prescribes complete faithfulness between married partners, however wretched the marriage?) Could it not be a sign, equally well, that God was restoring him to her love because she was willing to give him up? (Compare the story of Abraham and Isaac.) Could it not be the work of the Devil hoping to drive her to the worse sin of suicide?

The tribunal might scorn her talk of a miracle if she refused to consider any such questions seriously, or if she seemed so sick and distraught or so dogmatic a sectarian as to be unable to reason about such questions. But what if she seemed able both to feel very deeply moved and yet to be calm, critical, and dispassionate? What if she was willing to consider such questions carefully for a considerable time before making a final decision, and still she held in the end that she had good reasons for her beliefs?

Or take the case of Eclectic Edwin. Edwin is raised as an atheist with normal toilet training. He finds the absence of God as well confirmed by his college philosophy courses as by professionally expedient visits to church at Christmas and Easter. In order to be completely clear as to the falsehood of all major religions, he reads widely and finds his mind slowly changing. He concludes that there does seem to be some hidden Being responsible for the existence of the world. That to some extent personal predicates seem to be intelligibly attributable to this Being, whom it is convenient to call God. That in almost every age God seems to send witnesses to His existence; the witnesses often disagree as to the nature of God, but there is a hard core of ethical doctrine common to all of them.

That their lives are marked by *miraculous* doings – doings which, to those who already believe or who can feel curiosity about the belief that here is a representative of God, will represent new and extraordinarily good reasons for acting more confidently on the ethical teachings.[34]

Although they may dislike his conclusions, Edwin may conceivably strike our tribunal as a balanced, intelligent, and careful seeker after truth. He believes in the occurrence of certain alleged historical events on the evidence available and values these events as offering unusually good reasons for adopting a way of life different from his previous way. What is the tribunal to say? A tolerant philosophy like that of J. S. Mill, who rejected miracles, stipulates that a man must look at evidence *pro* and *con* as impartially as he can. He must make up his mind on the basis of what he takes to be the best possible reasons. He must be tentative about his conclusions and not seek to force them on others. (This kind of *faithful tentativeness* was discussed at Chapter I, Sections 10–12.) Edwin and our hypothetically amended Greene heroine fulfill these conditions. Thus their beliefs in the miraculous would seem to warrant the verdict from our tribunal that neither is necessarily correct, but both are philosophically respectable. Both are based on what, given the limitations of any human context, the agent has behaved rationally in taking to be good reasons. It is a sound axiom that, if people are tolerant, open-minded, willing to look at evidence and arguments, careful in examining them, mindful of the claims of intelligibility and overall consistency, then their personal evaluations – including those as to good and bad reasons in religious questions – are to be respected as rational. Concepts of *Miracles* worthy of the Judaeo-Christian *and* the liberal *and* the mystical tradition can retain an intellectually respectable place in the Life of Reason. They can retain it even in an age when Neo-Aristotelian physics and allied accounts of The Supernatural place a strain on our powers of historical imagination and sympathy.

NOTES

[1] *An Enquiry Concerning Human Understanding* (1748), Section X 'Of Minds'. See the 2nd edition by L. A. Selby-Bigge, Oxford 1902, pp. 109–31.

[2] W. Walker, *History of the Christian Church*, New York 1918, p. 491.

[3] 'The Concept of Miracle from Saint Augustine to Modern Apologetics', *Theological Studies* 15 (1954) 229–57. We do not wish to imply that Benedict XIV himself was influenced by Hume.

⁴ We are indebted to Dr. J. A. Robinson for comments on weaknesses in Hume's attack on miracles.

⁵ A very interesting exposition of why one very plausible interpretation of modern science undermines the latter belief is given by J. C. Carter, S. J., in 'The Recognition of Miracles', *Theological Studies* 20 (1959) 175–97. This article can be used as a helpful supplement to Nowell-Smith's earlier points about scientific laws and presumed violations of them. See also Friedrich Waismann's discussions of causality and modern science in *How I see Philosophy*, (edited after Waismann's death by R. Harré), New York and London 1968.

⁶ *Scriptum super Sententiis*, IV, d. 17, q. 1, a. 3.

⁷ Benedict XIV commented on Aquinas' distinctions: "But we for the sake of clarity prefer to say that major miracles exceed the whole forces of created nature and minor miracles exceed the power of corporeal and visible nature only." (Cf. Hardon, *op. cit.*, p. 234.)

⁸ *Summa Theologica*, I, q. 32, a. 1, ad 2m.

⁹ New York 1960, p. 94.

¹⁰ *Op. cit.*, p. 243.

¹¹ *Systematic Theology*, Philadelphia, American Baptist Publishing Company, 1907 (reprinted in London by Pickering and Inglis, 1956), Vol. I, pp. 117–19.

¹² *New Essays in Philosophical Theology* (ed. by A. G. N. Flew and A. C. MacIntyre), London 1955, pp. 244–45. Nowell-Smith's article first appeared in 1952 as a reply to Lunn's paper there of 1950. Both were in the now defunct Hibbert Journal. See Vols. 46 and 48.

¹³ Cf. Ralph M. Blake on Newton's critics in *Theories of Scientific Methods* (ed. by E. H. Madden *et al.*), Seattle 1960, pp. 121–22.

¹⁴ *New Essays in Philosophical Theology*, p. 253.

¹⁵ *The Idea of the Holy* (trans. by J. W. Harvey), Oxford 1923, pp. 66–67.

¹⁶ Ninian Smart's *Reasons and Faiths* (New York 1959) shows particularly well that "religious" and "believer in a deity or deities" are not synonymous descriptions. Cf. John King-Farlow, *Reason and Religion*, London 1969, Chapter II.

¹⁷ See for instance the more 'Naturalistic' contributions to A. P. Stiernotte's *Mysticism and the Modern Mind*, New York 1959.

¹⁸ Compare Father Hardon's article (note 3), pp. 232–35.

¹⁹ *Systematic Theology*, Vol. I, Chicago 1951, p. 106.

²⁰ *Ibid.*, pp. 108–09.

²¹ *Ibid.*, pp. 110–11.

²² *Ibid.*, p. 113.

²³ *Ibid.*, p. 114.

²⁴ *Ibid.*, p. 115.

²⁵ *Ibid.*

²⁶ *Ibid.*

²⁷ *Ibid.*, p. 117.

²⁸ *Ibid.*

²⁹ Cf. 'A revelation is a special and extraordinary manifestation' (*ibid.*, p. 168).

³⁰ Cf. *ibid.*, Vol. II, p. viii, where he replies to critics that his deviation from the Christian message is terminological, not substantive. Whether he is prescribing a non-traditional ontology or merely non-traditional 'symbols' is not a clear question until it is specified more clearly what sort of ontological commitments the traditional and the new 'existentialist' symbols carry. Tillich would, it appears, hold that the answers given

to *D* and to *S* (by *Answer S³*) take Christianity's traditional 'symbols', like angels, demons, and God the loving Father, much too literally and personalistically. Compare *Biblical Religion and the Search for Ultimate Reality*, Chicago 1955, pp. 23–26. He elsewhere speaks of "demonic" powers as really symbolizing "structures of evil" (*Systematic Theology*, Vol. II, p. 27) and as a "mythical expression of the self-destructive character of existential estrangement" (Vol. II, p. 172).

[31] *Proceedings of the Aristotelian Society* 47 (1946–47), 225–50.

[32] *Ibid.*, conclusion.

[33] This criticism of any Good Reasons programme which shies off objectivism is made with considerable force by E. M. Adams in his insightful book, *Ethical Naturalism and the Modern World View*, Chapel Hill, N. C. 1960, Ch. VI. This book deserves wider circulation among philosophers. (Cf. Tillich, *Systematic Theology*, Vol. I, pp. 19–20.) For the "field-dependent" programme of advocating relevant "good reasons" see S. E. Toulmin, *The Uses of Argument*, Cambridge, U. K., 1958.

[34] R. F. Holland takes a curiously related but quite unfortunately differing stand from ours in his influential essay 'The Miraculous', which is reprinted from *American Philosophical Quarterly* 2 (1965) at *Religion and Understanding* (ed. by D. Z. Phillips), Oxford 1967, pp. 155–70. He wisely stresses at first the importance of the individual's decision in interpreting a possibly miraculous event and of the conceptual or ideological background which the individual brings to such an event and decision (pp. 155–58). But he also strives to distinguish quite radically what he calls *the contingency concept of the miraculous* (p. 157) from what he calls *the violation concept* (p. 161). An account of how someone very surprisingly escaped death because of a most unusual but opportune concatenation of events that would not puzzle a scientist (*qua* scientist) illustrates the former. An account of how wine was found where there had been water, as in the Gospel description of the marriage at Cana, would illustrate the latter. Were we to witness the latter, Holland assures us, we would witness something both (a) *empirically certain* and (b) *conceptually impossible* (p. 167). He backs *this* assurance that Naturalist inquiry cannot always continue with pontifications like "Nor is it conceivable that there could have been a natural cause of it. For this would have had to be the natural cause of the water's becoming wine. And water's becoming wine is not the description of any conceivable natural process" (p. 168). This dogmatizing about what would *have* to defy science, thrown flat back in the face of Naturalists like Nowell-Smith, seems to be induced by (a) some curious 'criteriological' conservatism about how we could possibly go on identifying what we now CALL *wine*, *water*, etc. It is a kind of Neo-Wittgensteinian conservatism whose anti-scientific employment by Norman Malcolm against psychologists' empirical work on dreaming has, of course, been *devastatingly* criticized by Hilary Putnam–'Dreaming and "Depth Grammar"' in *Analytical Philosophy*, First Series (ed. by R. J. Butler), Oxford 1962; see especially Putnam on the (actual) past history of "acid" and the (possible) future history of "multiple sclerosis" at pp. 220–21. Putnam's remarks about such terms' ability to evolve in Sense while clearly retaining their main Reference apply beautifully to Holland on "water" and "wine". Holland's dogmatizing is also 'backed' by (b) his insistence on the unquestionable wisdom of his other radical distinction (reminiscent of G. E. Moore's way of giving a 'proof of an external world'), which is drawn inexorably "between a hypothesis and a fact" (p. 162). His way of drawing the distinction, it would appear, interestingly defies Lesniewski's *non-creativity* criterion for sound definitions. (See paragraphs 1 and 2 of our Chapter II, Section II.) It follows from Holland's way of drawing the distinction that sometimes one must *know* many facts about material objects and processes like snowflakes and snowstorms for *certain*

(pp. 162–63), and thus one simply cannot adopt anything like the' hypothetical' approach to the questions of metaphysics which we espoused in Chapter I. As he puts it: "And if there weren't things of this kind [snowflakes, snowstorms] of which we can be certain, we would be able to be uncertain of anything either" (p. 163). But this is just to misconstrue the serious psychological probability that one might well need at some time in ones development to *believe* that one was certain that one was seeing 'things' like snowflakes and snowstorms in order to doubt later on that one was really seeing 'things' like them. Holland misconstrues it by confusing it with a very dubious 'logical' or 'transcendental' sort of necessity that one should sometimes *know for a fact* that 'things' like snowflakes and snowstorms exist around one (pp. 162–163). Trying to salvage the grains of Holland's insight from the grandiose dogmas we would recommend in relation to Holland's talk of two radically distinct concepts of miracles a more flexible stance. People like Eclectic Edwin and our Neo-Greene heroine should be thought of as *reasonably* inspirable to agree that a miracle occurs by blendedly intellectual and emotional *belief-in* (psychologically) amazing 'ϕ-type' events that would not trouble a theoretical chemist or physicist at all about his currently favoured scientific laws and concepts if he also believed in the events. (There is an enormously high chance that a musical genius who is a much loved only son was killed in a multiple crash of airliners, but later the son turns out to be one of the two survivors out of the four hundred and thirteen passengers involved.) People like Eclectic Edwin and the Neo-Greene heroine can also be *reasonably* inspired to believe that a miracle has occurred by *belief-in* (psychologically) amazing 'χ-type' events which many reasonable believers would naturally take to be a specially loving form of Divine *intervention* ('*AD HOC*', so to speak) in Nature rather than just a specially moving expression of God's love for man in what God has *foreordained* all along. But highly reasonable believers need not consider even these events to be a decisive *demonstration* of God's existence to atheists present on the spot! These latter *believable-in* events of 'χ-type', ones like the notoriously odd business of the wine in Cana, would be of the sort which a reasonable Naturalist deep in science could well take, if he also took the events or something very like them to have occurred, as evidence that, e.g., radical rethinking about the possible effect of brainwaves on the molecular structure of liquids was incumbent upon the scientific community. The reasonable believer *might* grudgingly concede that a Naturalist *might* here be *sinfully* sceptical IF the Naturalist believes in the event *and* believes it to be a good reason for accepting theism *and* receives God's Grace *and* resists God's Grace by thinking about it hypocritically so as to save his pride, or the like. But a reasonable believer would (*qua* reasonable) think it best to leave it to his God and not to himself to judge a Naturalist in such a possible case. We finally comment that in place of Holland's radical distinction between two quite separate concepts of miraclehood, one can more profitably think of people like Eclectic Edwin and the Neo-Greene heroine as reasonably inspirable to conclude "That's a Divine sign – a miracle!" by a vast *continuum* of possibly *believed-in* events spanning the ϕ-type' paradigm that most naturally suggests to *believers* the specially glorious manifestation of God in what is always Divinely *foreordained* and the 'χ-type' paradigm that most naturally suggests to them some extraordinarily loving '*ad hoc*' intervention by God in the world that He created. If we interpret part of the parable of the prodigal son correctly (Luke XV, 11–32), the special feast given by the father as an '*ad hoc*', loving response to the (essentially unpredictable) decision of the prodigal to return indicates God's willingness to perform paradigmatically 'χ-type' miracles on, so to speak, an '*ad hoc*' basis, over and above the more 'ϕ-type' miracles which are part of a Divine plan as eternally envisioned. The always faithful son complaining of his father's special gesture towards the prodigal is like a believer who complains that he is not granted a 'χ-type' gesture, forgetful of God's repeated 'ϕ-type' gestures which should be miracles enough. For important light on some erroneous) philosophical underpinnings of Holland's and others' Moorean and/or Rylean and/or Austinian and/or Wittgensteinian and/or Strawsonian-*cum*-Neo-Kantian faith in Certainties about Facts, see Barry Stroud, 'Transcendental Arguments', *Journal of Philosophy* **65** (1968), 241–56.

CHAPTER IV

FROM *GOD* TO *IS* AND FROM *IS* TO *OUGHT*

I. CONVENTION AND WISDOM ABOUT "MEANING" AND "NECESSITY"

During this chapter and the next we hope to clarify and defend, in an initially perplexing *variety* of ways which bring together ethics and logic, a cluster of reasons for saying that "God exists" can be a *necessary truth* for a rational believer. More than one sort of necessity should turn out to be necessary. Clues as to the relevant sorts of necessity are supplied by considering some relevant senses or uses of "meaning". To say with Frege that "meaning" covers *meaning₁* or *Sense* and *meaning₂* or *Reference* is to begin well, but barely to begin! Nonetheless, if flexibly deployed by philosophers who can in the right context relate talk of a *word's* Sense and Reference in terms of its users' *typical work* and *intended work* with it, this distinction can beautifully reflect many of the ways in which we very naturally talk. Consider two well reflected things one might say. A militarist orator might retort to a vegetarian pacifist heckler at Hyde Park Corner: "By '*murder*' sensible and literate people have always meant [meant₁] *an immoral and illegal taking of a man's life*. They've not just meant [meant₁] *any case of just any old taking of life*." An Israeli officer searching for Martin Bormann might reply to a colleague in the Royal Canadian Mounted Police "By '*him*', sir, I meant [meant₂] *Bormann*, not *Eichmann*."

William Alston in one of the most important papers published on analytical philosophy of mind since the war[1] has called attention to confusion among analysts about two profoundly different kinds of theses. There are theses concerning what our present *concepts* of the human mind or its features now happen to be. There are theses concerning what the human mind actually *is* or its features really *are*. He speaks of this persistent confusion in analysis as one between *conceptual* and *ontological* theses. Alston emphasises the curious ways in which "refer" and its cognates as well as claims about analysing meaning are used by the perpetrators of the confusion.

Thus "refer", "reference", "mean", "meaning" and "analysis", if we understand Alston aright and if we may spell out a bit of what is still implicit in his essay, belong to a group of words which figure prominently in unfortunate conflations of enquiries like: (i) Do X's as we normally think of X's exist? (Perhaps analysis and science show our very concept of *mind* to be not worth cleaning up, to be now ripe for Ockham's Razor?) (ii) Given that something in reality which we can usefully continue to call X or *an X* or *the X* corresponds at least roughly to what we think and speak of as X or *an X* or *the X*, what is X or an X or the X – what are its most important characterizing properties in reality? (iii) How do we usually characterise X's? (What central cluster of qualities do we attribute to these alleged existents?)

Alston's complaint that Gilbert Ryle in *The Concept of Mind* (London 1949) and similarly confused critics of that influential book fail to distinguish *conceptual* and *ontological* theses is closely related to protests which we began to raise over fifteen years ago concerning a number of linguistic analysts' attempts to solve or *dis*-solve some traditional questions of ethics and philosophy of religion.[2] In protesting then we spoke of a confusion between *descriptive* and *prescriptive* theses in connection with "meaning" and some related words. Looking back now with detachment we could try to express our main concern about question-begging and confusion in alleged philosophical analysis by starting with some distinctions between crude but crucial descriptions of what is *Conventionally Aimed at Truth* and what is *Wisely Aimed at Truth*. (Compare: When a *religion's* organized structure has become corrupt, the conventional way of aiming at the service of God may no longer be the wisest, or be wise at all. See Saint Mark X, 17–31; Amos V, 20–27.)

(i) To understand the [conventionally truth-aimed] CTA-meaning of the word W in the language L is to understand the typical locutionary and illocutionary[3] uses of W among L-speakers, to understand the typically intended Sense(s) and sometimes the typically intended Reference (if any) of W when occurring in sentences that an L-speaker uses in order to state truths.

(ii) To understand the [wisely truth-aimed] WTA-meaning of the word W in the language L is to understand W's CTA-meaning in L and how, given the background of their starting with that CTA-meaning, L-speakers would *most wisely* use W in ways most appropriate to reality and in order to state relevant truths least confusedly and most insightfully – that is, how they SHOULD use it.

(iii) "If Q then R" is a CTA-'logical' truth, and a CTA-'analytic' truth, and a CTA-'necessary' truth if, crudely speaking, to deny "If Q then R" would be from the standpoint of CTA-meanings both to assert and to deny the very same thing in the very same sense at the very same time.[4]

(iv) "Q, and so R" is a CTA-'tautology' if, crudely speaking, "If Q then R" and "If R then Q" are CTA-'logical' truths, etc.

(v) "S is P" is a CTA-'logical' truth, etc., if "If this has the properties of [a/the] S then this has property P [or the properties of a/the P]" is CTA-'logical' truth etc.

(vi) "S is P" is a CTA-'tautology' if both "S is P" and "P is S" [or "A thing that is P has the properties of S, of the S, etc."] are CTA-'logical' truths.

(vii) Q is itself a CTA-'logical' etc., truth if denying Q would be for some R' (from the standpoint of CTA-meaning) both to assert and to deny the same thing R' in the same sense at the same time.

The rough-and-ready rules for describing WTA-'logical' truths, WTA-'tautologies', etc., may be derived in an obvious way from those of the CTA-variety. The philosopher *qua* philosopher, we would add, may be like the descriptive linguist, the 'non-normative' Anglo-Saxon style of lexicographer, the anthropologist and the sociologist in wanting to analyse plenty of CTA-meanings, CTA-'necessary' truths, etc. – but only as a *means*. A paramount final goal of properly philosophical analysis is to explicate the WTA-meanings of words which ought to matter greatly to men as rational, passionate animals. "Philosophy" and "philosopher" are among those words. "What is a philosopher?" is not *philosophically* answerable in a CTA-tighter version of such a CTA-meaning-minded attempt as "The kind of person who has a degree and lectures on people called *philosophers*-like Plato". Hence theses of truly philosophical analysis are very often worth calling "ontological as well as conceptual theses", "theses about Reference as well as Sense", "theses about how we ought to talk and think, not just about how we do".

Can there be any *necessary connection* between "God" and "Is" – or, better, between "God" and "real"? Can there be any *necessary connection* between "Is" and "Ought", "*Ens*" and "*Bonum*", "Reality" and "Value",

"Something which exists" and "Something which is good"? Or again, can we make sense of talk about God as a Necessary Being?

Confusions between some points about CTA-meanings and others about WTA-meanings have dogged too many of the most fashionable of recent attempts to answer these questions. Rather like some of the actual or strawmanly Sophists whom Plato's Socrates attacked in *The Republic*, the *Gorgias* and the *Theaetetus*, a good number of talented analysts after World War II tried to place philosophical problems against a background of strangely combined liberal-democratic, meritocratic, humanist, conventionalist and nihilist strands of belief. Nor does it seem to be a mere historical surd that the Second World War's ending could leave many anglophone intellectuals ripe for so much interest in the analysis of CTA-meanings and at the same time numerous Continental intellectuals so ready to admire certain of the Existentialists and the Dramatists of the Absurd for flirting with a tragic, nihilist vision of man. The claims we wish to make about *Good Reasons links* and allied *WTA-meanings' connections* between "This is a possible, but Divine being" and "This is an actual individual among the possible ones", or between "This is real" and "This is good" will make best sense when understood as *the rejection of a historically notable, but self-stultifying approach* to questions about "God", "Is" and "Ought". Not only has the approach been recently prominent, but some of its conventionalist themes have often recurred in our intellectual history and its sceptical roots are more easily scratched than seriously selected for extermination. Hence it is worth putting oneself temporarily into the perhaps rather heated position of someone who might come fresh in the 1950's to contemporary Anglo-Saxon and Continental philosophy. He then might become indignant about what strike him as being certain common, anti-rational assumptions of apparently quite fiercely opposed defenders of Reason. And understanding such sane indignation may take one a good step towards understanding the varieties of Divine Necessity.

II. LOOKING BACK WITHOUT ANGER: A CRY FROM THE FIFTIES

The problem of value cannot be relegated to a pigeon hole marked "ethics" and dealt with when philosophical questions considered more fundamental are already settled. Failure to grasp the full bearing which the problem has on all analysis largely accounts for the high degree of antipathy to "essence" curiously shared by certain exponents of linguistic analysis and certain champions of atheist *Existenzphilosophie*. Books like Urmson's *Philosophical Analysis* and Bergmann's *The Metaphysics of Logical Positivism*[5], reflect our increasing awareness that earlier positions of the linguistic movement were as metaphysical as the traditional philosophies which they attacked. The translation of Sartre's major work *L'Être et le Néant* into English[6] may serve indirectly to make it more clearly understood that contemporary linguistic analysis still rests on metaphysically controversial foundations (as sympathetic critics have already been pointing out). But much more important is the hint given by Sartre's dubious handling of "essence" and "value" that the metaphysical assumptions underlying what Bertrand Russell labelled "The Cult of Common Usage" are self-stultifying and self-contradictory. *L'Être et le Néant* should be prescribed reading for those linguistic philosophers who prescribe most earnestly the therapies of Ludwig Wittgenstein for dissolving philosophical problems.

Both the admirers of Wittgenstein and the devotees of Sartre have set themselves the task of exorcizing superstitions about "essence". But whereas many of the latter would decry an "essentialist fallacy" as a tragic misunderstanding of the human situation, many of the former would regard it as a tiresome, but very natural misconception of the way words work. Sartre attacks thinkers like Diderot for suppressing the role of God but retaining the concept of a fixed, 'preconceived' human nature; Wittgenstein teases those who share St. Augustine's belief that all words are the labels of ostensible entities. To call for a verdict of "essentialist *fallacy*" the Sartrian has to make open assertions about the kind of world we live in; but many linguistic philosophers hold they are simply pointing to facts that must, on reflection, be admitted by sensible folk of any conviction. Let us take three examples of the crudest sort of linguistic approach.

The slim volume *Aesthetics and Language*[7] claimed in all innocence on its baby-blue cover to offer "a fresh, unbiased scrutiny of the linguistic confusions of traditional aesthetics". Its first contributor, W. B. Gallie, launched an attack on Croce and Idealist thinkers. These, we learn, are typical victims of "the essentialist fallacy" in presupposing that a word like "Art" must stand for some *one* thing. The aesthetician's only valid functions, he concluded must be of a piecemeal nature, like upholding the differences between the art forms and assessing the applicability of comparisons and analogies. Any budding metaphysicians who seek the essence of Art are thus summarily dismissed. Consider another area of values: T. D. Weldon in his book *The Vocabulary of Politics* [8] claimed that political theory, too, has been vitiated by

the primitive and generally unquestioned belief that words ... such as "State", "Citizen", "Law" and "Liberty" have intrinsic or essential meanings which it is the aim of political philosophers to discover and explain (p. 11).

But actually "to know their meaning one need only know how to use them correctly, that is, in such a way as to be intelligible in ordinary and technical discourse" (p. 19). The assumption that all words are proper nouns produces "the illusion of real essences" and its uglier step-sister "the illusion of absolute standards". And compare the famous statement of the later Wittgenstein (*Philosophical Investigations* I, 116):

when philosophers use a word – "knowledge", "being", "object", "I", "proposition", "name" – and try to grasp the *essence* of the thing, one must always ask oneself: is the word ever used in this way in the language game which is its original home? – What we do is to bring words back from their metaphysical to their everyday usage.

The plausibility of these three examples rests on two foundations, one, legitimate and one which the "essentialist" is entitled to challenge. First, it takes a desperately dogged ostrich to deny that words like "art", "law" and "being" are used in a wide number of ways. Second, it is all too easy to graft onto a largely *descriptive* sense of "meaning" – "the way we do use and understand words" – a largely *evaluative* sense with a value something like this: "the way we should and would understand words if our concepts were appropriate to reality." Consider four examples of this latter sense. (i) D. H. Lawrence's widow Frieda says of those friends who still criticize her defiance of conventional standards for the sake of what she found *love* could be like: "I don't blame them that much. They don't know what 'love' really means." (St. Paul might say something similar about the meaning of "love" and his former colleagues among the Pharisees.) (ii) A travelling mystic who has reached a level of peace, detachment and joy that he had never believed possible says of an American Constitutional lawyer arguing with a Soviet Commissar (or a Humean arguing with a Sartrean) about what "freedom" really means: "Neither knows what 'freedom' really means – each side has a few useful clues but misses what's essential". (iii) A brash Londoner tells his country cousins: "You don't know what *comfort* MEANS until you've lived in TOWN." (iv) A once morbid and self-absorbed convert affirms he never knew what *happiness*, (or *gratitude*, or *fellowship*), really meant until a re-reading of both the Gospels and the Bhagavad Gita changed his way of life. This sense of "meaning" hardly fits Weldon's claim that to know words' meanings it is enough to be able to use them "in such a way as to be intelligible in ordinary and technical discourse". Weldon's approach might similarly lead him to condemn Kierkegaard for writing in *The Concept of Dread* (p. 82) "a precise and correct linguistic usage associates therefore dread and the future". "Correct linguistic usage" for Kierkegaard must mean here "a usage appropriate to reality". Fowler's "English Usage" and Dr. Gallup are *hors de combat*. But what ground is there for saying that, in effect, the three philosophers cited play on the evaluative connotation of "meaning?" Notably this: all three imply that once we understand how we do use words, we already have the answer to the question "How should we use them?" Otherwise, they could not conclude so confidently that once we understand the workings of our language we will have no right to claim that a legitimate puzzle or mystery remains; hence that we will no longer be justified in asking for the essence of thing named or the real meaning of the word we queried. Rather similar chains of argument have been employed against ethical "Naturalism", against traditional Christian equations between goodness and being or Aristotelian equations between goodness and the real object of human desire, and against the concept of God as an *ens necessarium*. Those who currently purvey such arguments may claim the support of G. E. Moore or Kant or Hume but their chief strength is to exploit the ambiguity of "meaning" (and so derivatively of "logical"), to dissuade us from the legitimate procedure of positing new entailment relationships to meet levels of experience which transcend the coarsest common sense.

The charge of "essentialist fallacy" like the charge of "Naturalist fallacy" can, therefore, sometimes be met with the simple retort: "but I am not looking just for a *meaning* in the 'descriptive' sense you imply."
Such a course would not have been immediately open to Plato for he is often guilty of extreme confusion about "meaning". But take another analysts' whipping boy, the target of positivists and crypto-positivists

from Carnap onwards. The appeal to metaphysical insight to justify *mis-usage* would be far more open, for example, to Heidegger – though he specialized elsewhere in obscurity on the question of value – if someone made such a charge against his essay *On the Essence of Truth*. For there he first expounds a variety of popular and traditional meanings of "truth", expounding what Wittgenstein would call their family resemblances. He then expresses himself dissatisfied with the inadequacy of popular opinion and feels called upon to soar to heights of metaphysical speculation in search of the essential meaning of truth. Perhaps indeed the feature that makes leading existentialists most repugnant to many linguistic philo-sophers is their typically "essentialist" procedure – despite some of their dramatized rejections of the role "essence" plays in systems like those of Plato and Aquinas. The analyst may complain that Plato's search in *The Republic* for the essence of Justice was barely more philosophically prim-itive and linguistically inept than Heidegger's redefinition of Truth; or than Kierkegaard's writings on Truth as Subjectivity and on "Angst" as dread of *nothing* (closely followed by Heidegger and Sartre); or than Camus' on The Absurd or than Marcel's and Buber's on "Thou". For an extreme example of "essentialism" one might note the pre-war Sartre's Husserlian enquiry: "is the imaginary function a contingent and meta-physical specification of the essence 'consciousness' or should it be de-scribed as a constitutive structure of that essence?" (*The Psychology of Imagination*, 201ff). Indeed the link with Plato is there. Not that they literally seek a παράδειγμα ἀνακείμενον ἐν τῷ οὐρανῷ but, like Plato in *The Republic*, existentialist writers always imply and frequently assert that the world we live in and our thoughts about it confront us with a *vocation* and a *challenge* to reshape and reform our concepts and so reorientate our outlook towards sources of what philosophers should value: Wisdom. This implication and the light shed by considering eval-uative uses of meaning should make it clearer that the "essentialist fallacies" of traditional philosophy arise not always from foolishly ignor-ing the loom of language, but sometimes quite legitimately from the trad-itional view of the world as a domain where questions about both fact and value can have true answers.

Michael Foster has spoken of a "humanist" view[9], Iris Murdoch of a "liberal" or neutral view of the world as being presupposed by most exponents of linguistic analysis. According to the latter view, as she put it in a broadcast talk on "Ethics and Metaphysics", morality does not "adhere to the stuff of the world".[10] This would certainly explain both the disjunction of *is* and *ought* in so many current analyses of ethics and the obscuring of the evaluative connotations of "essence". It would not, of course, justify the way some analyses play on the ambiguity of "ethics" and "meaning" in order to gain certain benefits from their "neutral" accounts of these terms – a sleight of hand necessary to maintain the appearance of talking about "morals" and "meaning" very much as the man in the street does, but of course with professional lucidity.

It might, however, be thought to follow that there are two self-consistent accounts of philosophy[11]: the traditional view whereby man's indissoluble (but "transcendable") bewilderment in the labyrinth of words reflects the value-ridden, vocational character of the world he meets in experience; and the "liberal" view of a neutral world where philosophy progresses, in Stuart Hampshire's words, towards becoming "a proper empirical study of the forms of language". But though the traditional view can at least be made self-consistent (while it will remain unacceptable to many), the "liberal" view does suffer from an inner contradiction which may without gross exaggeration be labelled an "essentialist fallacy". There is a certain degree of analogy with the self-contradictory procedures of atheist existentialists like Camus, Sartre and Simone de Beauvoir (or the Heidegger of *Sein und Zeit*) who devalue the world but still cling to a vocational account of philosophy. But there is more illumination in first considering how and why Sartre openly entertains something like an "essence" of man in the back parlor after loudly proclaiming the defenestration of "human nature" into the main street.

Sartre asserts in *L'Être et le Néant* (p. 76):

Il s'ensuit que ma liberté est l'unique fondement des valeurs et que rien, absolument rien ne me justifie d'adopter telle ou telle valeur. ... En tant qu'être par qui les valeurs existent je suis injustifiable.

Miss Murdoch in her book *Sartre* discusses his dubious shift from a technical, descriptive account of certain value terms in *Being and Nothingness* to a highly evaluative, popular account in his later works *What is Literature?* and *Existentialism and Humanism*.[12] But Sartre, (not so unlike the most self-righteously "neutral" linguistic philosophers), has already surrendered more significantly to objective value in that earlier work. Miss Murdoch may be correct in saying that concepts like "*être-en-soi*" and *"être-pour-autrui"* are hypothetical or mythological and do not constitute "a metaphysical theory of human nature". But what are we to make of his frequent insistence on certain *interpretations* of empirical phenomena as *correct* or *in*correct, notably that man *is* to *be seen* as a free agent however oppressive his circumstances? (See especially *L'Être et le Néant*, Part IV.) How are we to construe his assurances that the self is to be seen as a unity and not a collection of occurrences whatever some psychologists may say? (*ibid.*, Ch. II, ii.) This laying down of an interpretation or *"seeing as"* for what seems to be a man's *ambiguous* self-experience as *the right one* is all too like what is involved in positing an "essence". M. Naville replies in the concluding discussion of *Existentialism and Humanism* that Sartre has repudiated "human nature" but given almost exactly the same job to the phrase "human condition". And the stupifying expression "ontologie phénoménologique" does not obviate the harsh reality that Being and Nothingness repudiates "essence" and gives much of its job to "structure." Indeed Sartre is here forced to objectify his value judgments on the interpretation of experience in order to establish a basis for philosophizing and to make his account of value as an illusory aspiration sound at all plausible. For philosophy must presuppose that our experience can be rendered to some extent *intelligible* – is understandable in a way that is *worth* seeking to grasp. Concerning philosophy's advance with Plato F. C. Copleston pointed out:

the theory of forms presents us with a world which is not simply and solely a Heraclitean flux but a world shot through, as it were, with intelligibility (*Aquinas*, pp. 88–89).

Man can pose like Sartre or Hare as the autonomous Arbiter who allots value (and so intelligibility) to the world: but in order to prevent the chaos from overwhelming every basis for such a Pluralist Ontology as Ordinary Language obviously encourages he must, however implicitly, allow the wisdom of any sensible man's faith in his own free selfhood. And this is to raise value to the status of fact, to realise "heteronomy". Hume's greatest achievement was to show, not entirely wittingly, that the problems of causality and selfhood are at least partly evaluative problems, problems of the *right* or *wise* interpretation of experience; hence that without yielding ground to something like ethical intuitionism and objective value, philosophy is eventually driven from scepticism to hypocrisy or silence. The self cannot be descriptively "reduced" (by

Humean or Russellian standards of reducing things decently) to a "bundle of sensations" except by presupposing a self-deceiving self that performs such a reduction. The self cannot be descriptively reduced to "freedom choosing freedom", because these words presuppose, for their Sartrean significance, the good sense of positing an at least momentarily substantial and stable self that receives the attribute expressed by "freedom", or that conceptualizes and hypothesizes about its freedom.

Talk about a "bundle of sensations" (Hume, early Ayer) or about "freedom choosing freedom" (Sartre) may begin by seeming intelligible as talk about what are 'logical constructions' (somewhat like *the average plumber*) formed from a presupposed common *basis* of beliefs, about persons that *unify* bodies and conciousness. But when *persons* later turn out to be alleged 'logical constructions' formed from 'ground-level-givens' like sense-data, impressions and ideas, or like the For-Itself ever reconstituting itself by repeated choices and negations, etc., then the philosophical currency has turned into Toy Money for Bedlamites in Wonderland.

What bearing does this have on the suggestion that the "humanist" and "rootless liberal" outlooks of analysts involve something which might be called an "essentialist fallacy"? A fallacy is likely to be involved when a metaphysical viewpoint is simultaneously embraced as an integral part of an analytical procedure and excluded by the procedure's corollaries. It is typical that Wittgenstein in his long discussion at *Philosophical Investigations* (II, xi) of "seeing as" concerns himself with [CTA-]ambiguity and [CTA-]conceptual complexity – and not at all with ultimate justification for setting some limits to possible (valuable) ways of interpreting what is experienced. It is typical of many analysts, but really suicidal, for G. J. Warnock to write of Berkeley[12]:

He did not think of himself as inventing simply a *new* way of looking at the world, but rather as expounding the *right* way, the only way in which one sees things as they really are. But this, I think, is only to say that he, like other metaphysicians, had his illusions.

Michael Foster and Iris Murdoch have made sound cases that the approach of many linguistic philosophers is only compatible with a "humanist" or a "rootless liberal" outlook – but are such outlooks compatible with themselves? Of course, it follows from the popular disjunction of fact and value that there is no *right* way of looking at the world; yet, without ones positing a humanist or liberal outlook as the *right* one, and without attributing a basic soundness and high value to the concepts and speech habits of Ordinary Men in the name of that outlook, so many analytical chains of argument are not even dubious; they simply cannot get started.

Much as they might hate to be mentioned in the same breath, certain advocates of linguistic analysis and atheist *Existenzphilosophie* were led by their denial of "essence" and objective value into fallacies and tangles far more self-stultifying than Plato's. If a Republic of Letters is to bear investigation, it must cease to support itself by purveying what is officially forbidden fruit on an unofficial black market. The traditionalist can afford to face the charge of "essentialist fallacy" unmoved if he reaffirms the challenge of the world as posing questions of truth about both fact and value; reaffirms the Socratic challenge of philosophy as vocation to reveal vocation; reaffirms that man's indissoluble bewilderment in the labyrinth of words reflects the essence of the created world he meets in experience. George Herbert caught that essence more clearly than any philosopher in his poem "The Pulley", where God says of man in the world:

Yet let him keep the rest,
But keep them with repining restlessness;
Let him be rich and weary, that at least,
If goodness lead him not, yet weariness
May toss him to My breast.

III. FROM "GOD" TO "IS": GOOD REASONS AND JUSTIFYING EXPLANATIONS

How might some reasonable man conclude that Reason seems to him to require the existence of God? The lines cited finally by the frustrated philosopher of the Fifties from George Herbert's "The Pulley" and the link between fullness of rationality and an at least initial sense of need for a justifying explanation of the whole of things, including human history, supply the beginnings of one answer. A person who has reflected for a long time on Judaeo-Christian theism and on the claims of pure scepticism as well as those of ideologies and visions which compete with such theism in offering a justifying explanation, might spell out the argument for his conclusion with this, *THE JUSTIFYING EXPLANATION ARGUMENT*:

"(Premise One) I find that my manifold of experience [my apparently mystical moments, my sense of an Authority behind man's beliefs in real, objective distinctions between Good and Evil, Art and Rubbish, my experiences of a strange *union* or *communion* in prayer, my inability to accept death, cruelty or plain suffering as a pointless surd, my feeling of dependence [upon dependents upon dependents] and even my very restlessness before the final sort of "Why?" suggest both to my head and to my heart that there must be a justifying explanation for everything.

"(Premise Two) I find that some whom I greatly admire and respect as reasonable men conclude after their initial quests that it is pointless to look further for any justifying explanation – that this looking distracts one from reforming oneself and the world – but I also find others whom I similarly respect and admire concluding like me that these people have really stopped short of trying to answer Reason's most important question.

"(Premise Three) The mere concession that there must be *some* justifying explanation of history does not force any Deity upon the man who concedes this.

"(Premise Four) But exploration of various possibilities that reasonable men have been able to accept as the justifying explanation, and also consideration of sceptical attacks on them, still leave me convinced that belief in a perfect, person-like Creator supplies a very plausible kind of justifying explanation.

"(Premise Five) I have come to a stage where such belief in a Personal God seems to supply a justifying explanation vastly more plausible than anything in any other religions, ideologies and philosophies which I know of can offer.

"(Premise Six) I have also come to conclude that by this stage of my life my best chance of gaining substantially more wisdom and insight is to commit myself to this belief that can, it seems, supply so eminently more plausible a justifying explanation – to try to live tolerantly but *well* in harmony with *this* set of what William James called *eternal things*, while letting others choose any other tolerant way they find best.

"(Premise Seven) If *any reasonable person* finds that he agrees after long, open-hearted reflection with my Premises One, Two, Three and Six, and if *he* also thinks that metaphysical beliefs, $B_1 \ldots B_n$ supply by far the more plausible justifying explanation of history, then I would judge *him* to be wisest to commit himself to a tolerant faith in $B_1 \ldots B_n$.

"(Conclusion) Thus, if I consider *myself* to have been reasonable in assenting to Premises One, Two, Three, Six and Seven and in concluding that certain Biblical theistic beliefs $B_1 \ldots B_n$ clearly supply by far the best justifying explanation, I am least unwise and indeed most wisely *consistent* with my beliefs about *any reasonable person*, if I commit myself to tolerant but very real faith in the Biblical God."

This sort of reasoning[13] may seem to be set a contemptuous distance away from those deductive looking classics offered as *demonstrations* of God's existence – far, far from the sorts of Proofs sketched by Saint Thomas in giving his Five Ways or citing certain types of miracles . But Saint Thomas in offering intended demonstrations was trying to offer us the best possible reasons for belief in God. What really are the best possible (truth-seeking) reasons will vary with context. (Aquinas would agree with Aristotle that chains of geometrically rigorous reasoning need not be suitable paradigms for political deliberation.) If everything that a child now does suggests that he is clearly quite painfully sorry that he has hurt his father's feelings by saying 'I hate you' at bedtime, if the child is not only young but usually most affectionate and cooperative, what *better reason* does the father need for refusing to treat this conventional expression of serious hatred seriously? And what if working back from the Fifth of the Five Ways to the First a particular reasonable man finds that the *phenomena* focussed on by each Way can serve to call attention to one of many sorts of things that suggest the wisdom of The Justifying Explanation Argument for theism? That the Fifth focusses on a Nature which makes human history with personal agency and creativity and love all possible, whatever the suffering and pain, the Fourth on those comparisons of value which he's able – often reasonably and wisely – to make as if backed by a wiser Authority, the Third on the fact which he still finds stunning that there *is* something, a universe which seems to cry out to reasonable beings in it for a justifying explanation, the Second on the wonder-worthiness of the causal chains between dependent things, the First on the wonder-worthiness of change itself? What if also *some individual events* in his experience, rather than just what he takes to be the wonder-worthy *sorts* of events, strike the man as uncannily deserving of a profound awe and gratitude, as Miracles among miracles? All these can surely minister for a reasonable person to the claims of The Justifying Explanation Argument.

Some sceptics might suggest that such a person should take the ancestral spectacles off his nose so that the so-called 'wonder-worthy feelings' will subside or advise him that he should spurn the pressures of any such feelings ('*mere*' feelings!) in order to serve Reason. But the man might reply that he has indeed long lived without (or long pushed aside) those spectacles before in his search for truth, and all his own immediate ancestors were sceptics anyway. He might also reply that because a feeling – against the right background of reasonable openness and patience – can be a good reason for action, belief and commitment in the realms of morality, art, marriage, friendship and much else, it can certainly – against the right background – offer a good reason to a rational person for making a religious commitment. As we noted in Section Two, man's intellectual history has shown many a recent recurrence of those psychic rashes which meta-moralists can distinguish up to a point with such labels as *Pure Nihilism, Social Relativism, Non-Cognitivism, Individual Subjectivism* and the like. Later, in Chapter V, we shall argue the case for finally trying to purge the human mind of this family of Cults of the Incoherent. At the present point we ask: if reasonable people cannot fall back after study, questioning and reflection on what FEELS *good* or *bad, intelligible* or *unintelligible, logical* or *illogical, wise* or *foolish, just* or *unfair*, what can they fall back on? On the feeling that scepticism is least foolish, least unfair and least illogical? But what if that is by no means all reasonable people's feeling?

IV. FROM "GOD" TO "IS" – SOME FALLACIES ABOUT BEING A BEING

Traditional talk about God as (i) *Ens Necessarium*, (ii) *Ens a Se*, and (iii) *Ens Realissimum* can be illuminatingly analysed (from the standpoint of philosophical interest in WTA-meanings as well as CTA-meanings) in many ways. In the light of the concept of a justifying explanation these three terms seem specially tractable in the following ways.

(I) God is an *Ens Necessarium* because His perfections are such as to make belief in His existence seem to reasonable theists to be a requirement of Reason for them *qua* reasoners whose reflections on existence have developed in certain ways. His existence because of His perfections stands in need of nothing else as a justifying explanation. All other things whose existence reasonable theists know about seem to *require* or to *necessitate* (or to "cry out for") His existence, power and perfections ('Expohood'and

'Gooperdom') in order to give them ultimate point and value taken together as a whole.

(II) God as *Ens a Se* is unique in that He depends, it seems to the reasonable theist, upon no other individual as efficient-and-final cause (as justifying explanation) but all other known beings do individually and collectively depend upon God as efficient-and-final cause.

(III) An intellectual ideal associated with descriptions like "realissimum" and "most completely real" and "greatest fullness of being" is the ideal of being something *totally independent* for purposes of intelligibility, something which is its own efficient-and-final cause, its own justifying explanation, unlike "less real", "less substantial" things whose existence seems impossible or pointless except in relation to something else.

Perhaps these accounts of God as *Ens Necessarium, Ens a Se* and *Ens Realissimum* offer some live possibilities to those philosophers who are convinced that in some puzzling but important sense or senses "God *exists*" must be a *Necessary Truth* and *God* must be a *Logically Necessary Being*. The way for such possibilities has been prepared at least partly by our discussion at this chapter's beginning of WTA-meanings (*Wisely Truth-Aimed* meanings), WTA-'logical' truths and WTA-'necessary' truths. Aquinas, to repeat the familiar, (a) replied in the middle of his career to Anselm that "God exists" is a self-evident truth (*per se notum*) for those who have the Beatific Vision of the Divine Essence, but not for us in our present state; (b) argued 'relatively indirectly' compared to the Anselm of *Proslogion* II–IV (and more like the earlier Anselm of the *Monologion*) for God's existence and about His perfections by appealing to principles of Reason and to facts of Common Human Experience; (c) lost interest towards the very end of his life in philosophical *argument* (from Reason and Common Human Experience) about God's existence and nature – lost interest when he was enjoying what he took to be profound mystical experiences and forms of special communion with God. Thus Aquinas no less than Anselm would seem to support this thesis about the WTA-'logical' truth of "God exists": the more appropriate ones concept of God is to the reality – that is, to the WTA-referent of "God" – the less sense it would seem to make to deny or query "God exists". For then the more akin asking "Does GOD exist?" would seem both to asserting and to denying, or both to asserting and to questioning, the very same thing in the same sense at the same time. (We shall say more of this very shortly, in Section V.) Or again a concern with using words wisely so as to disclose what is important about reality could lead someone to speak of God as a Logically Necessary Being because the quest for any WTA-meanings seems to lead him eventually to the need for a justifying explanation of history: only that explanation, he concludes, can allow him to get to the bottom of questions like "What does 'Philosophy' really mean?", "What does 'Person' really mean?" and the like. As he would say: "Any attempt to fulfil the ideal of *Logical* Thinking at the philosophical level seems to lead me to the ultimate 'Why?' question. The only approach to a satisfactory final answer seems to me be the Justifying Explanation Argument. And that argument finally brings me from the initial ideal of *Logical* Thinking about how I should look at this and that phenomenon in the world (by way of concern to think straight about the world itself) to the proposition 'God exists'. Hence I say, perhaps in unexpected senses: *God is a Logically Necessary Being*."

But before pursuing the idea of God as an *Ens Necessarium* any further it is important to clear away misunderstandings that are rife today, misunderstandings often, we suspect, of a very elementary kind that make some would-be theologians – not least Death-of-God 'theologians' – fulminate against any traditional talk of God as AN *ens* or *A* Being at all.

V. FROM "GOD" TO "IS": THE MUDDLED FEAR OF CALLING GOD A BEING

Half-baked uses of Kierkegaard and Heidegger have had much to do with Paul Tillich's 'symbolic' and perhaps curiously atheistic major contribution to religion, *Systematic Theology*. But this work, as we saw in Chapter Three, is often bafflingly hard to interpret. Certain persistent fallacies which we think mar Tillich's reasoning have been mercifully spelled out as alleged strokes of insight in a much clearer way by a no less pretentious but much more simple-minded man, D. Z. Phillips, in his very recent work *Faith and Philosophical Enquiry* (New York 1971). Half-baked uses of Kierkegaard and Wittgenstein have much to do with Phillips' 'linguistic' and dubiously theist, though allegedly Christian, philosophy of religion. Since there is so much muddled thought now abroad about the possible blasphemy or *anti*-religious bent of calling God AN *ens* (A Being), it is worth dwelling for a few paragraphs on Phillips' book and what seems to be its likely relation to very powerful confusions encouraged by the enormous popularity of Tillich. (Tillich is still thought of by many as the 20th Century's greatest theological interpreter of Judaeo-Christian Scriptures and traditions.)

Faith and Philosophical Enquiry is a collection of 13 influential papers, first published between 1963 and 1970, which typify ingenious muddle-headedness, but which are like Tillich's writings in their importance as indicators of major modern trends. Phillips shares Tillich's penchant to speak for the Judaeo-Christian tradition as a whole, while eclectically avoiding anything that might seem *superstitious* (or even faintly 'supernatural') to defend in a scientific age.

Phillips' tactics put one in mind of Tillich's responses to old chestnuts like: "Now that we know so much about physics and biology than Moses or Jesus or Aquinas ever could, how can we consistently believe in a Transcendent Creator?". Tillich's relatively explicit responses throw much light on Phillips' real directions. Tillich would reply that such questions dealt a healthy blow to superstition and fundamentalism. Creation stories like Fall-of-Man stories are not literal but symbolic. Traditionalist clergy left them crudely and outdatedly symbolic. Updated symbolic and wise Tillichian theology teaches that anthropomorphic, traditionalist – e.g., Thomist – talk about God as a transcendent, purely spiritual, triunely personal *ens realissimum*, distinct from the physical universe created by Him, debases God by making Him a mere Supreme *Being* who creates and lovingly relates Himself to personal creatures. Traditionalist talk 'objectifies' God as a Being among beings. Such dying, unacceptable symbols must give way to live symbols: God is Being-Itself, not a distinct Transcendent Being. God is Ultimate Concern itself, not a concerned, personal Creator. God is beyond Existence and Essence and presumably beyond ever giving any earthly help to those old-fashioned enough to call upon His name in prayer. (Compare Phillips at pp. 103–05. *Worse* nonsense about prayer was offered in Phillips' first book, *The Concept of Prayer*, London 1965: for more sympathetic criticism see R. T. Allen, 'On Not Understanding Prayer', *Sophia* **10.3** (1971), 1–7.)

Phillips does not list any Tillichiana in his bibliography. But it is well worth bearing Tillich in mind when one feels lulled by many widely scattered and moving passages in *Faith and Philosophical Enquiry* which seem to be pronouncements of an ardent Kierkegaardian theist. For sudden echoes of Tillich and his emulators show that these appearances of Christian fideism are misleading. Phillips uses Kierkegaard's contrast of Eternal God and temporal man not, as first appears, for the Sad Dane's Supernaturalism, but rather for the earthier Cultural Relativism of Wittgenstein as interpreted by P. G. Winch.[14]

The objector who accuses me of denying the objective reality of God may have in mind a statement which I should support – namely the statement that God is not an object. That is a statement of grammar. Those who deny it, I suggest, speak of God in a way which is a logical extension of ways in which we speak of human beings. If God is a thing He is finite; and a finite God satisfies the needs neither of religion nor of theology" (p. 60).

The convenient quasi-ambiguity of the words "object" and "thing" here may put some off the scent – especially if they are already dizzied by whiffs of burnt offerings to Demythologization! It does indeed seem demeaning to a theist to call God a *thing* or an *object* as those words are often used in ordinary language. For the theist takes God to be both *personal* and *supreme*. In a similar way when Phillips typically says that God is not a thing among things or an object among objects (p. 85), or that God in His heaven is not an extra domain over and above our natural world, the Christian may interpret Phillips as saying something highly theistic. (Cf. Chapter III.) For the theist agrees to the extent that God is not *just* one being among many, not *just* 'something else' besides created nature: the Transcendent God is the uniquely perfect being, the only *ens a se*. But what Phillips really means in philosophical terms is that God is not a *Substance*, that God is not a *Transcendent Being*. (Phillips like Tillich seems to be confused here by two uses of "among". As our friend J. A. Jenkinson has put it in comment on Tillich, it is true in one way [Set Inclusion] that Maurice Chevalier was one among the millions of 20th-Century entertainers; in another way [Evaluative Levelling] it is not true that he was one among them.) Look again at the baited words: "If God is a thing He is finite." Suppose we write instead: "If God is any *substance*, if God is the *ens a se* and *ens realissimum* but nevertheless can be correctly given the label *ens*, if God is a distinct individual being, then it follows that He is finite." We would so have written out more clearly what Phillips means, which is presumably the first part of an *argument* of the form: "If *Q* then *R*, but *R* is incompatible with the needs of religion or theology, so (by *Modus Tollens*) *NOT-Q*"!! But why must God be finite if God is an individual or *ens*, or is a personal individual, or is a *thing* in the technical sense of a *Substance*? Possibly Phillips himself is conveniently misled by this demeaning flavour of "thing" or "object" in ordinary usage when we contrast mere things or mere objects, so sadly limited – ('finite') – because they are mindless, with conscious *persons*? Possibly also Phillips supposes like Spinoza (and Tillich?) that no substance *X* can be infinite in any religiously or otherwise important sense if it is *distinct from* another substance *Y*, even if *Y* is finite and dependent on *X*. Compare the child's fallacy of supposing that there cannot be an *infinite* (infinitely dense) series of numbers (fractions) between 0 and 1 because there is a number 2 which lies outside the infinite series. Being infinite need not involve being *all-inclusive*, any more than being all-inclusive in a finite domain involves being infinite. Phillips also seems to embrace the dogma that if *X* makes *Y* meaningful, valuable, purposeful, etc., then *X* cannot have any properties which are somehow faintly analogous to – ("logical extensions of") – any properties of *Y*. But this dogma is also fatal for even Phillips' philosophy of religion. He wants to say that God is the meaning of the world (Chapter III). He wants to say that both concepts of God and concepts of human institutions and events are intelligibly discussable by insiders. Thus God and man share the property that the concepts of each of them are intelligibly discussable by insiders (cf. Chapter II and IV–VII). Must *that* be denied too, on pain of demeaning God?

Another fallacy which is crucial to spot if one is to understand the source of many profoundly confusing, indeed at present very influentially confusing remarks spread right across Phillips' book and much of Tillich's *Systematic Theology* is the fallacy behind those already quoted words:

Those who deny it, I suggest, speak of God in a way which is a logical extension of ways in which we speak of human beings" (p. 60).

The major implication of this sentence in the whole passage quoted is shown by the way it directly precedes "If God is a thing He is finite". Thus we have the first part of an intended argument which unfolds *modo tollendo* as: "If *P* then *Q*, and if *Q* then *R*, but *R* is incompatible with the needs of religion or theology, so *NOT-Q* and thus *NOT-P*." In other words we have an argument to the effect that if the Medieval tradition of *analogical predication* in theology were accepted, then we would have to make God a thing in some anthropomorphically demeaning way. (Hume's attacks on Natural Theology are praised by Phillips more than once.) Hence we would next have to agree that God is finite, which is theologically and religiously intolerable, so that any talk of *Analogia Entis* must be scrapped by non-idolaters. Nowhere in the book is there a serious attempt to consider how and why many gifted and careful and *devout* Medievals concluded that analogical predication, controlled by applications of the *Via Negativa*, could make so much of both theism and theology possible to understand without any anthropomorphic sacrilege.[15] Indeed Phillips tends towards defaming those medievals when he writes

Religious mystery is connected with ... the prohibition against idolatry: that is against likening God to anything natural" (p. 142).

It is hardly surprising that Phillips makes hostile gestures towards the neo-Thomist E. L. Mascall's *Existence and Analogy*, and towards the Catholic neo-Wittgensteinian P. T. Geach's sympathetic chapter on Aquinas in his book with G. E. M. Anscombe *Three Philosophers*. The Anglican philosopher-theologians John Hick and Ian Ramsey are also chosen for castigation: for to Phillips' horror, we learn, Hick believes with the analogists that persons will enjoy an eschatological existence which will be literal existence and not totally unlike present personal existence (pp. 124ff). Personal immortality does not require demythologising and resymbolising to death! This, it seems, makes Hick like a *"superstitious"* mother who trusts in a Virgin Mary still living after physical death, to protect a baby from observable, physical harm. (Compare p. 103). Hick and Bishop Ramsey are also at fault, one gathers, for joining atheists like Kai Nielsen in criticizing the Winch-Phillips attempt to make features of religious ways of life only assessable by (and intellectually accessible to) people deeply involved in practising or promoting those ways.

Phillips, like Tillich, wishes to reject the theist tradition that God is a distinct being, a Creator, and to reject it in the name of making war on superstition and idolatry. And Phillips, like Tillich, sees no disastrous inconsistency between the 'Closed Circle' or 'Internal Criticism Only' approach to philosophy of religion and the 'Being an Insider I'm Free to criticize Any Superstitions like Personal Immortality or Divine Individuality' approach to theology. Nor does Phillips realize that the Wittgensteinian Family Resemblance approach to polymorphous concepts becomes unmanageable as an analytical method if too much *intransitivtiy* is allowed to the *relation* of similarity and there are too many *relata* so related. Realizing this and making good comparative use of many centuries' work on analogical predication *would* be a way of taking what is permanently valuable in Wittgenstein seriously for purposes of philosophy of religion. Phillips seems blind to this. So he finds talk of God as *a* Being, even as a *Supreme* Being idolatrous! There is much else to query in Phillips' form of 'Modernist' method. Whence comes the implied cross-cultural, cross-philosophical objectivity of *his* criticism of his rivals when his method is supposed so radically to isolate different sets of criteria for rationality as being internal to different approaches to the world? Here is a source of much rank inconsistency and possibly of some pure non-sense. "I'm safe in my Circle but you're not safe in yours!": this is the slogan between the lines, the theme song chanted implicitly throughout thirteen arrogant essays by various square-circular rabbits popping out from supposedly magic, allegedly Wittgensteinian, Kierkegaardian and 'Up-to-Date' Christian hats.

Nothing in the strident prose of Phillips or in the oracular eloquence of Tillich suggests that insight, rather than basic muddles about the different uses of words like "among", "being", "object" and "thing", and also strange confusions about understanding *P* and accepting *P*, about set inclusion and evaluative levelling, about analogous predication (or *likening A* to *B*) and evaluative levelling, has led to their rejection in the traditional belief that God is *a* Being, the Perfect Creator among His creatures in the realm of real individuals.

Like so many who reflect on the Creeds, we believe in *a* Being, God the Father Almighty...

VI. FROM "GOD" TO "IS" – CURRENT CONFUSIONS ABOUT EXISTENCE AS NECESSARY AND EXISTENCE AS PREDICATE

According to Terence Penelhum, one of the ablest analysts in philosophy of religion, the very idea of a self-explanatory being is absurd. Aquinas, he thinks, merely repeated the main error of Anselm's *Proslogion* II–IV in a different way. But it is Penelhum, not Aquinas who is repeating the most instructive errors when drawing his main conclusions in his well-known paper 'Divine Necessity'. The essay turns out to be almost a compendium of bad moves by other, less able analysts – but it is rounded off by one helpful beginning at the end.

Aquinas' own argument leads us from finite beings to a being whose existence does follow from his nature, and this entails that *if* we knew God's nature we *could* deduce his existence from it – and this is the mistake.... It is not our ignorance that is the obstacle to explaining God's existence by his nature, but the logical character of the concept of existence. ... Now for the morals: (i) It is absurd to ask why anything exists, because the only possible answers are in terms of the logically *im*possible notion of a self-explanatory being .... (iii) But unless you assume independently that a given being has a cause, you can always ask why it exists, i.e. what caused it. If you do assume it has a cause, you *ipso facto* make it impossible to ask why it is there .... For it is logically impossible to explain *everything* .... Theism cannot explain any more than atheism can. [Terence Penelhum, 'Divine Necessity', in D. R. Burill (ed.), *The Cosmological Arguments*, New York 1967, pp. 143–61 – those quotations are from pp. 153–55. Most, not *quite* all, of Penelhum's very popular errors in that essay are repeated in his recent book *Religion and Rationality*, New York 1971. See especially pp. 11–18, 35–47.]

Not surprisingly this passage is preceded by one proclaiming in the name of Kant and G. E. Moore the assertion that existence cannot be a quality at all (pp. 150–151). Not surprisingly this assertion is followed by the words

So it further follows that no existential assertion *can* be analytic .... [We have made] a logical discovery about the concept of existence, which sets it apart from other concepts: that no tautology can be existential is a consequence of this. (p. 151).

Nor is it surprising that the initial passage quoted from Penelhum is followed by the assertions (i) that "God has property *P*" cannot be self-explanatory (pp. 155–57); (ii) that God's existence and His nature or essence cannot be *identified* as the Scholastics wished because of "the logical character of the concept of existence" (p. 157); (iii) that "God's existence and nature 'can be' unique in the universe in being free of factual contingency", of causal dependence on anything else, "but the assertions of them share in propositional contingency with all other assertions of fact" (p. 159); (iv) that talk about *the Divine necessity* nevertheless *does make sense* when it is just talk about the unique non-dependence of God and His nature on anything else (pp. 159–60).

One of Penelhum's crucial compound errors is to identify all demands for explanations with "Why?" questions and all "Why?" questions with causal questions and all causal questions with what Aristotelians would call *purely efficient* causal questions. In the Judaeo-Christian conceptual scheme the 'Gooper'-properties of God are such that the answer to a "Why?" question requesting both an efficient cause and a justification can often be "Because God wills it and because – being Perfectly loving and wise, as well as all-powerful – God has made or has let this happen so that the greatest possible good will come about." The question "Why should God wish to let *this* happen in order – being Perfect – to bring about the greatest possible good?" may sometimes need to be answered by "I don't know how He – being perfect – knows that making or letting this happen is for the greatest possible good for everyone and everything, but God – being perfect – knows". That too can be a form of justifying explanation. But what if someone is so upset that *this* has happened and asks with non-causal and purely justification-seeking sorts of "Why?" questions: "But why should a perfectly good God have such power to make or to let *this* happen? Why shouldn't imperfect human beings have all the power they want to stop things like *this* happening, whether it's right to stop it or not? Why *should* there be a perfect God, even if one ought to exist, and why *should* He have the supreme power?" Then the answer within the scheme is simple and the sense it makes in the scheme should be analogous to that of correspondingly sound answers in others reasonable schemes. The answer is: "A perfectly good and loving being just *should* exist. And He *should* have such great powers. And a being with man's present drawbacks and weaknesses *should not* have anything too like such great powers." If the questioner continues to pose the purely justifying "Why?" and asks "Why *should* what is best happen?" the answer is that it *is* self-explanatory that (i) what should be should be, *and* that (ii) what can do what should be done can do what should be done, *and* that (iii) what does what should be done does it.

It could only be only a WTA-'necessary' truth that God *exists* or that it is best if Judaeo-Christian theism is true. But it is a helpful, curiously informative CTA-'necessary' truth also that "It is best that what ought to exist and happen should exist and happen" – and this is a WTA-'necessary' truth as well. To say that God's perfections and powers are such that what ought to exist does exist and what ought to happen is caused to happen just is to explain everything with the relevant blend of justifying and efficient-causal "Why?" answers.

Contrary to Penelhum's pontification it *is* logically possible to explain everything, it *is* reasonably thinkable that a being should be self-explanatory, it is *not* absurd to ask why anything exists – at least these demands are satisfiable within a Judaeo-Christian conceptual scheme where an entity with the right sorts of 'Expohood' and 'Gooperdom' is the right sort of thing to refer to when presented with the metaphysician's or the plain man's "Why?" that calls for both an efficient cause and a justification – that is, with a "Why?" that calls for a justifying explanation.

But what of other crucial assumptions in the unmistakably distinguished mind of one like Penelhum who *intends* to be so helpful to theism? One assumption amounts to the flat rejection of Aquinas' point that if one knew enough about a Divine Being's nature one might find it no less absurd (and absurd in the same way) to ask in the appropriately evolved language "Does a Divine Being exist?" than it would be absurd to ask at our present state of Anglo-Saxon linguistic evolution "Does a triangle have three sides?" But suppose, as Aquinas supposes, that angels could gain deep insight through what we might call 'mystical experience' or 'Beatific Visions' into the perfectly good and perfectly non-dependent power of God, into the fixity of God's will concerning certain values (including the value of the Divine existence), into God's intense love for eternal creativity, and more of the like, then the angel might well evolve a concept of God as *the x such that x now exists and x is all-powerful and x is non-dependent, etc., etc., and x passionately loves the role of eternal creator without cease.* For a soul with such insight would not the question "Might God cease to exist?" seem to have something approaching the semantic oddity of "Might there be cubic four-sided Euclidean triangles on Mars?" (Compare: "Might it not be that an *x* which always two-dimensional and three-sided somewhere is now three-dimensional and four-sided?") Now let Penelhum rehearse again the distinction between questions about CTA-meanings and WTA-meanings: perhaps the wisdom of Aquinas about "per se nota" and "quoad nos" will be a little clearer.

This would bring Penelhum back rather close to the two threadbare but still idolized punditries "Existence cannot be a property" and "Statements of existence, being statements of fact must be contingent truths, cannot be necessary truths, logical truths or tautologies".

These punditries like associated oracular cackle about "the logical character of existence" are still by far too often taken to be the henceforth eternal fruits of profound intuitions of Kant's and Hume's which have now been proven correct by Symbolic Logic.[16] Bertrand Russell's enthusiasm for the British Empiricist tradition, for his own adventures in Atomistic metaphysics and for axiomatising pure mathematics *qua* the basis of applied mathematics in the natural sciences had unfortunate results: partly because of its importance and power as a new formal system, *and* partly because of its brief but influentially too long supposed completeness as an axiomatic foundation for pure mathematics, the *Principia Mathematica* notation came to be thought of as *the* paradigm of Logic for symbolic systematisers to follow in most respects – C. I. Lewis' pioneering work on modal calculi was thought by many not to follow *Principia* in enough of those respects for his systems to be serious contributions to Symbolic *Logic*. More important still, the (Pluralist) *ontological interpretations* placed on the pure calculus of *Principia* and on its cousinly variants by Russell and those whom he influenced (including Moore, the early Wittgenstein, Carnap and *their* admirers) made it seem to the unwary as if formal articulateness and consistency dictated the acceptance of certain doctrines like "Existence is not a property/predicate/quality", "Statements of fact include all statements of existence", "All statements of fact are contingent truths". Russell drew the amazing conclusion that the fertility of his calculus (compared to formalizations of syllogistic) proved the meta-physics of Spinoza's and Bradley's Monisms and of Leibniz's Monadism to be hopelessly wrong: since he gave only certain Pluralist interpretations to his calculus (and never considered other possibilities adequately) this conclusion is hardly surprising![17] The great German mathematician and logician David Hilbert soon became convinced that the formal logical questions concerning the completeness and consistency of *Principia Mathematica*'s system as a foundation for pure mathematics would best be answered by *not* rushing like Russell to interpret the calculus. The formal properties of the calculus itself would best be studied if the syntax and the formulae were systematically divested of semantic associations. As is well known (but ill noted by some who pontificate on "the logical character of existence"), Hilbert's example of abstractness and precision in formalizing logical questions was not unhelpful to Kurt Gödel. In 1931 Gödel published the really profound logical result that no finite and consistent system of axioms, definitions and rules of inference like *Principia*'s could deliver all the truths *even of arithmetic as theorems*, axioms and definitions. Yet later in the 1930's empiricists like Hans Hahn and A. J. Ayer, who saw Russell's calculus as a tool for carving up metaphysical dragons, were still hoping to draw a rigid contrast between the analytic, necessarily true tautologies of mathematics, logic or semantics and the synthetic empirical hypotheses of the physical or social sciences.[18]

An admirable amount of bridging between Hahn and Ayer in the early 1930's and Penelhum's recent talk about "the logical character of existence" is provided by Antony Flew's anthologies of classic papers in 'Ordinary Language' philosophy – *Logic and Language*, First and Second Series (Oxford 1951 and 1953), *Essays in Conceptual Analysis* (London 1956) and, of course, *New Essays in Philosophical Theology* (co-edited with A. C. MacIntyre, London, 1955). Penelhum's paper, as we stressed, is almost a compendium of modern analytical confusions on the problem of relating "God" to "Is" and "Necessity". Papers that yield especially good illustrations of analysts confused by their admirable but inadequately critical attempts to learn from Hume, Kant and *Principia Mathematica* are Margaret MacDonald's 'The Philosopher's Use of Analogy',[19] (1937, reprinted in *Logic and Language*, First Series), J. N. Findlay's 'Can God's Existence Be Disproved?' (1948, reprinted in *NEPT*) and J. J. C. Smart's 'Can God's Existence Be Disproved?' (first given as a lecture in 1951, reprinted in *NEPT*). Consider some quotations which throw much light on how analysts have allowed themselves to become so amazingly boxed in by balderdash:

MacDonald writes:

Since existence propositions are never tautological it seems important to emphasise their difference from those which ascribe a predicate to a subject (pp. 88–89); in one sense "A man exists" and "*x* is human" do not mean the same since a true value for a propositional function would give a tautology while an existence proposition is never tautologous (p. 90); this may sound platitudinous. Have we not been told by Kant and certainly by Russell of the difference in logical type between existence and subject-predicate propositions? We have certainly been told that existence is not a predicate, which is true (p. 89).

Findlay writes:

We can't help feeling that the worthy object of our worship can never be a thing that merely *happens* to exist, nor one on which all other objects merely *happen* to depend. The true object of religious reverence must ... be wholly *inescapable* ... whether for thought or reality. And so we are led on insensibly to the barely intelligible notion of a being in whom Essence and Existence lose their separateness. And all the great medieval thinkers really did was to carry such a development to its logical limit (52); if an object merely *happened* to be wise, good, powerful and so forth ... it would deserve the δουλεία canonically accorded to the saints, but not to the λατρεία that we properly owe to God (pp. 52–53); What, however, are the consequences of the requirements upon the possibility of God's existence? Plainly (for all who share a contemporary outlook), they entail not only that there isn't a God, but that the Divine existence is either senseless or impossible ... necessity in propositions merely reflects our use of words, the arbitrary [sic] conventions of our language (p.54).

Smart writes:

For the first stage of the argument purports to argue to the existence of a necessary being. And by "a necessary being" the cosmological argument means "a logically necessary being", i.e., "a being whose existence is inconceivable in the sort of way that a triangle's having four sides is inconceivable". The trouble is, however, that the concept of a logically necessary being is a self-contradictory concept, like the concept of a round square .... No existential proposition can be necessary, for we saw that the truth of a logically necessary proposition depends only on our symbolism, or to put the same thing in another way, on the relationship of concepts (p. 38); An existential proposition must be very different from any logically necessary one, such as a mathematical one, for example, for the conventions of our symbolism clearly leave it open for us either to affirm or deny an existential proposition (p. 39). Existence is not a property. "Growling" is a property of tigers, and to say that "tame tigers growl" is to say something about tame tigers but to say "tame tigers exist" is not to say something about tame tigers, but to say there are tame tigers. Professor G. E. Moore once brought out the difference between existence and a property such as that of ... being a growler, by reminding us that though the sentence "some tame tigers do not growl" makes perfect sense, the sentence "some tame tigers do not *exist*' has no clear meaning" (p. 34).

Smart soon moves from a Moorean to a Kantian vein by saying that "exist" must be used to say that a concept applies to something and not to ascribe a property to a subject (p. 34). Compare Penelhum's saying at p. 151 of 'Divine Necessity', after paying hommage first to Kant:

Existence cannot vary in quantity or intensity, belong to some members of a class and not to others, or be interrupted and then resumed. Moore has brought out some of the peculiarities of the word "exist" in a very well-known paper.

Penelhum immediately concludes that existence "is not a quality at all". Very likely the examples of uses of "exist" that obsess Moore and his admirers obsess them in part because they and Moore have been much encouraged in their habits of philosophical thought by Russell's *interpretations* of his and Whitehead's calculus; in part because the use of these interpretations tend to be confounded with the use of Logic as a new formed discipline of great rigour – hence with *logical thought* in general!

So it turns out that while Penelhum makes a wise move in emphasizing the intelligibility of part of what is meant by "necessary being" – e.g., "being whose existence and nature are causally independent of anything" – he is too like the Hughes, Rainer and Crombie of *NEPT* who try to salvage theism from Smart and Findlay but tend to wallow in the old ruts of Shibbolethic obscurantism. He is too like the Crombie who writes

it is never true that we can involve ourselves in a breach of the laws of logic merely by denying that something exists (p. 114),

Penelhum is too like the Hughes who speaks on behalf of God's essential necessity and still adds

The theist had better not try to deny the statement that no tautology can be existential
… as we all know so well "existence is not a predicate" (p. 65).

VII. EXISTENCE AS NECESSARY AND EXISTENCE AS
PREDICATE: THE CONFUSIONS PROBED

VII.1. *Existence and Tautologies*

In loose usage the terms "tautologies", "truths by definition", "logical
truths", "analytic statements" and "necessary propositions" are practically interchangeable. Such loose usage is often partly a result of going
along with Ordinary Usage ('technically' a bit salted) and often partly
a result of quite undue reverence for the famous challenge of Hume with
which he closed *An Enquiry Concerning Human Understanding*:

If we take in our hand any volume; of divinity or school metaphysics for instance; let
us ask, *Does it contain any abstract reasoning concerning quantity or number?* No. *Does
it contain any experimental reasoning concerning matter of fact and existence?* No.
Commit it then to the flames: for it can contain nothing but sophistry or illusion.

We may seem, basking in the echoes of such rhetoric, to have a clear,
intuitive understanding of the difference between (1) questions about
existence and other facts, (2) questions of mathematics, deductive logic and
definition. But if we allow that tautologies are analytic, necessary, *a priori*
and the like, and wish to cling to Hume, we may need to consign many
seminal writings on modern logic to the flames as sophistry and illusion.

Consider the ways that we actually tend to talk about tautologies when
we are *doing* modern logic instead of philosophising and making appeals
like MacDonald and the others to modern logic as settling the issue.
Sentential Calculus allows us to derive from the universal applicability of
Truth Table Decision Procedures to its Well-Formed Formulas (wff.)
a very clear notion of what is meant by "Tautology", "tautologous", etc.
when applied to uninterpreted formulas of Sentential Calculus. But too
often analytical philosophers have shown little interest in distinguishing
pertinent *difficulties* which may arise when we move *from* (i) uninterpreted
formulas of Sentential Calculus to (ii) uninterpreted formulas of some
finitely axiomatised type of Predicate Calculus with Identity Sign – let
alone the pertinent difficulties which may arise when we try to move from
(i) and (ii) to (iii) quasi-'Natural Language' interpretations of formulas in
either Calculus. (Note that in English as a Natural Language, at least when

one is not doing philosophy, one often uses "tautology" to mean "empty, definitional word-play" or even, in looser moments, "triviality" and "truism".) A *tautology* of Quantification Theory *qua* a form of axiomatic Predicate Calculus with Identity Sign sufficiently powerful to formalise on interpretation much mathematical inference may be suggested (if one is perhaps overgenerously keen to make sense of "tautology" here) to be one or more of the following: (i') A proposition or formula which comes out true in the class of *ALL MODELS* or domains and forms of interpretation for a particular finite axiomatisation of Quantification Theory with Identity. (ii') A proposition which is an axiom or definition of a particular, uninterpreted, finite axiomatisation of Predicate Calculus with Identity Sign. (iii') A proposition which is a (clearly derivable) theorem of a particular, uninterpreted, finite axiomatization of Predicate Calculus with Identity Sign. The first account of "tautology" may be highly problematical for some Intuitionists since the range and membership-number of the class of ALL models may be problematical for them – might such talk seem to encourage commitment to a vague *totality* or (worse) to an *actual infinity* of models without proper consideration for the intelligibility of the commitment? But it would be acceptable as an account for some logicians and for some who wish to stiffen the slackness of Natural Language with vocabulary changes related to reflection on logic and meta-logic. Now the following could turn out to be tautologies by criteria (ii') or (iii') in many such finite axiomatisations:

(A) $(\exists x)\,(x = x)$

(B) $(\exists x)\,(Fx \vee \text{Not-}Fx)$

(C) $(x)\,(x = x)\ \&\ (\exists R)\,(x)\,(Rxx)$

(D) $(\exists x)\,(\exists y)\,(x \neq y)$

(E) $(x)\,(\exists y)\,(y > x)$

(F) $(\exists \phi)\,[(E!x)\,(\phi x)].$

There would be considerable reason in certain finite axiomatizations powerful enough for formalizing particular areas of, e.g., pure arithmetic to call such formulas, perhaps if uninterpreted and surely if given certain mathematically very useful interpretations, *existential* propositions as well as *tautologous* ones by tautology-criteria (ii') or (iii'). What could the modern analysts whose spoutings on symbolism and existence, etc., we have been citing want to say of these formulas (these tautologous and existential bogeymen) that would be consistent with their spoutings? What would they want so say if there were an existential-looking proposition the truth of which was shown to be undecidable within a particular system but decidable by meta-mathematical methods? (In 1936, a year before Margaret MacDonald published her paper, Alonzo Church increased the problems created by Gödel's incompleteness theorem for philosophers prone to indulge in loose talk about mathematical and logical truths as mere examples of analyticity, definitional truth, tautologousness, etc. Church published a rigorous proof that there is no *decision procedure*, no *mechanical test*, corresponding to the Truth Table test for Sentential Calculus, for establishing the validity of arbitrary formulas in first-order predicate calculus.)

We are *not* saying that such points about existential tautologies should encourage philosophers to praise Norman Malcolm's already mentioned exercise in fideism 'Anselm's Ontological Arguments' (*Philosophical Review* **69** (1960), 41–62). For what *language engagements* one should make or renew is something, as was discussed in Chapter One, that reasonable men must decide in fair measure as a response to the promptings of experience and to considerations of maintaining a coherent way of thinking. It is not good enough for an allegedly reasonable man simply to defend a language engagement as being part of his Form of Life. Consider the mathematician interested in symbolic logic who tells me it is a *tautology* of arithmetic when suitably axiomatized and interpreted that *there exists* at least one number, 0, by which no number is *divisible*. A reasonable man is more likely to be interested in *this* mathematician's existential tautology and *this* man's ideas about suitable axiomatisations than in the ideas of an equally consistent and formally gifted thinker who derives $(E!n')\,(n)\,[(n \neq 1) \to ($Indivisible n by n' & $n' = 1)]$ as an existential theorem of existential tautology of his interpreted system, formalism, conventions, etc. (But the reasonable man might also remember that such a theorem would seem no more useless to many 19th-century thinkers than would the non-Euclidean geometrical theorems of Bolyai or Lobachevsky. Perhaps there is *an* important sense of "indivisible" or "undividable" which excludes 1 as a divider.)

The dogma that an existential proposition cannot be deduced from a language that is in any way 'logical' must be set aside. And when our distinction between CTA- and WTA-meaning considerations is adopted after the dogma's funeral, the prospects for Aquinas' belief that "God exists" can be self-evident (*per se notum*) and can be reasonably called a necessary, logical or tautological truth about existence should look distinctly brighter. So should the prospects for talk of Existence and Essence being indistinguishable in the case of God. With regard to fears of any conceivable marriage between Existence and Essence, one should recall, of course, that modern logicians often make assertions of existence by using the Identity Sign – as in $(\exists x)\,(\exists y)[x \neq y$ & $(z)\,(z = x \lor z = y)]$; that often they also explicate the Identity Sign in terms of some version of 'Leibniz's Law' which refers to a totality of common PROPERTIES. Compare: $(x)\,(y)\,[x = y \leftrightarrow (P)$ $(Px \leftrightarrow Py)]$. A common interpretation of *P.M.*-ese thus seems to link many a thing's existence with its properties more freely than *Aquinas* or Kant might prefer. Consider also that it follows from standard, monotheist accounts of the Divine properties that $(x)\,(y)$ [(Divine-x & Divine-y)$\leftrightarrow$ $\leftrightarrow x = y$]. From the standpoint then of mere CTA-meanings we can already deduce that if something has the Divine properties, then only one thing has it – or that if 21 is the immediate successor of n in a finite string of integers then only 21 is that thing. Yet, reasonably enough, we feel no puzzlement about allowing ourselves to enter into language engagements which entail uniqueness of existence given that the existent has certain properties. We already undertake (reasonably enough) language engagements whence we derive the truth of "*P*". *P*: From mere knowledge of certain properties, we know that only *one* thing *could* have those properties. But then why would it be unreasonable to believe in the truth of "*P'*"? *P'* goes: A rational being, given certain extraordinary experiences of certain properties, would rationally enter into a conceptual engagement whereby he would derive that from mere depth of knowledge of the nature of those properties, if one has such knowledge, one would know immediately that *something* and only one thing exists which has those properties? Given the point of such a conceptual engagement concerning those properties as is involved in accepting *P'*, one might well reasonably cease to draw a distinction between *x*'s being *conceived* to have those properties and *x*'s being *known* to have them for any rational value of x.

VII. 2. *Existence CAN be a Property*

In the second Section of Chapter II we saw that one can sometimes helpfully employ a formal system in which the Existential Quantifier of the calculus is construed as binding (a) *merely* 'thought-up-things-and-thought-of-things' or 'individuals' as well as (b) actual individuals. We cited there Craig Harrison's work on certain *modal* systems in which the Ontological Argument can be formalized with existence as a property and one of its major errors diagnosed with surprising intelligibity.[20] But we chose there to opt for simple work in first-order predicate calculus – without the residual mysteries of modal operators. We saw that one can in effect, operate with a domain of entities (i) existing in the intellect alone, or (ii) existing in reality but unthought of, or (iii) existing both in the intellect and in reality. One can presuppose for consistency's sake that some form of preestablished harmony ensures that what goes on in intellects does not ever force one to quantify over any individual of which conflicting things have to be predicated or asserted. Let us suppose further that we dwell for the moment in such a domain; that it is small enough not to present relativity problems about time; also that the rigorous science of our fellows in the domain enables us to predict that at least one 'individual' (thought of thing *or/and* actual thing) comes into 'being' (being thought of *or/and* being actual) during each time interval t (of some small but measurable duration) – comes into 'being', or is 'new' in that during the previous time interval it 'was' neither *in re* nor *in intellectu*. Let us say then that during each time interval something 'new' enters upon subsistence or existence and something 'not-new' (which 'was' *in intellectu* or/and *in re* during the previous time interval $t-1$) disappears totally for the duration. It would then be quite sensible for us to hope, if our domain seemed to be getting rather *under*-populated by our tastes, that in the next time interval something *real* or *existent* would be added and only something *thought of* or *subsistent* would be subtracted. Someone with opposite tastes in population would be sensible to hope for the reverse. If the scientists could predict that at least ten thousand *tame tigers* ('individuals' of a kind hitherto non-existent and unthought of) would come into 'being' in the next thirty thousand time intervals, the Populatophobe would be elated if after two-thirds of that time if he found it true to say: "No tame tigers are (yet) real." But the Populatophile would be just as elated if instead he found then that he could truly say: "All tame tigers are (still) real." Moderates would prefer a situation in which they could (perfectly intelligibly) say: "Some tame tigers are real and some are not."

Moreover, a hyper-Populatophile with a special penchant for tame tigers might prefer to count all new tame tigers as *real*, be they existent or subsistent: he would presumably prefer to adopt largely the same *sub-stantiality-attitudes* towards existent and subsistent tame tigers as that which others hold only towards existents – so long as they came into 'being'. Or he might replace the "existent-subsistent" distinction by an "existent$_A$-existent$_B$" distinction in his idiolect to hook up with these unusual substantiality-attitudes.

Such tales should be mulled over by merchants of solemn nonsense about The Logical Character of Existence. The solemn doctrine that Existence is not a Predicate/Property/Quality gained considerable encouragement from the way that the Existential Quantifier was used in logical calculi like that of *Principia Mathematica* and from the ways in which these uses were mainly *interpreted*. For "x is green", "x hardens", "x is inky", etc., would thus preserve something like their 'surface grammar' when translated into 'canonical notion' as "Gx", "Hx", "Ix". But "x is real", "x is actual" and "x exists" would not become "Rx", "Ax", and "Ex" – rather they could all become "$(\exists x)(x=x)$" or be translated "$(\exists x)(\_x)$" for variety. Despite the counter-intuitive conflation of using "some" and using "exists" which would result, this point about how to do translation into 'canonical notation', given a certain interpretation of *P.M.*-ese, was not lost on those ever hopeful of canonizing their favourite brainchildren from the foreheads of Hume and Kant. They felt entitled by their belief that *P.M.*-ese had captured Depth Grammar, or had given man something closer to a language which could *picture* Facts properly or whatever, to talk with a swagger about their special knowledge of "the logical character of existence". This use of words like "logical" suggested that some technical point of logic with a formal decision procedure had been settled in their favour by the peerless position of *P.M.*-ese – even while new sorts of systems and interpretations were being obviously discussed. As Reichenbach, and many others have shown – [see Chapter II] – the illegitimacy of any such swagger on any such basis about the *philosophical* analysis of "existence" should have been admitted long ago.[21] "Existence is not a property" *ought* by now to look as dubious to Penelhums as "Objects can only be *named*".

Nor does it redeem all the confusions of the past to fall back rather like Penelhum on such 'non-technical' linguistic arguments as: "Real" is not a property because existence can have no degrees of intensity; "real" has no comparative or superlative; unlike "red" and "warm", "real" and "existent" are not connected with a quality; if the latter pair were connected with a quality we could say not only "This is redder and warmer than that" but also "This is more real and existent than that". It will not wash. Except in special dialects like those of used car salesmen at work "Unique" has no correct comparative or superlative. But does uniqueness cease to be a property when "unique" is used outside these odd dialects? Two cannot be more even than four. Julius Caesar could be the most stabbed but not the most killed of all Romans on the Ides of March. "Real" does not cease to be an intelligible when one speaks of the danger of civil war in Kashmir as now being even more real than the danger of foreign intervention. We do easily say "The danger is no longer very real" and we may find it odd to say "Ghosts are no longer very real", but does it follow that these two uses of the adjective "real" are completely equivocal? [22]

VIII. DOES "X IS A NECESSARY BEING" ENTAIL "X IS TIMELESS"?

The case we have tried to establish for the possibility of reasonable man's becoming reasonably convinced that God is a Necessary Being reveals our considerable sympathy with Aquinas' attempt to correct Anselm on this subject. But we find ourselves, as emphasized in Chapter III, anxious to be rid of certain commitments to Aristotelian physics and metaphysics which Saint Thomas was understandably and, for a man of his time, very bravely willing to make. Our version of *The Justifying Explanation Argument* offers no reason to construe God as a Timeless Prime Mover, nor did we wish it to do this. The first two of the Five Ways draw heavily on Aristotelian cosmology, the third draws both on Aristotle and on Stoic logicians' discussions of time and modality, the Fourth seems to draw more on Platonic and Neo-Platonic concepts of Eternal Values — not surprisingly they all lead to a Timeless Being. The Fifth Way would seem to minister much more naturally to the existence of a Temporal God with purposes and intentions which He temporally fulfils. But Aquinas' intellectual debt to the Greeks and Arabs made it all but impossible for him to see this. An important question remains: does Aquinas' Atemporal Necessary Being supply the justifying explanation of history supplied by the Biblical message of God's personal perfection and love? We suspect that it does not. We close this chapter with reflections on certain traditional Divine Attributes, reflections which suggest that if God is a Necessary Being because God's love and personal perfections supply His own and the world's justifying explanation then God is not an Unmoved Mover.

VIII.1. *Omniscience*

How can the *omniscience* of God be reconciled with human freedom? If God has foreknowledge of what everyone will do tomorrow, then how can anyone be said to have any choice about his doings? There is an elegant classical answer to this sort of question; it is an answer offered by Boethius at *De Consolatione*, Book V and endorsed by Aquinas at *Summa Contra Gentiles*, Book III, Chapter 61. The answer consists in saying that the bogey of divine *fore*knowledge is the product of a confusion between the atemporal world-view of God in His eternity and the knowings or not-knowings of man in time "which has its being in a sort of succession". Only if God were in time and so knew *today* what someone would do tomorrow, could His omniscience endanger his freedom. *Fore*knowledge is thus an anthropomorphic misnomer. The solution is, we repeat, classically admirable in its elegance; it carries a price, of course, that of placing God in the curious domain of the atemporal. Yet this is a price which Aquinas, with his admiration for Aristotle, would be especially happy to pay: it seems to clarify the Aristotelian view that God, to be perfect, must be purely *in act*; totally *without potency*. (Compare *SCG*, I, 16.)

There is an alternative solution to the problem of harmonizing Divine omniscience and human freedom. This solution, offered by Richard Taylor among others, accepts God as a temporal being and locates the source of our trouble in *omni*science rather than in *fore*knowledge. At any given time a certain sum of knowledge represents *all* there is to know. Included in that sum for an omniscient temporal knower will be all that is future that is totally determined by present causal factors. If some future events (like certain human choices) are not so determined, then, in respect of these events there just is nothing now to know: "if the future is partially undetermined ... an omniscient being would have to comprehend it just that way." [23] This solution also has an attractive elegance, but it does seem to require at least the following addendum if temporal omniscience is to measure up to Divine standards. Insofar as a temporal, omniscient being is also a purposer, omnipotent and the source of all other beings with power, His foreknowledge of the (wholly or partially) determined future of what is distinct from Himself is to be construed not so much on the model of our knowledge of what is distinct from ourselves *as on the model of our "knowledge" of our own intentions*. God's foreknowledge of tomorrow's sunrise is illuminated by a report of intention like "I know very well what I'll do with my next pay raise". But this addendum is not unwelcome: it stresses the Personal Character of God and it makes the world less like a machine with which Someone Supernatural timelessly tinkers (Lunn's Fable).

VIII.2. *God as Supreme Purposer*

Some years ago the Personalist theologian, E. S. Brightman, criticized those who shared his belief in a purposive God directing the universe, yet insisted that His eternity was utterly different from time. Brightman considered such talk unhelpful for his "empirical" approach to religion, which found evidence for faith in experience. If God's purposes bore no intelligible relation to our temporal human purposes, how could experience point to such a timeless purposer? More recently George Boas, in his Paul Carus lectures, has developed Brightman's empirical point into a more fundamental query as to the very meaning of teleology; he concludes in terms very generous to the opposition, that "teleology *had best* be used where it can be used literally", when theology is extended into cosmic planning, he holds, the planner or planners *had better* be modeled on the personal, historical God of Scripture rather than on a timeless metaphysical abstraction, (a Fundamental Ground, for example, or a Principle of Concretion).[24]

There are reasons, we suggest, for going beyond Boas' "had best" and trying to replace his chivalrous understatement with a hard (WTA-logician's) "must". A teleological explanation is naturally construed in Western theologians' talk as purpose-referential and intention-referential explanation. This is not to say that a *telos* for Aristotle in his account of causes has to be so treated. The Greek word may be construed as "finish", "peak", "consummation", "direction", "completion" and by other words less wedded to intention than the English "purpose". But Aristotle's God is not a Creator concerned with his creatures. Aristotelian teleology, unlike the Judaeo-Christian type, need not mesh with talk of judgment and eschatology, the Divine plan unfolding in history, salvation through Divine intervention, the Good Shepherd, and so on. In sharp contrast with Aristotle, Judaeo-Christian teleology is deeply committed to God as intending efficient cause, as interested in maintaining some worldly things and changing others. In other words, to speak of God as Supreme Purposer is for the religious purposes of our tradition to exalt Him as supreme among intending agents. Now it seems fundamental to the logic of *intention* that the intending agent be directed to, or engaged in, or considering an activity which is not yet complete for him. Certainly one can display intention in ones directedness to what one is *now* doing but that is because what one can here be spoken of as "doing" involves a temporal succession of states, each preceding another later state. "Am" cannot be the timeless present of orthodox theology in such an intentional context. It is a fair objection that God could intelligibly be said to be changing our *present* state of affairs intentionally without His own action (as opposed to its effects) being dated with the "*now*" of our Earthly time scheme. But this would be intelligible only on the following sort of model: Heaven is like a far off star whence God within His own time scheme acts upon our world intentionally. The time of our being acted upon is not the time of His action. But if one goes on to insist that Heaven itself has no time scheme at all, then one has no more suitable context for speaking of intentions in that region than in the realm of positive integers. Intention presupposes *some* time scheme of "before" and "after". This holds good whether we construe intention behaviouristically, or as the drama of a purely private stage, or partly as a matter of public appraisal. These points about intention are but corollaries to more general and obvious ones about persons and personal acts. Our concepts of person, personal purpose, personal consideration of what is best, personal decision and so on cannot, it seems, be uprooted from a context of conscious, temporal individuals; they belong in a setting of intentions and acts, the description of which must be characterized by relations like *earlier than* and *later than*.

It is at this juncture that some traditionalists would interrupt us on behalf of the Analogy of Being, saying we have overlooked an important possibility. Maybe, they would say, we can achieve a very dim understanding by analogy of the purposeful workings of an atemporal, non-human mind. Two questions arise about this suggestion: (a) Would such an analogy get us off our conceptual ground to any effect? (b) Why should we resort to it, when, if it did work, it would provide such an extraordinarily dim understanding anyway? As for (a) it is certainly true that we can speak by analogy or sense-extension of the purposes of non-human, non-conscious, temporal individuals like machines and missiles by presupposing purposeful men who make them. But the analogy for our purposes is a *cul-de-sac*. We do not want God to be like a machine that performs an alien purpose and cannot tell whether the successful completion of its routine achieves a purpose. Again, by a related analogy, we can talk of the purposes of atemporal, non-conscious things like axioms, definitions and concepts. ("The purpose of Axiom 3 is to exclude type confusions.") But neither analogy offers any flicker of intelligibility to the apparent contradiction involved in positing a purposing and self-consciously purpose achieving but non-temporal individual. Here the analogist's Way of Remotion seems simply to remove the Unmoved Mover. At least it seems so, if He is meant to be anything more than a bafflingly abstract type of Aristotelian final cause.

More important for those who want an intelligible account of theology is question (b). Why should we be so eager to press this unpromising analogy simply to keep God atemporal? The God of most Old Testament writers and the Heavenly Father of Christ's reported words sounds temporal enough – whatever the drift of later Hellenized comments like the introduction to St. John's Gospel. Certainly God is an *eternal* purposer in the Scriptures. But there the Divine attribute of eternity is quite naturally and venerably intelligible in the following temporal sense: God has always existed and always will exist through unending time and depends on nothing else for His existence. No other individual could trespass on the uniqueness of this *independent* temporal eternity: making God temporally eternal in this sense does not reduce Him to the status of His everlasting but ever dependent creatures.

Plato in *Republic*, Book II gives an excellent illustration of the initial thinking which leads some metaphysicians to prefer a desperate analogy to a Divine temporality. "Look at the wicked lives of the Olympian supreme beings", he says in effect, "they are so like people. Homer's Zeus and Hera are as fickle and untrustworthy as any humans. A supreme being worthy of imitation must surely be immutable, unchanging and ever reliable." The simplest way, as we later see in *Republic*, Book VI, to conceive of an individual as immutable, unchanging and ever reliable is to remove that individual from the spatio-temporal setting of human persons and construe the individual after the model of timeless figures, concepts and numbers: The Idea of the Good, The One and so on. "Geometrical figure" has been suggested as a root meaning of "EIDOS" which greatly influenced Plato. The aura of reliable necessity, which attends his Ideas, is particularly understandable in the case of one innocent of thoughts about consistent alternatives in formalization, one for whom the supposedly unique set of axioms and definitions governing the individuals of arithmetic and geometry have an absolute, necessary status. From this Platonic 'Leap' arises Augustine's atemporal God Who makes the world *cum tempore*. But an obstacle remains if, having depersonalized his supreme being, the metaphysician persists in supreme teleological talk. Following P. F. Strawson's acute discussion of atemporal Monads in Leibniz we may ask: how is it possible to treat a timeless individual, conceived after the model of concepts, "on analogy with individual consciousness?"[25] Worse yet for the theist, how can such an impersonal timeless being be fruitfully called worthy of imitation, when the analogy between the nature of that being and the nature of people is so obscure?

At any rate there is a perfectly good sense in which a Divine temporal being could be immutable, unchanging, reliable and thus worthy of imitation. The Divine temporal being must be utterly *unfaltering* in love, mercy, justice, sympathy, wisdom and so on despite the passage of time. It is unfaltering exemplification of such virtues as these through time everlasting which gives us the desiderated and imitable sense of the Divine immutability. We do not need the sense or non-sense which denies temporal succession to God's acts of love, mercy and wrath, yet asserts the agency and *intervention of* His love, mercy and wrath at different points in history.

VIII.3. *God as Omnipotent Purposer*

Judaeo-Christian theologians like Thomas and Maimonides, who claimed to find God's atemporal hand in Aristotle's *Physics* and *Metaphysics*, link the Divine omnipotence with atemporality by holding that God to be omnipotent must be totally in act and not at all in potency. There must, for instance, be no temporal lag, no gap of any kind between His willing and His will being done.[26] Any such lag or gap would detract from the

Divine omnipotence and perfection. Perhaps the best counter to this way of thinking would be to consider Boas' antitheistic attack on the whole notion of an omnipotent purposer.

In what sense of the word could an omnipotent being have any purposes whatsoever? We make plans not merely because the future is largely unknown but also because we know that it is a natural obstacle to the fulfillment of our desires. A stone does not need plans since there is only one thing it can do .... A human being has to make plans .... But an omnipotent being is like an impotent being; his actions flow out of his nature.[27]

Now there is something suspicious about an argument from which Thomas and Maimonides, on the one hand, can conclude that God the omnipotent chooser must be atemporal and Boas, on the other hand, can conclude that there are *logically* no omnipotent choosers.

Let us get the premises into an analogous form for disgorging their fallacy. It makes fair sense, if poor verisimilitude outside Maoist circles, to say that Mao can carry out any (logically significant) policy he chooses to adopt. If Mao really could implement with success any global policy he preferred and do so in as short or long a time as he saw fit, then he would be in a clear sense an all powerful global chooser and purposer. Substituting 'cosmic' for 'global' in protasis and apodosis, we would get the conclusion that he was an all powerful cosmic chooser. But we do not want omnipotent God to be just a cosmic Mao and the temptation here is to make atemporality His *differentia* in omnipotence. Resisting this temptation we must stipulate as the criterion of Divine omnipotence that not only can God bring about unaided any policy of His choice, but also that no agent other than God has choice or power of action but for God's freely chosen dispensation. This, not atemporality, is the needed *differentia* of Divine omnipotence by apparent Biblical standards.

Aquinas and Maimonides would object that if God is an omnipotent chooser there cannot be a time lag between His choice and its fulfillment: God has to be atemporal. This line of thought may rest at least partly on a confusion of what Peter Geach has called logically attributive and logically predicative adjectives. If a flea is red and a van is red then they are, roughly speaking, of the same colour. But a big flea and a big van are not, even roughly speaking, of the same size. When *"omnipotent"* qualifies a chooser, it is at least akin to one of Geach's logically attributive adjectives (good, big) in that we should not suggest criteria for power inappropriate to *choosers*. Perhaps a great deal of spurious mystification results from theologians' talking about the Divine omnipotence in a wildly abstract way and forgetting that *omnipotent* is, in its theological context, an adjective qualifying a personal individual. To argue like Boas that because God is an omnipotent chooser, therefore he cannot really be a chooser at all, is like arguing that because Fido is a big miniature poodle he is not really a miniature poodle at all. To argue like Thomas and Maimonides that because God is an omnipotent chooser, therefore He is atemporal, is, since choosers are intenders and intenders are naturally understood as temporal individuals, rather too like arguing that because Fido is truly a good dog he cannot be canine, because true goodness transcends canininity. The omnipotence of a non-temporal person is about as intellectually promising as the goodness of a non-canine dog.[28]

NOTES

[1] W. P. Alston, 'Dispositions and Occurrences', *Canadian Journal of Philosophy* 1 (1971) 125–54.

[2] 'From "*God*" to "*Is*" and from "*Is*" to "*Ought*"', *Philosophical Quarterly* 7 (1957), 136–48; 'Value and "Essentialist" Fallacies', *Thomist* 21 (1958) 162–70; 'The Logic of Cognitive States', *Mind*, New Series 67 (1958) 246–48. (Cf. *Reason and Religion*, London 1969, pp. 48–49, 142 etc.). Kai Nielsen's 'The Primacy of Philosophical Theology', *Theology Today* 27 (1970) valuably attacks 'value-free' dogmas about analysis and merits relating to the *CTA-WTA* distinction concerning "meanings" in this chapter. (Cf. Nielsen's *Contemporary Critiques of Religion*, Toronto 1971, pp. 6–10.)

[3] See J. L. Austin, *How to Do Things with Words*, Oxford 1962, pp. 82–119.

[4] See John King-Farlow, *Reason and Religion*, London 1969, Chapter III.

[5] J. O. Urmson, *Philosophical Analysis: Its Development Between the Two World Wars*, Oxford 1956; see especially pp. 14ff, 41ff, 167ff; Gustav Bergmann, *The Metaphysics of Logical Positivism*, London 1954.

[6] J. P. Sartre, *L'Être et le Néant*, Paris 1943. Translated by Hazel E. Barnes as *Being and Nothingness*, New York 1956.

[7] Ed. by W. Elton, Oxford 1953.

[8] London 1946.

[9] See his contribution '"We" in Modern Philosophy' to B. Mitchell (ed.), *Faith and Logic*, London 1957. See also M. B. Foster, *Mystery and Philosophy*, London 1957, for valuable arguments against philosophical fashions of the Fifties, as well as for useful points about the bizarreness of expecting rigorously checkable demonstrations of *Divine* or *Holy* Activity.

[10] See her contribution to D. F. Pears (ed.), *The Nature of Metaphysics*, London 1957.

[11] Certainly Miss Murdoch suggested that both are legitimate and tolerably strong metaphysical competitors in her contributions to *Aristotelian Society*, Supplementary Volume 30 (1956), *Twentieth Century* (Special Oxford Number, 1955), and D. F. Pears (ed.), *The Nature of Metaphysics*, London 1957.

[12] *Sartre, Romantic Rationalist*, Cambridge 1953, pp. 47–48.

[13] A predecessor of this argument caps the reasoning of *Reason and Religion*, Chapter VII, pp. 118–20 (cf. note 4). We consider this expanded version both more liberal in tone and more powerful in rational appeal. Premise Six is introduced because of reflection on the importance of William James' 'The Will to Believe' (which we discuss at length in Chapter VI). Premise Seven is introduced to reap the proper benefits of the self-applicable considerations on universalisability mentioned in our earlier *Apologia*, Chapter I, Section 10.

[14] P. G. Winch, *The Idea of a Social Science*, London 1958; 'On Understanding a Primitive Society', in D. Z. Phillips (ed.), *Religion and Understanding*, Oxford 1967, pp. 9–42. The latter was first published in 1964 and valuable criticisms of it appear in Alasdair MacIntyre's 'Is Understanding Compatible with Believing?' – see J. Hick (ed.), *Faith and the Philosophers*, New York 1966, pp. 115–33 – and in Kai Nielsen, 'Wittgensteinian Fideism', *Philosophy* **42** (1967) 191–209. Richard Rudner's treatment of *The Idea of a Social Science* in *Philosophy of Social Science*, Englewood Cliffs, N.J., 1966, helps to remove any doubt lingering in Winch's favour that perhaps his impressive breadth of scholarship in social sciences may rest after all on reasonable methodological foundations Cf. Jane Royal Martin 'Another Look at the Doctrine of Verstehen'', *British Journal for Philosophy of Science* **20** (1969) 53–67; Jane Royal Martin, *Explaining, Understanding and Teaching*, New York 1970, Parts I and III.

[15] For *analogical predication*, see E. L. Mascall, *Existence and Analogy*, London 1949, and the contrasting but no less historically sympathetic views of James F. Ross in 'Analogy as a Rule of Meaning for Religious Language', *International Philosophical Quarterly* **1** (1961) 468–502. Cf. Aquinas *De Veritate*, qs. 1–2; *Summa Theologica* I, q. 16; *Summa Contra Gentiles* I, 34. For discussion of current blindness to the importance of analogical thought and speech for *man* see John King-Farlow, 'Two Dogmas of Linguistic Empiricism' (address to the May 1972 meetings of the American Philosophical Association, Western Division), *Dialogue* **12** (1972), 324-335.

[16] For useful historical comment on this see A. J. Ayer at p. 10 of his introduction to his anthology *Logical Positivism*, New York 1959. See also the typical comments of R. Carnap on the supremacy of *Principia Mathematica* at p. 135 of this anthology.

[17] See John King-Farlow, 'Quantification Theory and Ontological Monism', *Zeitschrift für Allgemeine Wissenschaftstheorie* **4** (1972) 1–12. See also John King-Farlow and Juan Espinaco-Virseda, 'Matter, Form and Logic', *Rassegna Internazionale di Logica* **3** (1971) 93–104. Several points from these papers will be made in this paper – in relation to rather different questions.

[18] See Hans Hahn's 1933 paper 'Logic, Mathematics and Knowledge of Nature', translated by Arthur Pap in A. J. Ayer (ed.), *Logical Positivism*, New York 1959, pp. 147–61. Carnap's paper of 1930 'The Old and the New Logic', written shortly before publication of Gödel's incompleteness theorem, is also heavy in emphasis on the *emptiness* of tautologies (see Ayer, *op. cit.*, p. 143). W. V. Quine's essay 'Two Dogmas of Empiricism', originally published in 1951, was considerably motivated by distaste for the assumption that expertise in logic, despite Gödel's result of 1931 and despite logicians' lipservice to actual methods in science, still dictated loyalty to such mixtures of Kant and Hume as the rigorous separating of propositions into a dichotomy of ones equally irrational to question ('tautologies', 'analytic' or 'necessary' truths etc.) and others equally rational to question. Quine, unfortunately, like those whom he attacked, failed to draw the CTA-WTA distinction. But Morton White, a colleague of Quine's at Harvard in the 1950's who vigorously supported his attack on the analytic-synthetic dis-

tinction does try to draw something like the CTA-WTA distinction in the final part of *Towards Reunion in Philosophy*, Cambridge, Mass. 1956.

19 For a more detailed discussion of Margaret MacDonald's confusions about Existence, Tautologies, Predicates ets. see 'Matter, Form and Logic' (note 17).

20 C. R. Harrison in 'The Ontological Argument in Modal Logic' *The Monist* **54** (1970) writes at pp. 302–03: "There are, of course, well-known objections to the claim that existence is a property. Ultimately, these amount to a refusal to countenance possible individuals that are not actual. But consistent, complete systems of modal logic have been found which do make use of such notions. (N.B. – See, for example, two unpublished works by Dana Scott, 'Advice on Modal Logic', and 'Formalizing Intensional Notions'.) And since we are concerned in argument with what can be demonstrated rather than with what is simply true, we do not have to settle on criteria for deciding what possible individuals there really are before using a logic which allows them. For, if such a system is complete, a *provable* sentence is one which is true regardless of what possible individuals (or possible worlds) there are. Completeness, as usual, means truth in all interpretations. An interpretation is defined as a set W of possible worlds and a set I of possible individuals, and a function which assigns a truth value to every modal sentence at each possible world u in W. At a given world w in W, this function satisfies the usual conditions with respect to the connectives and quantifiers and in addition, we shall say that 'ϕ' is true at w if and only if for every U in W, 'ϕ' is true at u.

"The Ontological Argument lends itself particularly well to a first-order system in which the variables range over possible individuals. The formalization of the argument within modal logics of this kind is simple and direct, for the predicate of existence then has nontrivial application: there are possible individuals which are not actual. I shall employ one such system, due to Kaplan, Montague and Dana Scott. (This system is outlined in the two papers by Dana Scott alluded to above. There are differences in the two works in the treatment of non-denoting descriptions which, however, do not directly concern us here.) In it an interpretation includes a set of possible worlds, at which any sentence is either true or false."

21 Given a Monistic interpretation for ontologizing, the so-called 'existential quantifier' of P.M.-ese receives a type of predicative function. See 'Quantification Theory and Ontological Monism', cited at note 17. "Objects can only be *named*" (*Tractatus* 3.221), "There are no pictures that are true *a priori*" (2.225) and like relics of Logical Atomism would make most Penelhums smile. The time is ripe for them to smile also at the 'logically' refurbished Humean and Kantian antiques considered here.

22 For discussions of "real" in religious and theological language see John King-Farlow 'Religion, Reality and Language', *Pacific Philosophy Forum* **5** (1967), 4–55.

23 Richard Taylor, 'The Problem of Future Contingencies', *Philosophical Review* **66** (1957)1ff.

24 George Boas, *The Enquiring Mind*, Illinois 1959, p. 159. Our italics.

25 P. F. Strawson, *Individuals*, London 1959, Chapter IV.

26 Aquinas, *Summa Contra Gentiles* I, Chapters 14ff; Maimonides, *Guide to the Perplexed*, Part I, Chapter IV.

27 Boas, *op. cit.*, p. 139.

28 These reflections on God and timelessness were partly composed in 1960–61 when we were privileged to have George Boas as a colleague. We regret that Nelson Pike in his valuable recent work *God and Timelessness*, London 1970, omits discussion of Boas and Brightman, though his reasoning fits well with some of their thinking. Pike on his closing page (190) refuses to rule out any compatibility between "the doctrine of time-

lessness" and "a system of Christian theology", but also concludes that his historical and conceptual researches provide no reason for thinking that they *should* be combined. Unfortunately, writers like Tillich have made terms like "a system of Christian theology" vulgarly incapable of excluding practically anything. We suggest that our brief arguments here should be enough for those who value most the *person-like descriptions* of God in the Old and New Testaments as central to the Judaeo-Christian tradition. R. C. Coburn offers an excellent discussion at 'Professor Malcolm on God' *Australasian Journal of Philosophy* **41** (1963) 143–62, for those haunted by puzzles over Timelessness. James Kellenberger kindly cites and strengthens earlier arguments of ours in his recent book Religious Discovery, Faith and Knowledge, New York 1972, pp. 41, 45, 191 and 193.

CHAPTER V

FROM *IS* TO *OUGHT* AND FROM *OUGHT* TO *GOD*

I. SOME STEPS RETRACED: "GOD EXISTS" AS A NECESSARY TRUTH

In Chapter IV we allowed ourselves to cover a good deal of mixed territory in the hope of illuminating a cluster of importantly related confusions. Taken together these confusions often seem to discredit belief in the sort of personal God (whose 'Gooper'-properties are coordinate with 'Expo'-properties) that emerges from those strands of the Judaeo-Christian tradition which we aim to defend.

These strands are, we believe, wise and not wild ones. Nor is the whole tradition, we believe, deserving of a sanitary death by burial under the pyramid of certain well-meaning philosophers' chunks of highly conventional therapeutic analysis. It can be silly in some contexts to cling to traditional terms like "necessary truth", *"ens a se"*, *"ens necessarium"*, *"ens realissimum"* and the like. For often clinging to traditional jargon becomes an excuse for blindly upholding ossified conventions and for not thinking afresh about philosophy's central questions. But sometimes defending the wisdom of using such terms in no few contexts, especially given the case where rejecting these terms as senseless has all but become an ossified convention, elicits fresh thinking. It follows from the mixed explorations of Chapter IV, if we have been largely right there, that "God exists" is worth calling a necessary truth in at least four related and enlightening ways:

[A] "God exists" is a necessary proposition (WTA-'necessary' proposition), in that if we now have a perspicuous understanding of the CTA-meanings of "exists" *and* if we ALSO *had* a concept of God appropriate to the Divine reality, which we now do not, then the atheist claim against traditional Judaeo-Christianity "God does not exist" would seem to us to be extremely similar in important ways to (1) someone's both asserting and denying the same thing in the same sense at the same time;

also in some ways to (2) Epimenides the Cretan's saying "All Cretans always say what is false and I speak as a Cretan"; *furthermore* in some ways to (3) 'pragmatically', 'semantically' or 'syntactically' trying pronouncements like "Existence does not exist", "No words have any meaning and all sense is nonsense", "The one thing which would have to exist, if anything were to exist or be real (including words or speech acts), does not exist".

Corollary: Philosophy as the pursuit of wisdom is more concerned with WTA-meanings than CTA-meanings, but must of course be concerned with both.

[B] "God exists" as a WTA-'necessary' proposition is logically linked with "God's essence and God's existence are inseparable" which is also a WTA-'necessary' proposition. For if we now have a perspicuous understanding of the CTA-meaning of "exists" *and* if we also *had* very profound concepts of *God* and His most important *properties* P_1, P_2, P_3, etc., concepts appropriate to the Divine reality, which we now do not have, then the claims against traditional Judaeo-Christianity either (i) "God does not exist" or (ii) "God exists but does not have P_n" (would seem to us in important ways to be very similar to someone's asserting and denying in the same sense at the same time either (i) "There is an x such that F_1x and F_2x and F_3x, etc., and NOT F_1x and NOT F_2x and not F_3x, etc." or (ii) "There is an x such that F_1x and F_2x and F_3x, etc., and NOT F_3x".

Corollary: "Existence" and "reality" can be intelligibly and wisely used in suitable contexts as property-words.

[C] "God exists" can be a necessary proposition for many a rational person in that many a wise, reflective person can be convinced rationally by forms of the Justifying Explanation Argument that (i) the world almost certainly MUST have some justifying explanation that (ii) the Judaeo-Christian conceptual scheme offers so plausible a justifying explanation that he almost certainly MUST be warranted in now committing himself tolerantly to this scheme; that (iii) for a very limited and fallible being like man who must ACT and LIVE a LIFE that much closeness to certainty, if embraced with a certain sort of tentativeness and tolerance (discussed in Chapter One), is certainty enough for such a commitment.

Corollary: Talk of God as *a* Being and as *the Necessary* Being makes clear sense and is rationally defensible as wise talk.

[D] "God exists" is a necessary truth because so-called 'evaluative' claims about what is good, permissible, obligatory, wise, wrong, foolish, evil, etc., can be at least as much claims about hard facts as 'descriptive' claims about whether persons exist, whether persons have intentions and powers of choice, whether some person is physically or mentally healthy or ill, whether coal and flint are more alike than flint and deer or than English coal and Welsh coal, whether Picasso is more likely to remain highly esteemed as a painter than Bill Christensen, whether this alleged conscientious objector is being frank or is lying about his feelings on war, whether what young Robin is telling one is the tale of a mere dream she had or at least partly the story of something that actually happened in her waking life, whether what one reads in *Time* magazine about China is largely a mixture of distortion and fantasy or is really accurate reporting of main developments and most significant changes there from a clear-headed perspective. (Nor could we check out the truth of such 'descriptions' without granting the objectivity of many 'evaluations' about frankness, objectivity, relevance etc.) Relatedly we hold that belief in the truth of theism is NEEDED or NECESSARY if one is to look at the events of human history successfully – at them and their significance in proper perspective. Acceptance of God's existence and perfections is necessary if one is to see the world's history for what it is as a whole and to see the real sense of its developments and changes.

Corollary: Philosophizing or just plain sensible reasoning about the existence of God, mind, matter, artistic talent, weight or degree of resemblance, and much else of any importance simply does not permit any rigid distinctions between *facts* and *values*, *cases of IS* and *cases of OUGHT*, *descriptions* and *prescriptions*, etc. The attempt of philosophers to describe the real world *rightly* or *wisely* in a '*value-neutral*' way is self-stultifying. (Whether the description of something in the world is right, wise, balanced, illuminating, appropriate is *inter alia* a question about the world.)

Let us pass now to considering three objections to treating "God exists" as a necessary truth – objections based on (i) appeals to the alleged

meaninglessness of talk about bodiless persons: (ii) appeals to the existence of evil. After considering these objections we shall make two further
efforts to reveal the silliness of rigid distinctions between facts and values.
We hope that the latter efforts will enhance the theist's credit when he
moves in full circle from the last chapter's title to that of the present one:
"From *IS* to *OUGHT* and from *OUGHT* to *GOD*".

II. THE NECESSARY TRUTH CONTESTED:
PERSONS WITHOUT BODIES

Kai Nielsen has recently written in his *Contemporary Critiques of Religion*:

Not even moderate fideism is a defensible position ... it is not true that the admittedly
mysterious and problematic concept of God has sufficient intelligibility and coherence
to provide the foundation of a confessional group which is worthy of ones allegiance
(London and Toronto 1971, p. 135).

Nielsen wrote this after giving a résumé of what he takes to be the most
shattering arguments against theism for establishing such alleged unintelligibility and incoherence. He claims that the supposedly devastating
blow to theism

rests on no general theory of language; it is no more dependent on neo–behaviourist
or materialist conceptions than on verificationist ones. Rather it turns on the kind of
understanding we should gain by careful attention to our actual use of words in a
particular area. (pp. 119–20).

Despite Nielsen's sketchings of arguments and paradings of appeals to
Big Guns in the game of Revealing Revelation to Be Nonsense his honesty
makes it plain that he has doubts about the full soundness of some of
these arguers and arguments (p. 118). His assessments here as a very.
careful spokesman for atheism lead one to suppose that his party's single
decisive argument is very simple: "God exists" cannot be a necessary
truth or any kind of truth because what he calls 'God-talk', talk of
persons who lack flesh and blood but who are conscious, or who love
though they have no bodies, or who operate as bodiless agents, is talk
which makes no sense (pp. 114–28).

   Nielsen does treat the problem of God's being called a *timeless* agent,
lover, etc., briefly in these pages. And we have already agreed that *this*
habit of some theologians does pose unnecessary mysteries, besides seeming

alien to the descriptions of God as a person in the Bible. But this real problem for some theologians, we have suggested at the end of Chapter IV, is not a serious problem for more Biblically minded theists anyway, (We may be wrong to think unlike Augustine, Boethius and Aquinas, that a personal God cannot be timeless. But here the point between Nielsen and some theists is not at issue.) Nielsen's discussion – somewhat in the tradition of Hume – offers the theist two choices. Here is the dilemma. HORN (A): *On the one hand the supposed theist may be insincere about God's having no spatio-temporal locations* (is thus a wretched anthropomorphist!!), *and hence is not a genuine theist or 'God-talker'.* HORN (B): *On the other hand, the theist may really think that he has a bodiless Creator to talk about – in which case the theist defies the bounds of sense.* The faithful may perhaps thank God for an atheist arguer who will put his main case so lucidly and frankly. But the horns of Nielsen's dilemma are really so spectral, indeed so downright implausible that one faces another genuine pair of options. Either one should stop to write a whole book about the anthropocentrism in modern philosophy of language that creates the bizarre assumptions by which so able a philosopher as Nielsen is misled. Or one should be very brisk indeed in view of the wildly implausible and counter-intuitive things generated by these assumptions. For purposes of this book, the latter option seems to be indicated.

HORN A: Suppose one were worried by Horn B and resorted as a theist to saying that God's incorporeality or spirituality lay in His having a body of a special sort, an *aethereal* or *subtle* body which has spatio-temporal locations but which lacks the more burdensome features of what we or scientists call matter (cf. Nielsen, p. 125). We read in the Gospels, for example, of Jesus' appearing in a form that Nielsen might call *aethereal* after His death. We read of Jesus' so appearing and eating a fish, walking through a wall, inviting Thomas to touch His wounds, blessing food, speaking to friends and disciples, ascending into the sky and disappearing from men's sight. Suppose that God is such an aethereal being with spatio-temporal locations, able to manifest Himself to other more materially burdened sentient beings with bodies and scientific instruments (such as humans and, possibly, Alpha Centaurians) as often *or as seldom* as He likes. Such a supposition might horrify various theists and atheists alike as being utterly incompatible with talk of God's infinite perfections. But this might be silly. If talk of disembodied personal existence really made no sense, it would not be an imperfection in God not to be a disembodied person. *If* talk of *infinite space* really does make sense, then God's aethereal body can extend infinitely and be manifested wherever and in whatsoever forms He likes. And thus created matter does not get in His aethereal body's way unless He wishes it to. Witness Jesus' walking through the wall. (If talk of *infinite space* does not even make sense, then it could be no imperfection in an aethereal God not to be infinitely extended in space.) God can still be infinitely powerful, merciful, loving, wisie, creative, and so on. His having an aethereal body would not deprive Him of the 'Expo'- and 'Gooper'-properties that make God the justifying explanation of the world. "But how can God be infinite if he has spatio-temporal locations and matter also has such locations? If God is spatial and infinite, He alone can occupy space. There cannot be anything else in space besides a spatially infinite aethereal God". Compare the muddled sort of belief of the child, mentioned in connection with Phillips in Chapter IV, Section IV – the sort of belief that there cannot be an infinite series of fractions between $1\frac{1}{2}$ and 2 since, e.g., $2\frac{1}{2}$ or an infinite series between $2\frac{1}{2}$ and 3 lies outside the series. A rather gross concept of aether (as just more matter) and also a rather gross concept of matter as a Parmenidean chock-ablock *plenum*, leaving no spatial locations for anything else seem to be also presupposed by the objector. The Divine differentiae which would distinguish God's supposed aethereal non-material body from the material created world would include the one-way dependence of the temporally finite latter domain for its existence on the former temporally infinite domain. And why would God be less than perfect anyway if His supposed aethereal body were spatially finite, even if it could be spatially infinite, when He remains infinitely powerful, the sole Creator of all else, infinitely loving, wise and so on? (Indeed a God with an aethereal body might ease the interpretation of certain Old Testament passages for some theists: God walks in the Garden of Eden, appears to Moses in the Burning Bush and to Job out of the whirlwind, and the like.)

  J. O. Wisdom's *The Unconscious Origin of Berkeley's Philosophy* (London 1953) is said to put forth various neo-Freudian hypotheses about how Bishop Berkeley's attacks on *MATERIAL* Substance could result from childhood anxieties about toilet-training and faeces; is also rumoured to have been dubbed by Gilbert Ryle the *reductio ad turdum*. Possibly Kai Nielsen's extreme hostility to the very idea of God's being able to retain His perfections if He enjoyed an aethereal body sufficiently like matter to be said to have spatio-temporal locations would be said by J. O. Wisdom to throw fresh, important rays of light on the dark, residual problems of plumbing and civic rheology in Nielsen's fair town of Calgary or on the urban surplus of horse products during the Calgary Stampede.

HORN B: We have already mentioned with much praise Barry Stroud's 'Transcendental Arguments' (*Journal of Philosophy* **65** (1968) 241–56). Stroud usefully exposes certain verificationist assumptions about identi-fication and reidentification, assumptions which underlie the brand of Wittgensteinian fideism that Nielsen himself does embrace: faith in man's inability to think about events and individuals coherently unless man not only *begins with* but ever *continues with* a highly anthropocentric conceptual scheme. Further anthropocentric assumptions of Nielsen (who turns with surprisingly sudden enthusiasm to Wittgenstein and other Ordinary Language mongers at crucial stages in his exposition on pp. 116 and 127), have, we trust, been radically undermined by writings of our own on philosophy of language. [See 'Myths of the Given and the "COGITO" Proof', *Philosophical Studies* (U.S.) **12** (1961) 49–53; 'Dialogue Concerning Natural Metaphysics', *Southern Journal of Philosophy* **6** (1968) 24–30; 'Matter, Form and Logic', *International Logic Review* **3** (1971) 93–104; 'Quantification Theory and Ontological Monism', *Zeitschrift für Allgemeine Wissenschaftstheorie* **4** (1972) 1–12; 'Two Dogmas of Linguistic Empiricism', *Dialogue* **12** (1972), 324–335.] At any rate, 75 years ago when G. E. Moore was a young don he found it quite commonplace among his fellow philosophers for Absolute Idealist agonies of questioning to arise about the coherence and intelligibility even of predication, even of relational assertions intended to contingent, indeed even of any relational discourse, and also of talk about distinct individ-uals, places and times etc., etc. Moore saw that arguments purporting to establish any such incoherence or unintelligibility would require quite remarkably strong, indeed almost irresistible premises and inferences if they were to be reasonably judged fit to establish anything so counter-intuitive. The premises and inferences must be so intuitively or obviously sure that they could even be *trusted* to deliver the defeat of so much that seems so centrally intuitive or obvious. Unfortunately Moore, if we understand his varyingly interpreted texts, tended to confuse Fregean matters of *Sense* and *Reference* by making dogmatic remarks that he *KNEW* propositions about distinctly many hands' and trees' presence, about his lunches' temporally succeeding his breakfasts, and the like *to be true*. But what was as clear to him as anything could be clear, was not the *Reference or truth value* of his *dogmatic philosophical assertions* of Ontological Pluralism, of Matters' Existence etc. but the *Sense* and *intelligibility* of his *ordinary beliefs* that he had and saw hands which were quite distinct from the trees then in his sight, that he had already breakfasted at some earlier time on a table with a particular [spatial] length, and the like. Surely this rather Moorean point about the obvious *Sense*, not the obvious *Reference* of certain very familiar propositions needs to be made against Nielsen's scepticism no less than against the Humean and Bradleyan kinds Moore attacked.

As rather traditional Anglicans, and we are not untypical here of vastly many Christians, Jews and Muslims who pray or who have prayed earlier in history, we have led lives in which traditionally minded prayer to a loving God Who would hear and subtly answer ones prayers has been central. For many reasons, including philosophical ones, we have in Nielsen's earlier words paid "careful attention to our actual use of words in a particular area" (120), this area of prayer. There is the possibility that we *may* have been mistaken in our belief that a God with no spatial body has heard and often subtly answered us: it is part of our 'hypothetical' approach to theism to treat that possibility very respectfully. It is just possible, we allow by this approach, that we thought we held here an intelligible belief when it really had no sense or meaning. It is just possible that our (Ontologically Pluralist) beliefs about seeing *many distinct things* from bores to blackboards really made no sense at all. But when Moore's strictures to Sceptics are properly related to matters about a proposition's *Sense* (NOT its Fregean *Reference* or *truth-value*), the methodological problem facing Unsinn-Strategists like Nielsen is revealed to be all but incredibly more difficult than they have been able to realise. Nevertheless, as 'hypothetical' philosophers we shall admit that there is some measure of possibility that "God exists" can make no such traditional sense. How rationally to overcome some forms of concern about even this possibility is a matter we take up in Chapter VII, Section III.

III. THE NECESSARY TRUTH CONTESTED:
APPEALS TO EVIL

In this section we shall turn to the perennial charge that a theist cannot be both internally consistent and honest about the world. For, it is argued, there is too much pointless evil in the world for this to be compatible with a perfectly good God's existence. We offer here two studies indicating the weakness of the atheist case. One study points to the inadequacy of current attempts to make theism (if combined with such honesty) appear inconsistent. The second study shows how the traditional Western theist can always easily extend his domain of belief with Platonic, Hindu or Buddhist enrichments so that there no longer appears to be such tension in the domain between theist axioms and the Axiom of Honesty (a Biblical tenet) that the world is indeed a place where great mental anguish, moral depravity and physical pain abounds.

III.1. *Must Gods Madden Madden?*

Professor Edward H. Madden has in recent years been spending much wit and energy on attempts to show that naturalism is a vastly more rational position than any form of theism. The question we wish to raise here concern his two papers, 'The Many Faces of Evil' (henceforth *M.F.E.*), and 'On the Difficulty of Evading the Problem of Evil' (henceforth *D.E.P.E.*).[1] Both these articles deserve careful reading by philosophers of religion. Indeed, several of Madden's attacks on the inferential cheating and closed-mindedness of some of our era's leading religious thinkers should be welcomed by fair-minded theists, skeptics and atheists alike. We hope he will come to agree, however, that several of his own arguments are not good enough either; hence that an insistence on their improvement *or rejection* should be welcomed by fair-minded atheists, skeptics and theists alike.

  Question I. Would Madden say that he is capable of dispassionately considering this question of natural theology: "Are all or many of the events which we tend to attribute to inanimate nature really due to some hidden and unbelievably powerful personal agency or agents?"[2]
  Madden writes in *D.E.P.E.*

A feeling for the depth and pervasiveness of evil is so great in some people that Christianity is not even a live hypothesis for them. They can stand gratuitous evil if it comes from a naturalistic world that knows neither good nor evil or comes from a genuinely evil world, but they could not bear to hear from any providential source whatever that it is not really gratuitous evil after all – that there is some point to it.[3]

Some such tyranny of wrath and resentment over reason and relevantly detached reflection seems rather too often to underlie Madden's own procedures. In *M.F.E.* he lengthily quotes and endorses rather than argues for Ivan Karamazov's highly emotional claim that, since we know how innocent children suffer in this world, we should not consent to worship or even cooperate with a Creator, should He reveal Himself.[4] (Perhaps we are being offered an 'Emotive Disproof' as the real clincher?) Madden writes as if meditation on the claim would induce a "profound feeling" that *settles* the matter. "The price that is paid for ultimate harmony is too great, ultimate harmony is not worth its cost in human misery". This claim he seems to maintain against the possible existence (not just the gentlemanliness) of any divine causal agency or agents. Any somewhat well-meaning God, or god, it seems – even a limited deity[5] – must madden anyone because of the evil in the (possibly) very limited amount of world Madden knows. Must any possible deity with a possible grain of benevolence madden Madden into cocksure ontological rejection? If not, what kind, apart from a purely evil one, does he allow at the least to be a faint possibility? It is dubious in logical taste to ask the theist to take the naturalist's case seriously, if the naturalist is too *agitated* by evil[6] to take any theistic or quasi-theistic speculation seriously other than pure diabolism.

Question II. Do not a great many of Madden's claims about God and Evil presuppose incorrectly that some kind of formal or logical inconsistency has been established between theistically indispensable propositions about God and Evil?

At *M.F.E.*, p. 481, Madden tells one he will explain how all the most important of theist's "alleged solutions" to the problem of evil break down. He winds up:

I shall be explicit enough about the other alleged solutions also so that it should be quite clear why I think none of them succeeds. I shall conclude, then, that the problem of evil is insoluble and that this insolubility is a sufficient reason for not believing in any type of theistic God whatever.

A year before *M.F.E.* was published[7] Professor Nelson Pike had pointed out in print that there is no formal or logical inconsistency among these three propositions which he takes to be put forward by Hume's Philo as an inconsistent triad:

(1) The world contains instances of suffering.

(2) God exists – and is omnipotent and omniscient.

(3) God exists – and is perfectly good (p. 87).

To produce genuine logical strain among these three beliefs we need already to be sure that some such proposition as the following is true:

(6) An omniscient and omnipotent being would have no morally sufficiently reason for allowing instances of suffering (p. 89).

To make Pike's argument about Philo tighter we need to add "and perfectly good" after "omnipotent" in (6). To make Pike fully relevant to Madden, insofar as Madden is arguing against all "*omni*"-labelling theists [8], we need perhaps simply to replace "suffering" in (1) and (6) by "physical and moral evil". Insofar as Madden is tilting at what he calls "any type of theistic god whatever", we have such a vague, polymorphous set of possibles on our hands that it is very hard to be sure what would or would not be relevant. If Madden really wants to attack all possible theists he must argue among other things that the following propositions are logically incompatible.

(A) All or many of the events we tend to attribute to inanimate nature are due to some unbelievably powerful personal agency or agents, interested in our lives.

(B) Among and behind the different sorts of events we experience there are cases of physical and moral evil.

Clearly (A) and (B) are not *prima facie* logically incompatible, nor does it even strike us as improbable or hard to believe that both *could* be true together. For Madden to have any chance of an argument we must narrow down the field very severely and rather arbitrarily of what qualifies as "any theistic god whatever". To do this we add:

(C) There is at least one such unbelievably, powerful personal agent that is worthy of men's *worship*.

But here again a form of Pike's point is sorely applicable. In order to produce a *rational* tension between beliefs in (A), (B), and (C), we need to be sure of some things like these:

(D) A being worthy of worship could have no morally sufficient reason for allowing any moral or physical evil.

(E) A being worthy of worship would necessarily be able and be forced by his very nature ever successfully to prevent the existence of anything whose existence he would have no morally sufficient reason for allowing. It may be possible to prove (D) and (E) but at any rate Madden has not done so. Nor does it appear to us likely that he can do so or that anyone can – not even if one stipulates that the relevant worship-worthy sort of "theistic god" has to be of the utterly perfect, entirely omniscient and wholly omnipotent variety.[9] The greater the God the harder it is for us to judge His possible reasons! Madden might reply, if one may go by the opening paragraph of *M.F.E.*, that the onus is on the theist to spell out a solution to the problem of evil. But is it really self-evident that any such onus is on the theist? Madden thinks so because he thinks the "*omni-*"-labelling theist *must* admit that he is *prima facie* in trouble about "logical compatibility", *must* admit "the existence, *prima facie* at least, of gratuitous evil". But the upshot of the Pikean and neo-Pikean arguments which we considered is that skeptics who insist on such 'musts' and also theists who allow these to be foisted on themselves are (*prima facie* at least!) the victims of a serious logical error. Madden writes at *D.E.P.E.*, p. 62:

> The problem of *prima facie* gratuitous evil is clearly not a problem forced upon theism from an external frame of reference that different concepts of evidence and reasonableness. It is a problem wholly indigenous to the religious frame of reference and requires a re-examination of basic concepts within that system.

But the proper answer to this sort of question begging is a series of questions. What sorts of theism are really vulnerable to any such problem? Does it follow that because some theists think themselves vulnerable they all really *are* vulnerable? For where, *where* is the formal contradiction? Does it follow that, because the existence of evil is part of some religious frameworks of reference, a frightful philosophical problem about evil besets any rational believer in any sort of god? Is it not likely that many of the theists who think themselves so beset have been backsliding out of that frame of reference in one or both of two alien directions – to wit, (a) dabbling too deep in impersonal Hellenistic abstractions of perfections[10] that fit ill with the concept of a God as a personal agent, (b) drifting into extremes of anthropomorphism whence it seems that if an ordinary human being could have no morally sufficient reason for allowing something, then no personal agent whatsoever could have one?

Thus one type of intelligent theist might say that within his religious frame of reference talk of "*the* problem of evil" is misleading. There are many problems about evil within the frame, not necessarily philosophical problems: how to avoid doing evil despite one's propensities, how to endure unavoidable evils with dignity, how to avoid being driven into grossly anthropomorphic complaints about a god when one suffers evil, etc.,

Such a theist however, might well be interested also in some philosophical problems about gods and evil. (It does not follow that he would be callous if his approach should be of a detached intellectual kind.) He might, for example, want to achieve a relative advance in understanding why such a powerful and worship-worthy God would create or tolerate *this* kind of world. He might wish through argument to relieve people like Madden and Ivan K. of their obsessive feeling that the world must be too bad for there to be any worship-worthy God or gods.

III.2. *Evil and Other Worlds*

For the theist or sceptic who wishes to grapple further with the problem of evil let us put the question again in these words: "How could a perfectly good, eternal Person create, *ex nihilo* or out of anything else, a universe in which so much evil could arise?" In order to try meeting this question, to which so many Judaeo-Christian responses have seemed either unintelligible or harshly implausible, we propose to introduce very tentatively some pieces of precosmological and intercosmological speculation, then ask: "How well do the speculative pieces account for our planet's looking like the quasi-gardened garden of John Wisdom's 'Gods'?" How well, moreover, do the pieces fit the recent suggestion of a rather sensitive, yet sensible friend that this world often appears to be one "which stands almost in a Hell-like relation to some far better place, of which the refuse has fallen to Earth"?

Recent literature on the problems of Divine Creation and Evil includes some outstanding papers in the already noted anthologies of Flew and MacIntyre and of Nelson Pike,[11] From their diverse contributors let us cull some incompatible but thereby perhaps all the more useful starting points. (a) The proposition, "An omnipotent and omniscient being would have no morally sufficient reason for allowing instances of suffering", is not a self-evident truth, nor does it appear at all easy to establish; yet it is the sort of proposition which the atheist must overtly or covertly rely on to produce an incompatibility between "A perfect God exists" and "Evil exists in His Creation" (Pike).[12] (b) Even if we did allow that in some cases there is a rational justification for pain and suffering in terms of Retributive Punishment for sin, this would not explain why so many innocent children and animals incapable of sin should suffer; nor explain why disasters like the famous Lisbon earthquake bring the same misery and loss to the relatively just and the relatively unjust alike (Dostoyevsky, J. L. Mackie, Flew).[13] (c) If God is all powerful and all-good He would not have made sentient, rational beings prone to spiritual 'evils' like willing to lie or hurt others. An omnipotent God could easily have made all sentient beings sufficiently adjusted to our world so that they would not need pain to improve or instruct them; He could easily have made all sentient rational beings completely good, so that they would be not only unable but even unwilling to act sinfully (Flew, Mackie).[14] (d) Attempts to offer a morally sufficient reason for God's allowing so much evil by invoking each man's collective, inherited guilt through Original Sin are attempts that do gross ('counter-intuitive') violence to the moral instincts of reasonable and open-minded questioners. Moreover, attempts to explain away certain further evils as not due to Man's Original Sin, but rather due to the work of "evil spirits beginning before man began" have a desperately *ad hoc* ring. Indeed these attempts raise a still more damaging question: how could a perfect God find morally sufficient reason to let earthly beings suffer for and from sins committed by "evil spirits beginning before man began"? (Flew)[15] (e) The atheist asks what meaning can be attributed to love if God is said to love all His creatures infinitely much and yet to let men suffer and degrade themselves hideously instead of creating men completely good (Flew).[18] But the theist is entitled to a semantic reply in kind: the assertion that God could have made man completely good turns out, when carefully analysed, to lack intelligible content. The 'descriptions' of such kinds of cosmoi, where all men (or all similarly rational 'sapients') perform all their duties with effortless 'morality' and always exhibit 'virtues' without any interfering temptations, are too semantically deviant to be useful for either atheist or theist in the controversy over God and evil. For "moral discourse is embedded in the cosmic *status quo* (or even more narrowly in the planetary *status quo*)" (Ninian Smart).[17]

Since meditating on these five and other currently central and provocative incompatible assertions about God and Evil, we confess ourselves as 'liberal' Anglicans addressing others who wish to preserve and clarify what is best in the Judaeo-Christian tradition, to have become convinced of at least the *theoretical* desirability of trying to see how felicitously elements in the tradition can be combined with ideas of those religionists who believe in reward and punishment through reincarnation; how they can be combined also with ideas of those scientists who conclude that in, or beyond the enormous segment of the universe we can begin to study, there must be very probably other worlds where life, including life of sapients at least as rational as man, may flourish. In taking this view we are saying against Ninian Smart that theists should not merely dismiss the very idea of other far easier worlds as a feeble tool of the atheist attacker; theists should use the idea to their own advantage.

Speculation 1: It may well be that a perfect Creator would create cosmoi wherein mortal body-and-soul sapients never suffer either pain or any temptation to act viciously and even unpleasantly. In such cosmoi creatures would uninterruptedly love, aid and encourage one another in harmony with their neighbours and with their Creator. The speed of their journey to their ultimate destiny of full spiritual union with God would be decided not by their rejection of evil but by the degree of excellence they achieve from heeding their virtuous inclinations and sometimes choosing the more over the less virtuous. I do not agree with Smart that our moral and aesthetic concepts of goodness and value are so tied to one moral interpretation under our "planetary *status quo*" that many of us could not quite intelligibly value these sapients as leading lives of a very high moral and aesthetic order. (At least a few of us earthlings would consider Aristotle's moral paradigm of the man so trained and habituated as to be from now on beyond temptation, and the Bulter-Hume paradigms of the man in whom Benevolence and Self-Love are superbly adjusted to be at least as authentic cases of morality as the Kantian (?), Sartrean(?), Ninian Smartian paradigm of the autonomous, hideously tempted man, making mighty acts of will to stick things out.

Speculation 2: Now let us think of God as creating an example of what Smart would consider to be a more "cosmomorphic world", one where mortal sapients' thoughts and actions are more like those of the humans we know. Here again we find extremely strong natural inclinations among these creatures to love and respect themselves, their fellows and, especially, their Creator. These body-and-soul sapients occasionally suffer small pains and anxieties, but they eagerly help to distract and cheer their

neighbours when such 'evils' afflict them. Moreover each of these creatures, let us suppose, at a few times between the ages of 25 and 45 experience light and easily resistible temptations to act in ways that he
knows would, if they could effectively be acted upon, seriously pain and
hinder others and alienate himself – the agent – from his Creator. Each
sapient, moreover, is warned well in advance about these assumptions
and is taught how best to persevere. (We are assuming in the worlds of
S_1 and S_2 that sapients all have much stronger and more frequent empirical evidence than the class of Biblical earthlings would of God's existence
and of His concern for them.)[18] The souls of the relatively few who do,
despite the ease of resisting, succumb seriously to such temptations have
their souls eventually 'relegated' to union with bodies in a lower or "still
more cosmomorphic" universe. Those souls who at each lower stage of
union with sapients still make no serious effort to practise love and resist
temptations (even according to their now much more limited powers to
recognize and choose between good and evil) become the souls of sentient beings on Earth or even in worse worlds. Some even have to serve
'penal terms' of union with bodies of non-rational animals or idiotic
'botched' sapients. On the other hand, those descended souls who do
strive hard for good as they understand it are eventually 'promoted' either
to another, much richer, mortal life in a better world or to eternal disembodied communion with God Himself.

Speculation 3: Before creating anything God concluded it was right morally and aesthetically, perhaps almost 'obligatory', for Him as a *free,
creative person*, that there should be vast diversity in a Creation and that
an indispensable element would be variety in the multitude of free 'self-
realizing' persons. All are ultimately to realise themselves in full communion with God during the course of eternity, but at a speed largely determined by their own free decisions when afforded choices between either
(a) greater and lesser goods, or (b) good and evil. Among these persons
would be materially embodied souls: hence the Creation of the cosmoi of
Speculation 1 and 2 and then of the lower cosmoi for those who originally
allowed themselves to fail under optimal conditions for resistance. God
would not fail to *care* that such sapients would suffer in the lower
cosmoi determined by their choices. Indeed other worlds than ours may
have important counterparts to God's sending to mankind of saints, martyrs and prophets, of His guiding a Chosen People as an example. There

may even be cases of His sacrificing Himself in other worlds as a redeeming and freshly inspiring Christ to help persons master the powers of evil through such evidence of God's concern and through the grace proceeding therefrom.

These speculations seem to us, even if they are partly or largely mistaken in fact, to illuminate the conceptual contention that a perfect God could have a morally sufficient reason for creating universes in which freely self-realizing persons could bring sufferings and degradations, like those one knows in this planet, upon themselves by their own decisions. The co-existence of God and Evil has been traditionally and technically viewed by theologians as a 'Mystery', that is, not as a baffling absurdity but as an enigma towards whose unravelling human minds can make much progress, but only asymptotically. What we need to know of in connection with the enigma of God and Evil is the possibility of our making progress. Such speculations as these three, we submit, whatever their defects or other merits, do point to the logical possibility of such a practical possibility for making progress.

The atheist would make many protests, naturally enough. We consider only two here: (i) "But after listening to you speculate on conceptual possibilities I look again *a priori* at the concepts of power, good and evil. No God could have any reason for allowing any pain or depravity whatsoever if He had power to prevent it. Not even 'warranted' pain and 'wilful' self-degradation!" Well, to this there is the "iffy" answer that *if* our brand of theism is right in one primary respect, then the non-believer himself will eventually discover *a posteriori* how completely vindicating a good will come out of all evil! If this conceptual possibility of *a posteriori* vindication exists, at any rate we cannot be *a priori* mistaken. (ii) "These speculations are detestable philosophically since they raise but do not resolve grave problems about such philosophically muzzy things as Free Will, Spiritual Substance, Body-Mind, Retributive Justice and Memory's Relation to Personal Identity." But maybe it is philosophers who have made these notions seen far muzzier than they are. Many ordinary people often find them nothing like so muzzy. As noted before, if we were living somewhere between 1870 and 1920, think how many Idealist philosophers would be busy telling us that the concepts of Space, Time and Material Objects, or of Properties and Relations are hopelessly muzzy for philosophical purposes.

Finally, let us say a bit about why we think speculation on these lines should be considred not just as a possibility, but as a serious possibility. People like Flew, Mackie and Dostoyevsky's Ivan are thereby shown to lack the logical right to assume that ANY suffering (by children, animals, enormously virtuous adults, etc.), must be gratuitous or unjust. The doctrine of Original Sin finds a reinterpretation which makes each person his own fallen Adam. No individual's woes can be cited and attacked by would-be atheists as necessarily representing for all honest theists a set of disgracefully 'vicarious' sufferings which arise from such seemingly vile abstractions as Collective Man and Hereditary Guilt. Moreover, Hell and Purgatory can hence recieve more intuitively acceptable interpretations in terms of metempsychosis and hope of eventual self-realization. Condemnation to Hell becomes a fall into a worse role in worse worlds. Degrees of Purgatory become degrees of improvement in one's future roles and world. Without resorting to foggy symbolism one can assert the existence of a material Eden and yet assert it untroubled by our earthly hypotheses about the evolution of our own species or by our earthly searches for jawbones of our own Missing Links. The judgment that God could have peopled all inhabitable universes as in Speculation 1 does not it should now be clearer, entail the judgment that God could have no morally sufficient reason for not creating worlds progressively more like our own and even others far less pleasant. The meta-speculation that all three Speculations have interesting partial analogies in hard fact does not have the possibly intelligible, but implausible and desperately *ad hoc* character that men like Flew and Mackie would claim. For the *hoc* at which the speculation is directed after long and painful reflection is what is so long familiar; our world, our *hoc*, is like Wisdom's garden, but *worse*! For it both seems in familiar parts to be so plausibly explained as a morally and aesthetically concerned Creator's kindly handiwork, and seems in familiar parts, as our friend would have it, to be the Hellish leavings of a better place.

Perhaps (we do not say "of course"), the Judaeo-Christian tradition can be fruitfully interpreted with such a speculative ad-mixture both of science and of ideas from sects within sects of Orphists, Buddhists and Hindus. The fruitfulness, we have suggested, may only be of a defensive, philosophical character. But it may also have for the natural theist a value for constructive, religious meditation as well.

IV. THE NECESSARY TRUTH REAFFIRMED:
"NO 'IS' WITHOUT 'OUGHT' IN THE OFFING"

The 'hypothetical' theism that we advocate, including its Justifying Explanation Argument, involves a commitment to the objectivity of many values. These values include (if one pays due heed to contexts) the *wisdom* and *foolishness*, *importance* and *triviality*, *worth* (or *relevance* for wisdom) and *pointlessness* of various statements and also of various inferential moves and positions which are offered inside or outside of philosophy. These values include the *reasonableness* and *wrongheadedness* of men and of the ways in which they form beliefs or arguments, the *morality* of seeking the truth and rejecting falsehood about many matters that one judges to be important. Admission of the objective *value* of something or many things is no less essential to a rational conceptual scheme than admission of the objective *existence* of something or many things. Admitting *either* truths about what is *or* truths about what ought to be seems so closely linked for rationality with admitting the other at once that Saint Thomas certainly seems to be *at least partly* on the right track in believing that *"ens"* and *"bonum"*, *"ens realissimum"* and *"ens optimum"*, *"esse"* and *"bonum esse"* are (i) different in CTA-Sense but identical in Reference, (ii) convergent in WTA-meanings. For example, he writes at *Summa Theologica* I, *q.* 5, First Article:

everything is perfect so far as it is actual .... Hence it is clear that goodness and being are the same really. But *goodness* expresses the aspect of desirableness, which *being* does not express. (Cf. F. C. Copleston, *Aquinas*, London 1967, pp. 148–51.)

Detailed exploration, we suspect, would show in Saint Thomas' favour that the Voluntarism which we charged in Chapter One with *religious irrelevance* is furthermore conceptually incoherent (CTA-meanings and WTA-meanings considered). We suspect this because Voluntarists have tried to analyse 'Gooper'-predicates and related value terms in a way that makes them radically too far *subordinate* to 'Expo'-predicates and associated terms.

Modern analytical philosophy abounds in talk about the impossibility of deriving an "OUGHT" from an "IS". For example, W. D. Hudson has recently edited a thick anthology, *The IS/OUGHT Question* (London 1969). It includes at pp. 120–34 J. R. Searle's essay of 1964 'How to Derive "Ought" from "IS"' and many of the numerous criticisms which that so frequently debated paper provoked. It also includes at pp. 259–71 Searle's reply to his critics in his recent book *Speech Acts* (Cambridge 1969, pp. 175–98). The question at issue in the centre of this current storm seems to be whether what many consider a clearly 'non-evaluative' premise like (1) "Jones uttered the words 'I hereby promise to pay you, Smith, five dollars' " can through the mediation of other 'non-evaluative' steps like (1a) "Under certain conditions C anyone who utters the words (sentence) 'I hereby promise to pay you, Smith, five dollars' promises to pay Smith five dollars" entail what many consider 'evaluative' conclusions like (3) "Jones placed himself under an obligation to pay Smith five dollars" and (5) "Jones ought to pay Smith five dollars". (See Searle in Hudson, *op. cit.*, p. 121.) In his final defence of the soundness of his arguments against all previous critics Searle writes:

When one enters an institutional activity by invoking the rules of the institution one necessarily commits oneself in such and such ways, regardless of whether one approves or disapproves of the institution. In the case of linguistic institutions, like promising (or statement making) the serious utterances of the words commit one in ways which are determined by the meaning of the words. In certain first–person uterances, the utterance is the undertaking of an obligation. (*Op. cit.*, p. 262.)

We suspect that Searle confuses ones awareness of ones obligation to *people as people* (and thus of duties towards their dignity, feelings, trust, expectations, etc.), as an obligation which creates at least a *prima facie* case for being obliged not to flout their prized social rules just for flouting's sake, with the over-esteem for *rules as such* that he claims to eschew (pp. 262–63).

Let us now try to derive an "Ought" from an "Is" that will be in many kindly ways, though not *necessarily* in all ways, equally generous to Searle and his critics.

Premise 1. This body of arguments from Searle's pen now exists and is available to us and so also does a large and growing corpus of counterarguments from his critics. *Conclusion* 1: *Either* we have a body of argument from Searle of a kind worth investigating about an important subject *or* we don't. *Conclusion* 2: *Either* those of Searle's critics, who believed that we do have such a 'consideration-worthy' body of argument, had good reason to work on it and were thoroughly warranted in spilling ink in trying seriously to get to the truth about this matter or they lacked genuinely good reason to take it so but rather understandably thought they had and were somewhat warranted, *or*/they lacked good reason and were not warranted, *or* etc. *Conclusion* 3: *Either* they engaged in something we ought at least partly to respect, whatever their mistakes, *or* we ought to feel warranted in questioning the point of so much 'literature', *or* etc.

If someone grants that we have just offered a sort of argument but seriously questions whether this attempt at deriving an 'OUGHT' from an 'IS' really is a worthwhile attempt, *or* whether it is even at least worth considering to be possibly promising as an deductive enthymeme or a non-deductive Good Reasons argument, *or* etc., then he shows in a different way how stating the existence of this argument commits one within a rational conceptual scheme to the necessity of also stating that therefore at least one of a disjunctive set of related categorical "OUGHT" statements about the argument must be true. It ought to be taken seriously, or ridiculed, or ignored, or left to the reader's discretion, or whatever. "There is no 'IS' without an 'OUGHT' in the offing." To admit that something exists is, *of course*, to admit that some non-trivial TRUTH about what ought to be so, or to be done or left undone, etc., or ought not to be so or done, or left undone, etc., holds with regard to that instance of existence. To grant that such a *disjunction* of "OUGHTS" is true is PERHAPS to grant the truth of something worth calling a *tautology*. But it *also* to grant the truth of at least one substantive "OUGHT" state- among the DISJUNCTS. This utterly familiar, unsurprising fact is ignored only at the philosopher's peril: without it he is prone to embrace rigid dichotomies between facts and values, and thence to think of facts as 'harder' or more 'real and objective' than values, and thence to embark upon some 'value-free' analysis of 'objective reality' and hence to do thoroughly bad metaphysics.

V. THE NECESSARY TRUTH REAFFIRMED:
"FOR AN 'OUGHT' IS AS HARD AS AN 'IS'"

Metaphysics may sometimes be usefully considered as the Janus with Ontology and Epistemology for its two faces. It tries to show us what there is, what the fundamental 'realms', or 'sorts', or 'models' of Being are really like. It tries to show us what it is to *know*, or at least to *believe most rationally*, in such a way that the certainty, or at least the plausibility, of an ontological claim about the world as part of an intelligible cosmos can

be determined. Since metaphysics, so considered, is the search for a humanly attainable wisdom about reality, it turns out to be nothing less than
philosophy itself – at least if we stay close to the traditional and etymological significance of philosophy as *the love of wisdom*. If anyone claims to
be "talking metaphysics", or more simply to be "doing philosophy", he
must agree to certain ontological and epistemological assumptions about
the objectivity of value. He must agree to them, that is, or else agree that
the kind of 'metaphysics' and 'philosophy' he pursues is rather too like the
kind of 'philately' you pursue when you try to borrow a standard postage
stamp; rather too like the kind of 'nuclear fission' you pursue when you
try to crack a nut.

There has long been a din about the thesis that moral and related value
judgments are not only not *derivable* from descriptions of 'hard' enough
matters for 'cognitive descriptions' but are themselves not 'factually'
enough generated by 'hard' enough data for them to *be* 'cognitive' (true-
or-false) at all. This pernicious step-child of "IS"-"OUGHT" separation-
ists is incompatible with right thinking on "God exists" and merits
investigation. Moral and related value terms, it is allowed, may have descriptive criteria: for example to say "Dubbs is cruel" is certainly to say
something verifiable about his behavior. Nonetheless, the thesis continues,
the moral term "cruel" also has an evaluative *force*: when I say "Dubbs is
cruel", I say that he behaves in certain observable ways *and he ought not to*.
Saying that he ought not to, according to the non-cognitivist, is not stating
some further fact about Dubbs or anything else. "He ought not to", to
rehearse the familiar, is an expression of feeling (Ancient Ayer), a form of
attitude-declaration-*cum*-persuasive-manipulation (Standard Stevenson),
a sort of prescription or command (Early Hare), a kind of resolution
(Vintage Braithwaite), and so on. For there just is no further sort of fact I
could intelligibly be meaning to state about Dubbs when I say he is cruel,
other than observable facts like his ignoring his wife, beating his dog, and so
on. (There is, to rephrase their view, no "OUGHT" needed to explain
moral discourse, only the "IS" of spatio-temporal objects plus feelings,
behavioural following of language rules and other conventions, non-
linguistic behaviour, thoughts, dreams, images, and so on which we are
still tragically unable to analyse out completely as more subtle sorts of
spatio-temporal chunks or relations and properties thereof.) Sometimes
the non-cognitivist stance seems too uncomfortable to admirers of ordi-

nary language. It is too much not to be able to say that moral judgments *qua* moral ones are true or false, as the man in the street does. But then one can try the expedient of saying that they are true or false, provided we do not take the truth criterion to be correspondence with some objective "OUGHT" independent of human feelings and goals; moral and related value judgments are true if they can be upheld by the reasons which people, conventionally called "sane and sensible" in our society, conventionally say are "good reasons" for holding a moral view. Such reasons would be promotion of happiness and of social harmony. (A somewhat rough-and-ready admirer of Toulmin, Baier and Nielsen might say something like this. But we would imagine that *their* obvious respect for persons as *persons with needs* forbids *them* to stop there.)

For the benefit of recalcitrant linguistic analysts, who want to draw still closer to ordinary men and be still more outspoken cognitivists, a new approach was suggested by Peter Glassen.[19] No clear answer can be given to the question whether moral judgments are cognitive until it has been properly framed. "Are moral judgements cognitive?" has, he holds, no clear answer. But "Are moral judgments intended to be cognitive and are they so understood?" does have a clear answer. For most people are found to believe that moral judgments assert something, that they are true or false, that one can be right or wrong about them, that they can be proven or disproven, that they are capable of having objective validity. Thus the cognitivity of moral judgments can be established by listening to the way non-philosophical people talk.

Glassen gives a number of good examples to prove his claims about popular speech. This, in itself, is welcome since it may counteract the kind of *a priori* linguistics whereby ordinary speech is systematically misconstrued to fit non-cognitive theories. But what is the *philosophical* import of this demonstration? Cynthia Schuster, a rather neo-positivistic sounding non-cognitivist, offers the reply that nothing philosophical is proven against non-cognitivism since this 'positivist' doctrine is a *prescriptive epistemology*, not a *descriptive sociology*.[20] The positivist's prescription rests on a decision, but not, she hastens to add, on an *arbitrary* one. One decides, she tells us, what to call 'knowledge' after weighing the *advantages* and *disadvantages* and the *relevant considerations*. These factors are far from being coterminous with the speech habits of the ordinary man, which are the property of sociologists anyway. Reichenbach is thanked by

Schuster for his positivist point about "decisions". Stevenson is cited by
Schuster with private evidence as being a non-cognitivist who holds his
doctrines in this spirit. So Glassen's arguments, she concludes, are irrelevant to the philosophy of morals and related values.

Glassen seemed to offer too little to take us from the *is* of how we do
talk to the *ought* of how we should. Since Glassen was addressing himself
to philosophers, he presumably presupposed they recognised the value of
ordinary language. But Schuster seems to prove too much for non-cognitivism's good. Since "advantages", "disadvantages" and "relevant" are
'evaluative' terms, though not necessarily moral ones, *moral* non-cognitivism seems to be bought at the price of recognising *other* realms of objective
value. Perhaps one could slip out of this by saying that what we are to accept as *advantageous* or *relevant* is to be determined by convention; or perhaps by another prescription, resting on another decision, resting on some
other conventional standard or some other prescription – until the cognitivist ceases to cry "Arbitrary after all" in the exhaustion of an infinite regress.
But Schuster tips her hand suddenly and saves the cognitivist such trouble.
She cannot resist saying that Glassen is *"downright irresponsible"* to call
moral propositions cognitive when he offers no testing methods for their
truth. She cannot resist adding: "Ironically it begins to appear that logical
positivists are the only responsible philosophers" (pp. 97–98). These last
two statements must seem to her to be *true*: for, as Glassen is generous
enough to *expect*, *she* would surely not put them forward in a journal as
mere ejaculations of abuse and adoration. Yet they also sound like two
moral judgments. (a) As a matter of known moral fact, we are being told,
we ought not to call any propositions cognitive without offering methods
of verification. (b) As a matter of shown moral fact, we are being told, we
ought to follow the example of logical positivists – of morally and otherwise responsible men who denied there were any testing methods for
moral judgments, and so denied there were any moral facts to know.

This high spot of the exchange makes Non-Cognitivists sound rather
too 'dialectical' – or even insane! Let us dip into their pond once more.

It may have already begun to appear possible that acknowledging our
common awareness, however dim, of objective value amounts to a
necessary postulate of philosophical commerce. But to make this
less controversial let us consider certain arguments by W. D. Hudson
himself (in an independent paper and not the anthology recently mentioned

on *The IS/OUGHT Question*), in favour of what he calls 'subjectivism'.[21] The concealed implications of this doctrine seem to be the 'objectivity' of *chaos*, the 'subjectivity' of beliefs about a *cosmos*. To say something about what the cosmos is *really* like, be it in obviously scientific or in obviously metaphysical discourse, is to make a value judgment about how we should interpret our experience. Although Hudson queries the objectivity of *moral* value judgments, it is only on the exasperatingly familiar assumption that no other related intrinsic value judgements are serious candidates for objectivity either. For he treats non-moral value judgments like "Strawberries are nice" as self-evidently subjective "expressions of feeling or taste". Since his arguments for subjectivism rest on linguistic analogies, a certain amount of linguistic analysis is first required to see whether they are good analogies from a CTA-linguistic point of view. Then can it be determined more fairly whether the analogies (granted certain assumptions about the wisdom of how we do now talk) also offer good reasons for his philosophical thesis. What is it for an analogy to be philosophically valuable? The answer would illuminate many fundamental questions!

Hudson first argues, against what he takes to be the ethical objectivism of Bertrand Russell and Paul Edwards, that the following comparison shows factual reasons to confer no more objectivity on moral judgments than on "mere expressions of taste or feeling".

"Strawberries are nice."	"Bull-fighting is wrong."
"Why?"	"Why?"
"Because they are sweet."	"Because it causes pain."[22]

Hudson claims he is simply fighting Edwards with his own weapons, but he appears to assume that there is real *point* and *value* and *wisdom* in the way people around him talk about morality. If they gave factual reasons for moral judgments but not for expressions of taste, then there could, presumably, be point to the view that moral judgments are significantly like statements of fact. (Had Edwards' argument no bearing on the issue, whether valid or not, why bother to refute it? Why not dismiss it for irrelevance?) But if the comparison shows that we can just as easily give reasons for "Strawberries are nice" as for "Bullfighting is wrong", then 'subjectivism' must by his lights be somewhat confirmed. If we can show the analogy to be highly specious, then it would seem that by Hudson's own assumption he should treat objectivism rather more seriously. Unless, however, he has postulated this value judgment about *point* in ordinary language as something he recognises to be true or has postulated some other value judgment about appropriate, sensible, reasonable procedure that is relevant, there would seem to be no point except of love of idle logomachy in his advancing the analogy. And, unless his readers believed in the truth or wisdom of something like his value postulate there could be no philosophical commerce with them.

At any rate, the analogy breaks down for a combination of at least four reasons:

(A) It is regrettable that Hudson's sort of subjectivism confuses *expression*-like utterances of feelings with statement like utterances about feelings. It is statements and commands which elicit such kinds of "Why?" as occur in his examples. Ayer's careful distinction of *evincing* from *stating* in *Language, Truth and Logic*, where he holds that moral judgments belong among expressions of feeling, makes him reject the misleading title of 'subjectivist'.

(B) "Strawberries are nice" can easily be used to communicate any one of at least four possibilities or different amalgams of them. (i) "How I enjoy strawberries!" Where we have an ejaculative expression of feeling, the more *ejaculative* or *expression-like* it is, the odder it is to ask "Why?" (ii) "I enjoy strawberries a lot." The speaker describes or states his feelings *about strawberries* with the politely impersonal "Strawberries are nice", when asked what fruit he particularly enjoys. If a very recent, very foreign visitor, cautious about what is *strange* food to him, asks him "Why?", this question is quite appropriate. The foreigner wants to know if the sort of edible thing that makes him eager or gives him pleasure is anything like what arouses and gives the speaker pleasure. (iii) "You'll generally find that people like strawberries." The speaker makes a statement about a great many people's feelings, not necessarily his own. When someone asks his advice what to serve after the main course at a banquet, the speaker may say "Strawberries are nice" in this way. (iv) "Any person with good taste would enjoy them" or "You (one, they) ought to enjoy them". Here the junior gourmet makes a value judgment, quite possibly of an objectivist kind: it's a poor, foolish, ignorant, unnaturally under-endowed sort of person who doesn't like them. Just so the senior gourmet considers a judgment about which sherry is really nice or nicer, this Spanish one or that Californian, not really a matter of personal or general taste. It is a matter of decent, or knowledgeable, or cultivated, or expert taste.

(C) "Why?" is even more ambiguous in cold type. With "Why$_1$?", one can ask *argumentatively* for a reason (that is a justification). "I don't see that's so. Support your claim with a reason. *Justify* it!" With "Why$_2$?" one can ask *enquiringly* for a cause. "I'd appreciate knowing the cause of cause of that's being so." With "Why$_3$?" I ask *enquiringly* for an amplification or clarification: "I'd like to hear more. What is it about strawberries that you like?", "I'd like to get your view clearly. What is it about strawberries that one ought to appreciate?" There are also all sorts of *crossbreeds* – such as argumentative varieties of "Why$_2$?" and "Why$_3$?", an enquiring variety of "Why$_1$?", and so on. Each calls for a somewhat differing sort of "Because..." statement, and a somewhat differing use of "*reason*" – "reason" being a word here that Hudson throws around with no regard for nuances in the cluster of most obviously relevant contexts of use for {"Strawberries are nice," "Why?"} and for {"Bull-fighting is wrong." "Why?"}.

(D) If the speaker should say "Strawberries are nice" to convey possibility (ii) that he personally happens to like them, then "Why?" will most naturally be taken as an enquiring request either for a cause or for a clarification. In answer to "Why$_2$?" he tells the cautious foreigner what it is about this dessert unknown to such foreigners that causes his knowledgeable appetite to perk up whenever it is served. (He gets a *causal sort of reason* like the reason for one's headache being that one left the window closed.)[28] In answer to "Why$_3$?" from a curious but unchallenging country cousin, who cannot abide them and never knew of anyone who could, the speaker could explain what it is about them, their sweetness, that he likes. (The enquirer gets an amplifying reason.) But in case (iv), we have a value judgment by which a gastronomic objectivist could tendentiosly assert that everyone with any claim to sensible taste should like strawberries. "Don't throw them away! Strawberries are too *nice*!" Here we are more likely to get an argumentative "Why$_1$?" in return. "What possible reason have you to say we all ought to like them?" *A justifying reason is called for if argument is to be joined.* Hudson confuses the issue by repeatedly speaking of all such conversations as "*arguments*" (pp. 533–34). If they are understood as arguments, then they are most naturally construed in the cases of both strawberries and bull-fights

as the assertions of objective value judgments, followed by an argumentative "Why₁?", followed by a justifying reason. But Hudson also says
that, in such conversations, B is "really" pressing A to say more precisely
what he is for or against (p. 532). If so, the printed conversations are
not most naturally construed as arguments but as somewhat odd, almost
dangling, uses of indicative sentences, followed by requests for amplifica-
tions, then followed by clarifying 'reasons'. When A says "Strawberries
are nice", however, he is (most often) most naturally taken in this case as
saying he likes them (he is *all for* them) and then explains what he likes
about them and what he *is for* about them. Yet when A says "Bull-
fighting is wrong" he is (most often) most naturally understood not just as
saying he dislikes it, is against it, but as saying that *everyone ought* to be
against it. He then says next more precisely what it is about bull-fighting
that he disapproves of and that everyone else *should* disapprove of.

Hudson's comparison of the conversations offer but a specious
analogy. On the odd occasions when "Strawberries are nice" occurs in
an *argument* it is most likely to have been intended and understood
as a general objective value judgment, not as subjectivist's expression
description of personal taste.[24] In this case the fact that a justifying
reason is naturally given for both "Strawberries are nice" and "Bull-
fighting is wrong" can hardly be said to tell even linguistically against
objectivism. But, while it is not very likely outside pugnacious junior
gourmets' circles that the conversation about strawberries will be much
of an argument at all, it is quite likely that the interchange on bull-
fighting will begin a serious moral argument. When "Strawberries are
nice" is advanced in its most natural way, relative to a following "Why?",
the 'subjectivist' way (ii), then "Why?" most naturally requests a causal
or an amplifying sort of "Because..." statement. When "Bull-fighting
is wrong" is advanced in its most natural way relative to a following
"Why?", the objectivist way (iv), then "Why?" most naturally demands
a justifying sort of "Because" statement. Again, when the conversations
are taken fairly naturally, but somewhat less naturally, as clarifying
discussions we again find an important divergence. In one conversation, the "Because..." statement most naturally states simply what it is
about strawberries that I like, in the other the "Because..." statement
most naturally states what it is about bull-fights that I dislike, and that
I certainly *ought* to dislike, and that everyone else *should* dislike. Despite

his attempt to solve philosophical problems by linguistic analysis, Hudson has completely missed the posit of common wisdom which makes "Why?" and "reason" shift here in use and purpose with a context.

Thus, if we start with the tacit value-postulate that there is a certain point and wisdom in the way we talk, we conclude an analysis of Hudson's discussions with an explicit reason to believe that proper value judgments are much more like objective claims about the weather, which we will often back with factual justifying reasons, or with a justifying appeal to good [truth-seeking] reasons, than like expressions and descriptions of our more raw and guttish feelings, which we usually or *normally* do not try to prop up with reasoning.

The failure of the analogy is worth establishing even if we agree that the common wisdom needs no little purification. For, from quite a range of value postulates about ordinary language, we can conclude that the linguistic ineptitude of Hudson's analogy offers good reason for believing no longer just in the objectivity and cognitivity of *some* value judgment (or particular value postulate) but in the objectivity and cognivity of some *moral* value judgments. But suppose the analyst has no initial value postulate. Suppose he accepts nothing like Socrates' doctrine that examinations of our confused talk about Piety, Courage, Justice are worth attempting since they lead to clear recollection (*anamnesis*) of partly forgotten values; nor like Aristotle's belief in the language-reflectedness of human rationality when he said that the doctrine that *pleasure is not good but something evil* is a silly doctrine because "We agree [in such matters] that what everybody takes to be the case, really IS the case"; nor like Wittgenstein's view that everything (in Ordinary uses of Natural Languages) is in order as it is ; nor like Gabriel Marcel's conviction that a grasp of much which is implicit in our ordinary ways of talking is badly needed, since it leads to a more explicit, if extraordinary, account of how we should relate to other men and God. What then? If we really discover that an analyst holds simply nothing of the kind to be true, then we wonder why he calls himself a *philosophical* analyst – or why he tries to *reason* at all.

Such alleged philosophers are people that *exist* and so, as people whom they seek to influence, we *really ought* to wonder why they carry on like this. The theme returns: "No 'IS' without an 'OUGHT' in the offing"! It is "OUGHTS" in the offing about everything in existence that may lead the puzzled but reasonable man by way of The Justifying Explanation argument to "GOD EXISTS". If the arguments of this chapter about spirits, *and* about Evil, *and* about values are basically sound, then "God ought to exist" is clearly backed by "A Perfect God CAN exist". He can exist and can reasonably be inferred to exist necessarily. Promising a return to "OUGHT", "IS", "CAN" and Non-Cognitivism in Chapter VII we may safely close with at least a touch of growing confidence in this second theme "For an 'OUGHT' is as hard as an 'IS'".

NOTES

[1] Edward H. Madden, 'The Many Faces of Evil,' *Philosophy and Phenomenological Research* 24 (1964) 481–92; Edward H. Madden and Peter H. Hare, 'On the Difficulty of Evading the Problem of Evil', *PPR* 28 (1967) 58–69. For purposes of economy we shall treat Professors Madden and Hare as one substance, Madden, being two persons in one unholy binity.

[2] Cf. John Wisdom's 'Gods' in A.G.N. Flew (ed.), *Logic and Language*, First Series, Oxford 1951, pp. 187–206.

[3] *D.E.P.E.*, p. 63. Cf. *M.F.E.*, 487, last para.

[4] *M.F.E.*, pp. 488–89.

[5] Cf. Madden's 'Evil and the Concept of a Limited God', *Philosophical Studies* (U.S.) 18 (1967) 65–70. We reply to this paper in 'The Liabilities of Limited Gods', *Philosophical Studies* (U.S.) 20 (1969) 46–48.

[6] Cf. Madden's words at *M.F.E.*, p. 487, about himself in a froth when offered a dim defence of Buchenwald. That the defence offered by the particular individual was dim *not* show that far greater good could not come even from such tragic evil.

[7] Nelson Pike, 'Hume on Evil', reprinted from *Philosophical Review* 72 (1963) in Pike's anthology *God and Evil*, Englewood Cliffs, N.J. 1964, pp. 85–102.

[8] I.e., supporters of a God who is *omniscient, omnipotent, all good*, etc.

[9] Cf. Pike, pp. 88–89 and 98–99; also A. Plantinga, 'The Freewill Defence', in Max Black (ed.), *Philosophy in America*, New York 1964, pp. 204–20; also M. B. Ahern's 'God and Evil – a Note', *Sophia* 3 (1967) 23–26 and A. Plantinga, *God and Other Minds*, Ithaca N.Y. 1967, pp. 115–55.

[10] Cf. the final section of our Chapter IV.

[11] A. G. N. Flew and A. MacIntyre (eds.), *New Essays in Philisophical Theology* (London 1955; henceforward *NEPT*). Nelson Pike (ed.), *God and Evil*, (Englewood Cliffs, N.J. 1964; henceforward *G&E*).

[12] *G&E*, pp. 88ff.

[13] *G&E*, pp. 6ff and p. 68; *NEPT*, pp. 146ff.

[14] *NEPT*, pp. 152ff; *G&E*, pp. 55ff.

[15] *NEPT*, pp. 147–48.

[16] *NEPT*, pp. 96–99.

[17] *G&E*, p. 112 and pp. 102ff., *passim*.

[18] Cf. a section of our 'Religion, Reality and Language', *Pacific Philosophy Forum* 5 (1967) 4–55 at 41–43. The sorts of speculations offered here may give the natural theist hope that, since such a mixture of a world has to be accounted for by theistic

hypotheses, one need not grant with Pike that, although Hume in *Dialogues*, Section X fails to establish the incompatibility of God and evil, he shows in Section XI that empirically based theistic hypotheses (as opposed to Faith or *a priori* arguments) cannot plausibly lead us to God since this world is so full of evil; that is, the natural theist is entitled to be suspicious of Pike's concession to Hume on Section XI in *G&E*, pp. 101–02. (See Chapter VII, Section II.)

[19] Peter Glassen, 'The Cognitivity of Moral Judgments', *Mind* **68** (1959) 56–68.

[20] C. Schuster, 'Glassen on the Cognitivity of Moral Judgments', *Mind* **70** (1961) 95–98.

[21] W. D. Hudson, 'The Alleged Objectivity of Moral Judgments', *Mind* **71** (1962) 530–34.

[22] *Mind* **71** (1962) 531.

[23] Writers who *still* hope to postulate a rigid distinction between all *causes* and all *reasons* need to take causal sorts of reasons more seriously. It is surprising to find G. E. M. Anscombe writing "It will hardly be *enlightening* to say: in the case of the sudden start the 'reason' is a *cause*; the topic of causality is in a state of too great confusion" (*Intention*, Oxford 1958, p. 10). For she later writes: "What is so commonly said, that reason and cause are everywhere sharply distinct notions, is not true" (p. 24). And this point is highly enlightening, as Hudson's errors show. But if the statement of the point is enlightening, so is the first understatement. For another extreme (more exciting) see Donald Davidson, 'Actions, Reasons and Causes', *Journal of Philosophy* **60** (1963) 685–700.

[24] Objectivism about values is, of course, not a view confined *a priori* to paradigm cases of what we call peculiarly *moral* matters; politics, aesthetics, ways of reasoning and other matters are open to objectivist appraisal. Gastronomic objectivism is, perhaps, a black sheep, but it is a black sheep *of the family*.

CHAPTER VI

PROBABILITY AND 'THE WILL TO BELIEVE'

INTRODUCTION

The 'hypothetical' approach to questions of faith and metaphysics, which we have advocated all along since Chapter I, suggests that it is a search for probability rather than an insistence on certainty which should characterize the philosopher of religion. Such a search for probability goes with the very kind of open-ness to new concepts, new values, new forms of thought and visions which the (so closed-minded) Pharisees and Sadduccees would have needed to be ready for the traditionally based, yet shatteringly novel messages of Jesus about Spiritual Redemption, Prudent Unworldliness, the Resurrection, the Real Presence and the Trinity. Such open-ness would have left the later Christian clergy and laymen far better able to benefit from the most valuable ideas of Galileo, Spinoza, Darwin, Marx and even (with a pinch of salt) Freud, Carnap, Quine and the later Wittgenstein.

At this stage, accordingly, it seems desirable to probe the notion of *probability* a good deal harder, not least to probe the rationale behind certain much misunderstood theories of probability called *subjective* or *personalistic*, that derive from F. P. Ramsey. Such a double probe will be undertaken in Section I and Section II of this Chapter VI. In Section III we shall try, from this probe of probability and subjective theories, to draw some conclusions about how most wisely to refashion William James' 'The Will to Believe' and Pascal's Wager in the interests of rational religion.

I. METAPHYSICS AND PROBABILITY

I.1. *Probability and Father Dwyer's Blending of Aquinas with Wittgenstein*

In 'Thomistic First Principles and Wittgenstein's Philosophy of Language'[1] Father Peter Dwyer SJ has put forward some suggestions, both learned and exciting, for increasing friendly commerce between admirers of Saint Thomas and admirers of Ludwig Wittgenstein. Recognizing that there is considerable philosophical diversity within each set of admirers and that some fine philosophers already belong (with obvious reservations) to both sets, Dwyer concludes:

Thomistic first principles complement and correct the philosophy of Wittgenstein by drawing attention to the fact that language has an objective criterion of meaning which is, in the last analysis, independent of what we might say about reality.[2]

We share Father Dwyer's faith both in the fruitfulness of doing metaphysics and in the importance of modern linguistic analysis, though we do not entirely share what appears to be his optimism about some of the later Wittgenstein's philosophical tendencies. For some of these tendencies seem to demand that analytically minded admirers of Aquinas should not simply seek to complement and correct them, but rather join forces with analytical humanists to discredit and rebut them. First, we shall follow a discussion related to Dwyer's on metaphysical *objectivity* with some suggestions about the importance here of the concept of *probability*. We go on to pursue an investigation of words like "probably" in the light of some current positions in philosophy of language. Some further conclusions are drawn about the uses and abuses of "probability" and "good reasons" in metaphysical discourse. Here we mean metaphysical discourse concerning issues which Thomists and other metaphysicians rightly continue to raise today as *objective, factual, cognitive* issues about which human beings can profitably argue and make rational decisions.

Father Dwyer restricts his comments to Wittgenstein's *Tractatus Logico-Philosophicus*[3] and the posthumously published *Philosophical Investigations*.[4] These works are widely divided in time and in respect of some crucial philosophical views, but Dwyer's scholarship succeeds in suggesting continuous lines of possible sympathy between Thomism and the evolving Wittgenstein. We think that his strongest case for a parallel between Thomistic metaphysics and the *Tractatus* lies in two features that he covers: (a) Wittgenstein's insistence (drawing from Frege) on the proposition (not the word) as basic unit of meaning has its parallel in many a Thomist's stress on *acts of judgment*[5]; (b) Wittgenstein's Tractarian belief in an inexpressible but manifested isomorphism between the logical structure of the propositions and the objective structure of facts, or something like this view, has a more cautious analogue in

Thomist metaphysics; Wittgenstein's caution about the expressible, however, has its analogue in Thomists' distinctions between 'transcendental' notions and the limitations of 'predicamental' expressions.[6] With regard to Thomism and the *Investigations*, Father Dwyer makes an interesting case that the Thomist and the Wittgensteinian can learn from each other in the difficult task of analysing psychological verbs, a proper understanding of whose use is crucial for understanding the human situation.[7] (Wittgenstein's *questioning* of certain established ways of treating such verbs, we would add, is a monumental contribution to philosophy.) He also rightly argues that a modern Thomist, concerned with the variety of human judgments and other mental or linguistic acts, can profit greatly from Wittgenstein's attacks in the *Investigations* on the extreme narrowness of the *Tractatus* in its recognition of significant forms of communication between rational beings.

There are quite a number of puzzling assertions in the *Investigations* (or possible, even plausible *interpretations* of them) which Dwyer ignores or passes over quickly, although they suggest much that is not only inimical to Thomism but obstructive to any serious metaphysician's attempts to ponder *deeply* and *undogmatically* on the nature of things. For any serious attempt to ponder deeply and undogmatically on the nature of things must involve accepting *and frequently stressing* the possibility that some of our ordinary ways of talking and thinking about the world may be radically misguided. It must involve accepting the possibility that reason and intellectual honesty may after great reflection lead us to put forward theses of "revisionary metaphysics"[8] as truths about ultimate reality. It cannot subscribe *in advance* (*a priori*) to the idea that a metaphysician's revisionary argument MUST rest on a linguistic muddle. It cannot say IN ADVANCE "What *we* do is to bring words back from their metaphysical to their everyday use"; or "the results of philosophy are the uncovering of one or another piece of plain nonsense... we are destroying nothing but houses of cards"; or "philosophy may in no way interfere with (or explain) the actual use of language; it can in the end only describe it".[9] St. Thomas would not say of a society which revelled in affirming the consequent or consulting witches that each instance of this, being a language game in a way of life, "is in order as it is" and that there are no higher rational ideals to strive for. We assume from Dwyer's remarks about *objectivity* and *explanation* that he would share Aquinas' disdain for the restriction of philosophy to such descriptive linguistic therapy. Nevertheless, we are surprised that he does not lay more stress on the philosophical *folly* such positions involve and their incompatibility with the respectable ideal-cum-partial-actuality of a *philosophia perennis*. Elsewhere we have sought to explore the curious results of accepting certain neo-Wittgensteinian premises and values.[10] *Caveat emptor*: with all respect, we suggest that Dwyer beware lest his Thomist first-principle, that *being is intelligible*, be elsewhere perverted, as a bar against conceptual revision, to read: *if this is the way we have generally understood things to be, that is how they must be understood*.

It is on the score of "objectivity" and the *Investigations* that we think Father Dwyer speaks too little and perhaps, therefore, misleadingly. For a Wittgensteinian might reply that it is ridiculous to think of the Thomist with first principles as having any necessary *complement* – let alone any *correction* – to offer the author of the *Investigations*. Such a philosopher might say:

"Language has an objective criterion of meaning", writes Dwyer, in suggesting that *here* Wittgensteinians can learn from Thomists! But Wittgenstein is the very man who finally PROVED that this claim about objective criteria must be right. Just reflect on his account of public rules and criteria for meaningful discourse, on his relating of intelligible language-games to communal ways of life.[11] It is Wittgenstein who finally showed the nonsensicality of scepticism and subjectivism, who delivered modern Thomists from the Pyrrhonist-Cartesian challenge they never fully met. Again Dwyer says that this *criterion* he speaks of "is in the last analysis, independent of what we might say about reality". But it is only thanks to the detailed arguments of the *Investigations* against the logical possibility of *logically private* languages that the "objectivity" and "independence" of linguistic criteria are fully established.

It must be conceded to such a Wittgensteinian, that the influence of Wittgenstein's teaching in the 30's and the mid-40's at Cambridge seems to have contributed greatly to the fall from philosophical favour of private sense-data (*qua* foundations of empirical knowledge), of sceptical perplexities about other minds and the like. Many English-speaking philosophers have thus been brought *much closer* to what many Thomists would consider a *properly* objective empirical basis from which to philosophize. Were Aquinas now with us, he might well utilize several of Wittgenstein's arguments against scepticism, scribbling them in the margins of St. Augustine's *Contra Academicos*, declaring openly that such arguments (or some forms of them) complement Thomism very usefully.[12] The *Philosophical Investigations* are very hard indeed for one to interpret as a consistent whole, ever feeling sure of being true to the author's mercurial intentions. Recently, however, several devotees of this book have (unwittingly?) suggested by their writings that in his later work Wittgenstein simultaneously took one step forward towards accepting an objective world shared by all men and tractable for human reason, and one step back with the other foot. The suggestion seems to be confirmed by the recent publication of Wittgenstein's lectures in 1938 on philosophy of religion.[13] Let us next contrast two incompatible but 'objectivist'-looking positions, (X) and (Y).

(X) The theist and the sceptic can reasonably disagree about a matter of *fact* i.e., whether God exists or not. Although it is a factual dispute it cannot be settled by calculations or scientific experiments; as with tricky disputes in law, psychoanalytic interpretation, morality, or artistic evaluation, each disputant, if reasonable, *builds his case* by calling attention to certain patterns or to absence of patterns his opponent should expect. They can exhaust a large supply of relevant material, sympathize with and understand each other well. Some will be convinced, but others may be both impressed and still rationally disagree and continue to argue sensibly about claims like "God exists". This position was put forward by Wittgenstein's friend John Wisdom in his classic "Gods",[14] an essay which opened the gates to more intellectual contact between analytically trained believers, agnostics and atheists – contact made difficult in the heyday of Logical Positivism. A position like that of "Gods" seems to leave scope for what Aquinas would call *the natural light of reason*, for much mutual understanding and growth in sensitivity, for intellectual room to manoeuvre by reasonable men of good will contesting metaphysical, political, theological, moral and aesthetic issues. The natural light of reason may not always bring easy agreement, far from it. But, well used, it can make communication and debate over such issues a mark of human increase in understanding and dignity. This is a far cry from the view of some (who treat St. Thomas' *summaries* of arguments for *believers* as Manna enough for all) that the natural light of reason, when combined with obvious empirical premises, will show anyone demonstratively in at least Five Ways that God exists – that anyone without blind sinfulness, gross stupidity, or extreme prejudice will have to accept the arguments without question. But it does allow the theist to say that judging by experience and this natural light many a relatively unimpeded man can find *admirably good reasons* for believing in God, although the impediments are many and admirable non-believers are many. Some such position is needed, we suspect, as a foundation for a liberal, agapeïstic society if it is to contain believers *and* non-believers living in harmony and mutual respect, yet willing to *argue* rationally about ultimate realities. We have attempted to expand on, and refine such a position elsewhere in earlier chapters.

(Y) Of course, we are human animals inhabiting an 'external' (objective, physical) world, communicating succesfully about many matters with others of our society thanks to communal language rules, able also to communicate successfully about many matters with people outside our society whose ways of life are fairly similar to ours. We can with much effort make considerable gains in understanding very different forms of life and belief; conceptual analysis can go fairly deep in elucidating forms opposed to ours. But these facts do not enable us to make ('transculturally') objective judgments about which forms of life and belief are wiser, better, more rational, etc.

What has to be accepted, the given, is – so one could say – *forms* of life.[15] Forms of life taken as a whole are not amenable to criticism; each mode of discourse is in order as it is, for each has its own criteria and each sets its own norms of intelligibility, reality and rationality.[16]

An examination by philosophical believers and non-believers of supposed *grounds* for belief is pointless; *reasons* and *evidence* are not to be considered *in support of* such fundamental beliefs for ways of life.[17] Human reason reaches bedrock on such fundamental questions: there is no arguing about the *given* at this level. People are indifferent, intrigued, repelled, converted etc. But it's not the sort of thing, as we should now recognize *a priori*, for the outsider to evaluate in intellectual terms.[18]

Position (Y) encouraged by some strands in the later Wittgenstein's unsystematically formulated and posthumously published work, would be the proper target for detailed attack by Dwyer on the score of 'reality', 'intelligibility' and 'objectivity'. Indeed, we hope this survey and drawing of distinctions about Wittgenstein's movement from suggestions about objectivity of structure in the *Tractatus* to claims for the cultural relativist's ultimate 'objectivity' of life-forms in the *Investigations* will prompt him to publish further comment. For our own part we suspect that any argument claiming to establish (objectively!) that certain matters of theology, morals and metaphysics cannot be objectively disputed must eventually be reduced to one of two concessions[19]: EITHER (i) the disputes make no sense because the forms of life and belief are too irrational from an objective standpoint to be counted as generating intelligible propositions (a *move* from the Investigations' respect for the *'given'* life-form back to something like a violently incompatible form of Logical Positivism); we do have an objective standpoint, therefore, for evaluating such issues as pseudo-issues. OR (ii) human reason can formulate at least one meta-language which treats the object languages' claims sufficiently sympathetically and comprehendingly for us to say that by objective criteria *properly binding on all men of different forms of life* such disputes are insoluble and unarguable by reference to such criteria or any intellectually honorable criteria. While (i) is a step BACK AND AWAY from Wittgenstein, (ii) seems to be a *reductio ad absurdum* 'Wittgensteinian fideism'.

Between the sentimental Scylla of commitment to 'Wittgensteinian fideism' and the intellectual Charybdis of craving for 'undeniable demonstrations' there flow the softer, more multifarious currents of *probability*. It is these currents which should now attract the attention of believers in God and in metaphysics and in the natural light of human reason: let us try to show reasonable dissenters first-rate reasons to believe that most probably a theist view of man's estate is the wisest and closest to truth which men can attain given their endowments and limitations. If we talk primarily in terms of probabilities rather than proofs we are more likely to get rational communication. For talk of "probabilities" and "good reasons" bespeaks a belief in the importance of individuals' power of personal judgment and choice in matters of religion and of metaphysics generally. Justly or unjustly the words "proof" and "demonstration" suggest forms of *coercion* and *inevitability* which would make a mockery of reasoned personal commitment to God.[20]

I.2. *Some Possible Objections on Metaphysics and Probability*

In order to become clearer about the usefulness of "probability"-talk to believers in the natural light of reason, it is worth examining in some detail our idea(s) about our sense(s) of or use(s) of "probability" in the light of some current approaches to meaning. We shall have to beat some prickly and aridly dusty linguistic bushes while climbing over bleak and jagged conceptual terrain. To make such a trip appear less likely to prove unrewarding, we want to close Section I of this chapter by considering certain likely objections to bringing probability into natural theology and metaphysics. But it is mainly because the concept of probability is so crucial for a tolerant life of reason *and* faith that we shall grind away at misunderstandings of the question "What is probability?"

First Objection: "It is scandalous to speak of the probability that God exists when God, unless a mere idol, is a Being Who necessarily exists." [21] *Reply*: As Aquinas pointed out against Anselm, the 'intrinsic' self-evidence of affirmations of God's existence is not known to us who cannot grasp God's essence. What does need discussion in "probability"-talk at the 'meta'-level is the proposition "God exists" or the proposition "God necessarily exists" in the object language of Faith.

Second Objection: "To fall back on probability is to deny the possibility of proving God's existence – and to deny it *a priori* at that!" *Reply*: From a probabilistic standpoint one *may* deem it quite probable that one or more of the Five Ways or other traditional proofs can be reformulated in some form of a very valuable Justifying Explanation Argument resting on empirically true premises and sound WTA-'necessary' propositions. But one seriously leaves open the logical possibility, rather reasonably in view of past human errors, that something may be amiss. Or one can think of the 'Cosmological' type of theistic argument as more like an expression of insight concerning the world we know and judge about intelligibly, an insight that we seem to realize rationally an inescapable need to posit a Divine *ens causa sui* beyond the world Who makes the existence of such an intelligible yet contingent world possible. [22] The insight may be spelled out with a convincing ring in an attractive-look-argument – but the possibility remains that the apparent insight is at least partly misinterpreted or delusive, the spelling-out is unsuitable, the attractiveness is open to fair suspicion.

Third Objection: "Faith in God requires perfect trust and love, how can one show such things for a Being Whose existence one considers only probable?" *Reply*: taking a rational *risk*, by committing myself if I think there are really excellent reasons for believing in and loving such a Being, although I might just possibly be mistaken. (Such is a *rational* Leap of

Faith.) There are, after all, 'revisionary' possibilities about one's wife's or mother's existence or about one's own continuous existence and identity. (See our comments in Chapter I.) Recognizing these as intelligible possibilities need not prevent one's loving a woman or oneself to distraction! Why need it in the case of loving God?

Fourth Objection: "'Probability'-talk is only appropriate for discussing what Carnap[23] calls Internal Questions, questions that arise *within* an already accepted conceptual scheme, in which the criteria of probability (such as degrees of experimental confirmation or relative frequencies) are specified for deciding Internal matters. External Questions, about how best to modify the scheme must be settled pragmatically not probabilistically. To ask whether or not to include God within one's scheme is to pose a stupendously *non*-experimental External Question." *Reply*: This sort of objection arises from an unduly narrow view of the reasonable range of "probability"-talk, as will be shown in Section II. Typical narrowness is shown by Carnap's view, cited later, that all 'probability'-talk is either *relative frequency-within-a-theory talk* or *degree-of-confirmation-within-a-theory talk*. Let us refresh our thought by pointing out the obvious intelligibility and clarity of saying: "Given the facts and connections and insights that we have been considering, it would most probably be extremely wise and reasonable to insist on structuring our conceptual scheme so as to place a unique Divine Being right at its centre from this time on." Let us fortify it further from memory. In earlier chapters, we have seen that the conditions of fruitful discourse in a tolerantly but also responsibly liberal society, also the fallibility of men in any group falling short of the celestial, make it wiser for metaphysicians to advance their claims *primarily* in terms of hypotheses and probabilities rather than inescapable proofs. We saw that allegiance to such a primacy of emphasis does not rule out the possibility that there are strong arguments for important metaphysical claims which are graspable by the natural light of human reason. Nor need this allegiance rule out genuine personal commitment to the love and service of a Divine Being. (After all, a Divine Being Who made men rational enough to grasp the possibility of their making mistakes almost anywhere would not want them to deceive themselves about the implications of this grasp.) To assert the primacy of probabilities, and thus to admit that one *may* be wrong, and hence is willing to consider arguments, is to encourage scope for the natural light of reason to operate in quarters now darkened by 'neo' or 'crypto'-Positivism on the one hand and by so-called Barthian or Wittgensteinian fideism on the other. Rational theist metaphysicians have a lot to be grateful for in the anti-fideist writings of William Warren Bartley III's *The Retreat to Commitment* (London 1964) – as in the writings or a Mill, a Madden, or a Nielsen. From the long analysis of "probability"-words and their possible senses that will emerge we may extrapolate this sort of plausible use:

To say reasonably of a metaphysical proposition MP that there really is a very significantly strong probability that MP is true, is to say that, after careful, informed, intelligent, appropriately dispassionate and open-minded intellectual reflection on the relevant empirical and W.T.A.-'logical' considerations, one has remarkably good grounds and notable justification by the light of reason, as a direct seeker of truth for truth's sake (whatever the other benefits), to accept MP and to act upon it. Yet it is also to admit that one may be possibly mistaken about MP, that, even if true, its correctness may be partly hidden from many other reasonable beings. For they have a right to pursue truth independently. In believing and acting upon MP oneself, one must respect this liberty of conscience.

Fifth Objection: "But what becomes of *knowledge*, if *probability* takes central place in religious and metaphysical assertions?" *Reply*: For many practical purposes, reasonable belief in the extremely high probability that a crucially central proposition is true may warrant a man's saying loosely that he knows it to be true. ("God exists." "There is no God." "Minds can exist in separation from matter.") But when there is a philosophical discussion going on and reasonable disagreement between intendingly reasonable men, then assertions of knowledge and certainty can become an obstacle to equable communication and also to intellectual humility. Let the warring metaphysicians on many sides of many famous fences stop and thank Heaven (or human reason) for Probability and "Probability". With the natural light of reason less dimmed and shaded, maybe we philosophers shall reach more conclusions together. Well, *probably*, or should we say "Perhaps"? Probably! Yes, probably.

II. 'PROBABILITY' AND SEMANTIC THEORIES

An excellent place for analysing "probability"-talk – talk involving words like 'probable', 'probably', 'likelihood' etc. – is the thrice published position of Stephen Toulmin.[24] A major target in all three versions has been the whole range of probability theories termed *subjective*. Whatever the possible drawbacks of Toulmin's claims, they are vigorously and readably formulated. Moreover, what is more important, they exemplify the ambition of a philosopher of science and a historian of science, who is also a meta-moralist and a true lover of commonsense and linguistic analysis, to begin clarifying our intuitions of continuities in the use of 'probability' when applied to various areas of commonsense and philosophy and scientific judgment. Let us take as initial text the end of Toulmin's chapter on Probability in *The Uses of Argument*:

There is, after all, no radical discontinuity between the prescientific and scientific uses of our probability terms …. The punter and the actuary, the physicist and the dice–thrower are as much concerned with degrees of acceptability and expectation as the metereologist or the man in the street; whether backed by mathematical calculations or no, the characteristic function of our particular, practical probability-statements is to present *guarded* or *qualified* assertions or conclusions (p. 93).

There seems to be some truth in these words, but how great or small is it? That becomes a puzzling question on reflection. What does this conclusion over 'the *characteristic function* of our particular, practical probability-statements' show about the *sense(s)* or *meaning(s)* or even the uses of 'probability', 'probable', etc.? Perhaps more illumination can be gleaned from Toulmin's allusions to J. L. Austin's early account of *performatives*[25] and later on to "abstract nouns formed from gerundive adjectives"[26] Insofar as some analogy with guarded 'performative' talk like 'I swear that (*ceteris paribus*) P' *or* 'I promise that (*ceteris paribus*) P' holds good, presumably Toulmin means that in the contexts of our using present and future tensed sentences at least, not the pragmatic but the semantic content, the very *meaning* of "probability"-talk is its cautionary commitment *function* operating on the rest of the affirmation. (Not surprisingly Toulmin becomes involved in some dubious and untidy wrangles about past tensed sentences containing "probability"-talk. Problems also arise about *truth values* if the 'performative' analogy is pushed too far for assertions in any tense.[27]) Whether or not this is consistent with his meta-ethics, the allusion to gerundive adjectives and related nouns seems at times to be meant by Toulmin to clarify the *univocity* of "probability". "Probably", it seems is said to be sufficiently like a clearly 'evaluative' term, such as "good", for the following principle to hold: the various sorts of grounds for grading or evaluating something as "good" or as "probable" are not to be confused with what is meant by expression of the grading act or evaluation itself. If we share Austin's own later suspicions in the 50's about the viability of such allegedly clearcut categories as 'performative', 'constative', 'normative' (cf. 'gerundive', 'descriptive', evaluative'), we must be dubious about the adequacy of Toulmin's analysis of what words like "probability" and "probably" mean. But at least Toulmin has led us *deep* into the thickets we must confront for understanding "probability". We hope that the following discussions set against the background of Toulmin's remarks will lead us at least to a partial discovery of which senses or uses of "probability" metaphysicians will and will not want in which sorts of context.

II.1. *"Probability", "Meaning" and Semantic Theories*

Toulmin too often talks as if the words *"meaning"*, *"use"* and *"function"* were all philosophically perspicuous and as if giving a clarifying account of any one of these would do the same thing for the other two. For example he writes:

"probability" has a perfectly good meaning, to be discovered by examining the way in which the word is used in everyday and scientific contexts alike.[28]

Set this assertion alongside his previously quoted claim about "the characteristic function". Moreover *"force"* seems to be all but equated with *"meaning"*, *"use"* and *"function"* when Toulmin speaks of *"gerundive"* terms.

From the standpoint of J. L. Austin's *How to Do Things with Words*[29] and from that of J. R. Searle in 'Meaning and Speech Acts'[30] we need to distinguish carefully between "locutionary", "illocutionary" and "perlocutionary" uses of sentences in which a word like "probable", "probably" or "probability" occurs. Austin stressed that at the level of the locutionary use of such sentences one already has the 'meaning' or 'sense and reference' of the words involved together.[31] Uttering or writing such sentences meaningfully is not to be confused with what (or with the force of what) we are doing in expressing them, although there are extremely important relationships between locutionary acts and various "conventionally" related "illocutionary acts" such as describing, promising, swearing etc.; nor may either type of "act" be confused with achieving any "non-conventional" effects brought about by expressing them. Such "non-conventional", or "perlocutionary" effects would be ones like deceiving, frightening and angering.[32]

From this standpoint it seems natural to complain that Toulmin has tended to confuse questions about the meaning of sentences in which such words as "probable" occur with questions about what we are (usually as opposed, say, to ironically) doing in calling a hypothesis *probable*. And so the argument would go for 'probable', as it has already gone with "good" and "true".[33]

Suppose it is often, or even always the case that what we are doing in calling a hypothesis *probable* with a single-verbed categorical present indicative sentence is either to present a guarded conclusion or to make a guarded commitment, what does this show about the meaning of "probable"? After all "probable", "probability" etc. are equally at home in a host of different linguistic environments, These include "If only it *were* at all probable!"; "Is it really probable?"; "Which is the more probable?"; "If it were probable, why would I be here?", And a healthy number more.

What Toulmin is doing is to distinguish between taking the meaning (or the primary meaning) of "probable" to be a function of just one sort of illocutionary use and making it a function of a small subset of such uses – a family of uses that he associates with *his* vague use of "gerundive"! Neither approach could give us the whole story. But, worse still, he would have put the cart before the horse, even if he considered very many illocutionary uses. For he has failed to see that what we are doing in calling a hypothesis *probable* is a function of the meaning or meanings of the word "probable". By concentrating on categorical indicative sentences in which "probably" rather than "probable" of "probability" occurs, Toulmin suggest that the effect of the adverb on the force of such sentences reveals the primary meaning of the noun and adjective. But we shall find reason to infer that "probability" is often used with something as its reference – that, therefore, paraphrasing categorical indicative sentences in which the noun "probability" could appear with others restricted to the adverb "probably" leaves one with a sentence that obliquely points to such a reference after all.

In favour of such an argument more formal philosophers interested in linguistics could say two things *inter alia*: (a) It seems more intuitively plausible (since the sentence-types readily intelligible to humans like English speakers with a finite vocabulary are generally infinite) to say that for such humans individual word meanings (sharing a 'fundamental' level, perhaps, with grammatical rules and semantic projection rules)[34] are "prior" to sentence meanings – "prior" in enough ways for it to be desirable to treat word-meanings as primitive items or notions in a comprehensive semantic theory. (b) Consider such linguistic environments as "Is P really (probable)?" and "If only P were at all (probable)!" and "If P's (probable), then Q's very (probable)". Here even offering such a crude, crass stab at a near synonym as the adjectival expression, *able to meet evidential standards answering to some relevantly live interest*, seems to offer a far more acceptable translation procedure for handling the adjective "probable" than a Toulmanish-sounding one which would prompt us to engage in such whole-sentence-translations as : "Do I guardedly predict *P*?", "If only I guardedly promised *P*!" etc. It might be replied that a procedure fairer to Toulmin and his gerundive sallies would call for, e.g. "Ought I really to go and guardedly predict *P*?" to translate "Is *P* really probable? But this would seem to require us to treat "*P* is really probable" as fairly equivalent in CTA-meaning to "I really ought to go and guardedly predict (or promise) *P*". And that sort of thing would seem to lead to too many similarly counter-intuitive results.

But with the philosophy of language now in such a healthy state of flux it would be rash indeed to claim that the kind of argument just offered against Toulmin in the tradition of Austin and of Searle should treated as the last word, even if it received a measure of blessing from more formal critics. For one thing, let us consider the conclusion of many that word-meanings are in some crucial way or ways 'prior' to sentence-meanings and notice the sort of intuitive premise given about relatively far more acceptable procedures of translation for sentences including words like "probable", "true" and "good". Surely both conclusion and subsidiary premise will strike many philosophers as being much better grounded than the major Austinian doctrinal premise, that semantic studies should be fundamentally grounded on the distinction between the three kinds of 'linguistic acts'. To give examples, such important contributors to both philosophy and theory of linguistics as Ziff, Katz and Fodor[35] have considered Austin's ideas with interest, yet they seem to attach no such deep theoretical importance to Austin's distinction between 'acts'. We assume (and often with sympathy) that one among their reasons for this is that they shy away from using what would sound like scientifically precise technical terms in connection with 'acts' because it often would seem very hard to tell how to VERIFY at all decisively which and how many Austinian 'acts' or sorts of 'acts' are being performed in the course of a particularly observable linguistic utterance.

For another thing, W. P. Alston and L. J. Cohen have shown how eclectic and careful philosophers, who do take Austin's talk of "acts" much more seriously, can still wish – for differing reasons – to impact a

great deal of what Austin would consider illocutionary use into fundamental ('fundamentally prior'?) accounts of meaning. Consider the following attempts by Alston to give basic accounts of sentence-meaning
and word-meaning.[36]

A meaning of S_1 is S_2=df. Sometimes S_1 is used to perform the *illocutionary act (s)
that S_2 is usually used to perform* ... *A meaning of W_1 is W_2=df.* In most sentences
in which W_2 occurs, W_1 can be substituted for it without changing the illocutionary
act potential of the sentence.

Alston goes on to the comment:

If this is the line along which meaning should be analysed, then the concept of an
illocutionary act is the most fundamental concept in semantics and, hence, in the
philosophy of language.

Alston shows himself quite aware that we are a long way from having
all the adequate tools for theoretically "characterising uses of words"
or "analyzing illocutionary acts", but he remains optimistic both about
our present abilities to distinguish illocutionary acts for "practical
purposes" and about our future theoretical abilities. While we find it
hard to share wholly in either form of optimism, we should not be
amazed if he and similarly deviant neo-Austinians came up with the
needed tools; the reasonable philosopher of language must accept and
even welcome the state of flux we mentioned; and one of several among
present rival approaches to language, or some or all of several present
rivals, or something as yet largely untried, may lead to extraordinary
gains in clarity and in our power to account systematically for linguistic
phenomena. (Perhaps they will gain much from the interest in *suppressed*
performatives of formal linguists like J. R. Ross.) Presumably any form
of sympathetic AND acceptable reconstruction of Toulmin's analysis of
'probability' now seems most likely to be specifiable in the event that an
illocutionary 'semantic theory' like Alston's could be made more broad
and yet rigorous. But it would have to be a reconstruction, not a mere
resurrection. Grounds of both completeness and consistency make us say
this. As for completeness, an Alston-type theory would have to account
for the very wide "illocutionary-act-potential" of sentences in which
words like "probable" and "probability" occur. The making of guarded
predictions and conclusions could, perhaps, be considered to be among
the few most important of such "acts", but they would still only be
among the few most important many among important ones.

As for consistency, no self-consistent attempt at revival could allow Toulmin first to talk on the one hand about "*probable*" as "a term which keeps invariant force through a wide variety of applications", to talk with a uniqueness-urging definite article about "the meaning of term 'probability'" or "the characteristic function" etc.; yet to say on the other hand: "It is idle to hope that what is true of claims of the forms 'It is probable' will be necessarily true of claims of the forms... 'It was probable'".

These incompatible ways of talking about "probability" do mirror Toulmin's natural insightfulness into a complex manifold. It is this which makes his ideas so well worth trying to evaluate. But an account of "probability" which is to be compatible with a worthwhile semantic theory must reshape such inconsistently expressed thoughts into an intelligible harmony. It must, moreover, cope with the legitimacy of the locution that Toulmin cannot consistently handle: "It's probable that *P*, very probable, but just *possibly* it's false." This cannot be characterized just as a guarded assurance that *P*, followed by a less guarded one, followed by a very, very guarded assurance that *Not-P*. In such a case, we suspect, one should allow that the locution "It's probable, etc., but etc." is used to speak about the relative strengths or weights or merits of the evidence *for and against P*. The reply "No, it's not probable that *P*, not very probable, anyway, as *you* say", cannot be very naturally construed as a guarded denial of *P* or a query about *P*; it must be understood as a reply, at least in some contexts, that says something about the grounds for believing *P*. Toulmin recoils in horror from talk about the *designatum* or *reference* of "probability". But in context "The probability that it will rain" can be used to designate, stand for, etc. the grounds for believing that it will rain, the strength of those grounds, and the like. And "Probably it will rain" is often used to say pretty much what "The probability that it will rain is great" is used to say more ponderously. We hope that all this will emerge more clearly soon in II.4. But first we shall consider *Some Possibly Golden Eggs among Toulmin's Obiter Dicta* in II.2 and then *Some Lexicographical and Etymological Factors* in II.3.

II.2. *Some Golden Eggs Among Toulmin's Obiter Dicta*

Toulmin's approach may prove especially valuable for facilitating *(Alpha)* informed analysis of the *criteria* for applying different modal terms in different fields and also possibly for *(Beta)* the construction of formal explications of the *force* of modal terms when used to enhance the (dominatingly non-declarative) performatory aspect of indicative sentences.

(Alpha) To say, in any field, "Such-and-such is a possible answer to our question", is to say that, bearing in mind the nature of the problem concerned, such-and-such an answer deserves to be considered. This much of the meaning of the term 'possible' is field-invariant. The criteria of possibility on the other hand are field-dependent, like the criteria of impossibility and goodness.[37]

The same distinction between force and criteria applies to the modal term 'probably'. Toulmin is surely right in suggesting that too many philosophers assume there is only one kind of way to establish the probability of claims – whatever the field; whereas quite different ways will be appropriate in discussing claims about tennis reports on Davis Cup form, Fröhlich's theory in physics and Piero della Francesca's artistry. Toulmin seems equally right in suggesting that the neglect of field-dependence for criteria may lead to the false assumption that a favoured set of criteria must constitute *the* designatum of probability: thus force and criteria may sometimes be so confused as to offer something worth calling, *guardedly*, a genuinely repulsive form of the Naturalistic Fallacy.[28] But to grant Toulmin this is not to grant him the view to be later questioned that the modal terms 'probably' and 'probable' have a *unique* force.

(Beta) Ordinary usage and scientific talk of "probability" are referred by Toulmin to Austin's work, on the performatory force of "I know". He thus, in effect, exposes the limitations and insensitivity of much formal work on modal logic. Rudolf Carnap, for example, tells one in *Meaning and Necessity* that

Our task will be to find clear and exact concepts to replace the vague concepts of the modalities as used in common language and in traditional logic. In other words, we are looking for explicata for modalities (Chicago 1947, p. 174).

This explication he proposes to provide in terms of 'semantical L-truth'. In a somewhat more recent work *Time and Modality* (Oxford 1956) A. N. Prior discusses a number of modal systems which might be applied to puzzling talk of future events. Carnap advocates only modal formulae which when well-formed must qualify for the semantical predicate "true" or "false". Prior uses many valued logics but with the notion in mind that a well-formed formula about the future may be neither true or false now, yet it will become true or false later on.

Neither Carnap nor Prior envisages the possibility that very often the modal '*explicanda*' of our discourse need not always be declaratively analysed but treated as almost 'purely' performative in force and as requiring a formal treatment far removed from truth table techniques. After Toulmin's work on "probably" and the application of his moral here to "possibly" and "necessarily" it is no longer respectable for those who would include modalities in formal semantics to delay working out a logic for performatives taking "that" clauses. Part of the minimum machinery needed for some of this could be as follows. We need (a) the sort of signs we have elsewhere called "qualifiers" [39], which would express degrees of commitment and which would remove the qualifier-bound formula from the calculus of truth and falsity. We need (b) external rules to govern the commitment links between qualifier-bound expressions, rules sufficiently thorough to obviate the paradoxes Quine has raised for modal inference. We need (c) 'internal' rules to establish what sorts of propositions may and may not be bound with qualifiers to result in well formed formulae. To give examples for a very simple model:

(1) 'P', a true or false proposition could be strongly guaranteed as '$|P|$' and progressively more weakly guaranteed as '$||P||$', '$|||P|||$' etc.

(2) '"$|P|$" → "$||P||$"' but not *vice versa* should be a commitment rule.

(3) '$|P \& Not\text{-}P|$' and '$|P \lor Not\text{-}P|$' should be excluded as ill formed – commitment to tautologies and contradictions is *a priori* improper. Such a Performative, or Commitment Logic might, when richly developed, turn out to have interesting application to legal concepts. It might prove especially fertile for legal puzzles relative to Russell's Theory of Description.

The relevance of such crude formal models, when properly developed, to understanding religious ritual acts, including religious vows, and related degrees of responsibility, might be surprisingly helpful. But this is a question for a very different place of prolongable pursuit.

II.3. *Some Lexicographical and Etymological Factors*

As noted in II.1, Toulmin turns to what he calls *the gerundive* model of words like "rightness" and "validity" to explicate the probable. He claims that attempts to define what is probable in non-evaluative terms face all the pitfalls of Moore's Naturalistic Fallacy. For Toulmin "probable" seems to belong to the same evaluative family as "valuable", "right", "valid" and "good". (See *The Uses of Argument*, pp. 68–70.) This does not help Toulmin's own claims that "probability" is certainly clarified by his talk of analyses of sentences in terms of making guarded assertions, however. For unless it can be established, as is most unlikely, that anything he calls a *gerundive* term has a unique force, it seems hasty to conclude that "probable" has both a gerundive ring and thus an invariant force. Nor does Toulmin clarify the relation between his talk about what is "gerundive" and his talk about what is "performative". He might need to be very careful here in order not to undermine with two models his claim against Urmson, Carnap and others that "probability" is not an ambiguous term.

Before we jump to any unguarded conclusions, however, let us look more closely at the origins of "probable" and cognate words. Instead of repeating Toulmin's rather *a priori* anthropology in the matter of learning probability talk, we need to do some harder linguistic or lexicographical research.

In modern English there is a large number of contexts, where "probable" and "likely" may be used to do the same job – a number sufficiently large to warrant our calling them synonyms.[40] In a number of Indo-European languages we find a word akin to "probable" plus a synonym akin to "likely" or we find only a word akin to "likely" which has to do the major work of "probable" in English. The 1958 edition of the *Encyclopedia Britannica* tells us that "the original meaning of the word 'probable' is, roughly, 'approvable'". Another word, it tells us, with the same connotation is "likely". "Probability", said Locke, " is likeness to be true." In Latin "*probabilis*" and "*verisimilis*", in French "*probable*" and "*vraisemblable*" are synonyms; German has only one word "*wahrscheinlich*" ("true seeming"). We may supplement these observations by noting that Latin "*verisimilis*" and English "*likely*" appear to lexicographers to be older than "*probabilis*" and "*probable*", hence perhaps they originally were in the same (maid-of-all-"probability"-talking) situation as "*wahrscheinlich*" is presently in German. That in classical Greek many judgments of probability were made with the verb ἔοικα basically meaning 'resemble' and its cognate adjective εἰκός which

came to mean 'resembling the true', and hence 'probable', 'reasonable
to believe'. That in the Slavonic branch of Indo-European languages
Russian has two synonyms: (a) *"veroya 'tniey"*, gerundively connected
with the verb *"ve'rit"*, to "believe" or "credit" as *"probabilis"* is with
"probare" in its sense of "approve", "allow", "credit", "esteem"
(b) *"pravdopodobniey"*, like *"verisimilis"* in formation, (cf. *"Pravda"*,
truth).

If, as Austin suggested, etymology often offers crucial help to linguistic
analysis, and if, as Toulmin holds, accounts of "probability" must be
related to common-sense probability talk, then we have a two-fold task
on hand. Common-sense probability talk in English may usefully be
treated as having its two main roots in the etymology of "probable"
and "likely". English, French and Latin "-ble" suffixes, as Mill is sometimes still held to have forgotten to his cost concerning the *desirable*,
may be gerundive indicators as well as capability indicators. In the
English of 1485 we find a use of *"probable"* as meaning "capable of
demonstrative proof" – Latin *probare* could mean *prove* as well as *approve*.
But much more commonly since the sixteenth century "probability" has
signified *"worthiness of belief"* and *"what is worthy of belief"*. The
Oxford Universal Dictionary has it for 1576 "something which judged
by present evidence is likely to be true, to exist or to happen". On the
other hand "likely", a word with obvious ancestors in Old English and
Old Norse, could be used to mean either "similar to" and "resembling"
or " truth-like" and "probable" as late as Milton's time. Thus to explicate
common-sense *"probability"*-talk in English we should investigate: (i)
the gerundive notion of *being worthy of belief on the strength of present
evidence*; (ii) the perhaps historically more primitive notions of *being
like the truth, true looking, resembling the truth and seeming to be true*.
(For the latter compare the Greek ἔοικε and English "so it seems",
frequently used to mean *"probably"*.) The alleged gap between "Is" and
"Ought" trembles again: *being like the truth* and *being like what may usually
merit belief* are not psychologically associated by accident.

Truth Resemblance. A cursory look at the logic of "looking like",
"resembling". "seeming to be", and even "being like" does not appear to
help Toulmin's thesis that the quasi-performative use of probability
judgments is *the* use or *interesting use*. Nor does it appear to help his
charge that "improbable but true" is always a solecism. For take these

expressions: "x looks just like y but of course they're different"; "x resembles y terribly closely but they're not the same individual"; "Pa seems to be Swedish, he looks and sounds Swedish, but he's really a Pole", "he is so like his twin brother, don't confuse them!" Just so a proposition may be said to seem very like, sound oh so like, closely resemble, look exactly like and be ever so similar to the truth – but really to be incorrect. In fact the point of using such locutions is sometimes just to lead up to the denial. On the other hand, sometimes the purpose behind the use of these locutions is at least guardedly to reject the denial. And to the extent of this *sometimes* the logic of "looking", "being like", "resembling", etc., does favour Toulmin's pronouncements on probability. For sometimes we say, as Anthony Quinton and Wilfrid Sellars[41] have noted, "he looks ϕ", "he's so similar to y", "he appears to be ϕ" just in order to express a guarded commitment to his being ϕ or being y. But a "sometimes" is not an "always": the uses of "looking", "resembling", etc. would suggest that "unlikely but true" and "probable but false" are not always solecisms as Toulmin has repeatedly insisted. This is only a suggestion, and one can afford to burrow deeper.

"Probability" as Gerundive Term: To call p probable is of course not always just to call it "worthy of belief". On the one hand, a fiery imitator of Tertullian and Kierkegaard may preach that the most improbable claims of his creed are those most worthy of belief. On the other hand, to be probable is often to be worthy of belief because of that present evidence which for practical purposes is the best one can go by. Toulmin takes great exception to W. C. Kneale's saying that Marco Polo's claims were improbable but true. *Either*, Toulmin replies, "were" should be replaced by "seemed", *or* "were improbable" should be construed as a piece of disguised Oratio Obliqua. Yet Kneale's seemingly straightforward locution needs no such doctoring if we understand "improbable" in the following straightforward way. To say that Marco Polo's claims *were* improbable is simply to say that because of and judged by the best evidence practically obtainable in the context indicated by "were", his claims were not belief-worthy. The non-present tensing of the verb may often indicate the context of reasons and judgment to be very different from the present one. Such indication is direct, and not a piece of disguised Oratio Obliqua, when "probable" words are so understood. But in the case of " *is* probable" it does often seem outrageous to follow this up with an outright denial.

Why? Because often it is indeed puzzling if without explanation someone *now* rejects a proposition, while claiming that the best evidence *now* available suggests it is worthy of belief!

But even this present tensed conjunction is intelligible in some contexts. For one thing, it is intelligible on the assumption that the commendatory force of "probable" and "best evidence" has become for the speaker somewhat *ossified*. (We use a term from Hare's *The Language of Morals*.) Suppose the man in the street says "Well, quite probably there will be a – tomorrow, but I don't really think so". He may mean that the reasons for believing so are conventionally very respectable but he mistrusts conventions. Now there is less 'ossified', more natural alternative. This has serious importance. He may mean that the reasons for believing so are ones he *generally* regards as excellent grounds for belief in cases of this sort – but he just has a hunch that here is an exception worth pressing against a general rule that is worth expressing. Here, *pace* Toulmin on solecism, the speaking up for the rather unusual need not involve speech that is somehow illegitimate or unintelligible.

II.4. *Some Senses of "Probability"?*

Toulmin has harsh words for those like the J. O. Urmson of 'Two of the Senses of "Probable"' – see M. MacDonald (ed.), *Philosophy and Analysis*, Oxford 1954, pp. 191–99 – and the Rudolf Carnap of 'The Two Concepts of Probability' – see H. Feigl and M. Broadbeck, *Philosophy of Science*, New York 1953, pp. 438–55 – who have tried to distinguish different senses of "probability". Carnap especially angered Toulmin by proposing that we distinguish "probability$_1$" (a formal degree of confirmation – a purely formal *logical* relation between evidence and hypothesis) from "probability$_2$" (a relative frequency). Unfortunately for a torch bearer of the *Wienerkreiszeitgeist*, Carnap thought that our actual CTA-usage of "probability", even among present-day scientists trying to make rational decisions, must present a mere *explicandum* to be replaced by a suitable concept or concepts from the Unified and Purified Sciences of the Methodological Elite; the Methodological Elite must be philosophers of physics. This approach tends to put a damper on further scientifically, practically, mathematically and epistemologically existing discussions of CTA- and WTA-meanings of "probability" – meanings which may warrant a state of progress through ferment. Also Carnap thus exposed himself to *some* measure of fair criticism from Toulmin – as perhaps when he says at *The Uses of Argument*, p. 93:

Where one in fact, to cut away from the mathematical theory of probability all that it owes to our prescientific ways of thought about the subject, it would lose all application to practical affairs.

Take three typical outbursts by Toulmin:

(i) But unless we are once again to confuse the *grounds for regarding something as probable* with the *meaning of the statement that it is* probable, we need not go on to say that there are consequently a number of different senses of the words "probable" and "probability".[42]

(ii) In the first place, the abstract noun "probability" ... is a word of such a type that it is nonsense even to talk about it as denoting, standing for, or meaning anything ... there is no special thing which probability-statements must be about, simply by virtue of the fact that they are probability–statements.[43]

(iii) To attempt to define what is meant by the probability of an event in terms of such things (as frequencies) is to confuse the meaning of the term "probability" with the grounds for regarding the event as probable ....[44]

If Toulmin is to be believed in several emphatic places, the word "probability" has but one sense, and wise answers to a question like "What is the statement that there will probably be rain this evening ABOUT?" can never be answers explicating what the abstract noun "probability" stands for or designates or denotes – they can only be common-sense answers like "the evening's weather". In what follows we shall suggest that, at least at the level of a good many English-speakers' crude, but rather strikingly rational intuitions, the word "probability" does seem to have more than one sense[45]; also, at this level, which a semantic theorist ignores at the danger of turning out to be bombinating in an idiolectical or purely imperative vacuum, such a question about a "*probability*"-statement's 'aboutness' can often, if not always, be informatively answered: "Well, yes, it's partly about this evening's weather, partly about X" where X is some quasi-synonymous expression for "probability" such that many an English speaker would normally agree that "*the probability that P*" can be said to "stand for" or "denote" the X that P.

Here then are three meta-facts about the sort of linguistic facts that leave us dissatisfied with Toulmin's pronouncements on the Sense and Reference of the noun "probability". (A) The following utterances U1–U6 in which "probability" occurs would strike us in various – not ALL – philosophically untainted contexts as being neither very unclear nor very oddly worded English utterances. (B) The following substituends for U1–U6 would strike us as similarly respectable and chaste in the right contexts. (C) In an interestingly large subset of the contexts in which we might utter U1 or U2 or U3 and so on, it seems that at least one or one-or-more of the substituends would enable us to say equally well what we wanted to say in uttering U1 or U2 and so on. (Each substituend SN, it seems, would amount to the same thing as its corresponding UN in SOME not very strained context.)

U2	*What is the probability that they committed suicide?*
U1	*There's a strong probability that they committed suicide. (In reply to U2.)*
U1S1	*There's a strong likelihood that they committed suicide.*
U2	*What is the probability that they committed suicide?*
U2S1	*What's the degree of evidence that they committed suicide?*
U2S2	*What is the strength of the evidence that they committed suicide?*
U2S3	*How good are the reasons for concluding that they committed suicide?*
U2S4	*How justified are we in concluding that they committed suicide?*
U2S5/6	*How probable/likely is it that they committed suicide?*
U3	*I'm afraid it's (definitely) a probability that they committed suicide.*
U3S1	*I'm afraid that there's a high degree of evidence that they committed suicide.*
U3S2	*I'm afraid that the strength of the evidence for saying that they committed suicide is considerable.*
U3S3	*I'm afraid that the reasons for concluding that they committed suicide are definitely strong ones.*
U3S4	*I'm afraid that we're well justified in concluding that they committed suicide.*
U3S5/6	*I'm afraid that it's (definitely) probable/likely that they committed suicide.*
U4	*What is the probability of one's drawing a black ball from the bag first time?*
U4S1	*How great is one's chance of drawing a black ball from the bag the first time?*

U5   *Since there are 99 balls and one black the probability is only one in a hundred.*

U5S1/2/3 *Since there are only 99 etc. the probability is exactly one per cent/ exactly 0.01/ exactly 1 in 100.*

U6   *Before the invention of synthetic hormones and estrogen the probability of a hereditary syphilitic's remaining sterile was slightly higher than 99 times out of 100.*

U6S1/2   *Before etc. the relative frequency/ frequency of etc. was etc.*

U6S3   *Before etc. one had every reason to believe that in slightly more than 99 cases out of 100 a hereditary syphilitic would remain sterile.*

U6S4/5/6 *Before etc. the high degree of reasonableness for expecting a hereditary syphilitic to remain sterile could be expressed numerically as slightly more than 99%/0.99/99 out of 100.*

These examples by no means exhaust the sorts of linguistically and philosophically interesting environments where "probability" can occur. We would surely find further semantic enlightenment, especially if we looked at more cases of "probability" being used without the definite article. An exploration of environments for other members of the "probable"-family might turn up a still further significant divergence of types of acceptable substituends. But this sample by itself should suffice to make anyone with an English dialect fairly like common ones unhappy about Toulmin – and about no few dictionaries! If we set aside "likelihood" as a generally acceptable, but perhaps diminishingly felicitous synonym for "probability" down the stretch from U1 to U6, we derive from what looks like a healthy, if crude, intuitive interpretation of these examples at least the following senses or interpretations-for-use of "probability": (i) degree of strength of evidence for a belief/hypothesis etc. or value of the reasons/grounds for such, (a) expressible numerically in some contexts, (b) not expressible numerically in others; (ii) HIGH degree or GREAT strength of evidence for a belief or hypothesis etc. or HIGH value of the reasons/grounds for such, (a) expressible numerically etc., (b) not expressible numerically etc.; (iii) the actual historical frequency of certain events in relation to others; (iv) the belief-worthiness of a hypothesis expressible numerically in relation to the frequencies covered under (iii); (v) the 'iffy' ratio relating certain potential events or sets of events to certain other potential events to be expected if some train of events were initiated; (vi) the belief-worthiness of a hypothesis expressible numerically in relation to the 'iffy' ratio covered under (v).

Relying on such crude but promising intuitions, then, we would tentatively expect the dictionary of a sound semantic theorist to offer us at least six crude senses of "probability" along somewhat these lines. Looking at *The Shorter Oxford English Dictionary* we find that there are only three entries, despite its giving far more attention than we have to "probability" WITHOUT the definite article;[46] that our (i) and (ii) seem confused together by its entries as are (iii) and (iv), (iii) and (v) and (v) and (vi). Toulmin of course often seems to want only one sense and he is so keen on playing lexical Procrustes that he follows a wise move with an extremely implausible one. First he draws a distinction, roughly of a kind the S.O.E.D. needed for separating our (iii) and (v), between (a) "the frequency with which events of the kind we are considering happen in such circumstances" and (b) "The proportion which the event under consideration represents of the number of alternative possible happenings."[47] Then, having actually indicated differing contexts in which we WOULD normally take such expressions as (a) and (b) to be synonyms for "probability", he rejects (a) and (b) as possible senses of "probability" in any context. He dismisses them, presumably, because in defiance of intuitively relevant examples like ours he wants to insist that for ALL occurrences of sentences involving "probability" (a) and (b) must represent mere grounds[48], i.e., (a) and (b) can never be synonyms for "probability". Such, to borrow a shaft from Wittgenstein, can be the cost to philosophers of an obsession with one sort of example even when one is quite aware of others. Such also is the price of believing that, because sometimes the use of an expression only implies the existence of something obliquely, therefore, it is never used to state its existence or to refer it directly.[49] A good reason may be as real as a good horse: Toulmin's emphasis on "probably" in simple, categorical indicative sentences as a means of denying reference to "probability" is like paraphrasing "He rode *this horse* to *London*" with "He came *here* and came *on horseback*" in order to deny that "London" and "this horse" have any reference.

For similar reasons we should want to call it intuitively promising to say, in opposition to Toulmin, that in many contexts of use the words "the probability" in a sentence can be allowed to designate, denote, stand for, or refer to something. It does not always, we agree with him, refer to one and the same thing and perhaps in some contexts talk about its Reference would mislead. At any rate, the words "The probability" are often enough used to stand for or refer to the strength of reasons, or the degree of evidence, or the high degree of evidence, or the actual frequency, or the conditional proportion (the 'iffy ratio'), etc., etc. The abstract noun "probability" is NOT likely to be of such a type, it would seem for all Toulmin's protests, that we shall NEVER speak of it as denoting, or standing for, or designating or referring to anything at all.[50] When it comes to the questions "What are probability-judgments about ?" or "What do they all express?" we should perhaps not follow Toulmin in always turning our backs. Answers like "Well, usually they are about (or they express) one or more of several things such as..." look like being sometimes well in order.

Our reappraisal of Toulmin's account of "probable"-words has been highly tentative and piecemeal in approach. This is partly because now is a better time than ever before for metaphysically minded philosophers of language to adopt such an approach. Whatever our queries, doubts, criticisms, we entirely agree with Toulmin that an interest in attempts by the mathematically and logically gifted to construct formal theories of probability should be supplemented, at the very least in the case of philosophers, by a keen interest in the sorts of sentences where ordinary people and relatively unphilosophical scientists use words like "probable", "probability", and "likely". (Whatever our queries, doubts and criticisms, we hope that these explorations may induce some readers to take another look at Toulmin himself both on ordinary language and on the history and philosophy of science.)

II.5. *The Contexts of Many Subjective Theories of Probability*

There are, we can see, crucial locutions to which Toulmin accords no careful treatment. For instance "This idea is likely to succeed/is a probable winner, but we cannot rule out the chance of its falling through" is not a solecism. Nor is it confused to say: "It's quite improbable that anyone will be killed but of course it's not certain." Nor is it remotely confusing to say: "Probably he won't get the slightest scratch, but bring along the iodine just in case." However high the probabilities of what is uncertain may rise, there may turn out to be contexts where the opposite possibilities cannot be discounted by a reasonable AGENT. What is it to say that (whatever the probabilities against q), the *possibility* remains that q? It is often, in Toulmin's own words, "to say that, bearing in mind the nature of the problem concerned, such-and-such an answer deserves to be considered."[51] In the contexts of such legitimate locutions as these an analysis of probability judgments simply in terms of guarded or qualified assertions seems glaringly inadequate. To say "probably p, but possibly *not p*" is not to assert p with mild qualification and then assert *not-p* very, very guardedly. It is surely more often like saying (a) that the known grounds for believing p are of the respectable sort that should generally pay off; but (b) that all the same their value is not so strong or universal as to merit our simply ignoring the Risk of the opposite contingency in our choices and actions.

It is the contexts of such locutions, contexts where decisions must be made in the face of risk and a residual posit of serious uncertainty, that interest leading *subjective*, or *personalistic*, theorists of probability. These contexts and not the 'tinsel crown' of designatum (inner feelings of strong or weaker confidence) for the Probable have supplied the main motivation for the writings of men like F. P. Ramsey, L. J. Savage, and Patrick Suppes.[52] Such theorists are concerned with belief as expressed not by inner voices and feelings but by observable behaviour, hence the tribute paid to Ramsey by his successors in subjective probability theory. As Toulmin puts it:

There is certainly no reason why mental words should figure at all prominently in books on logic; especially if one thinks of belief, with Russell, as something having as one aspect "an idea or image combined with a yes-feeling". The important thing about drawing a proper conclusion is to be ready to *do* the things appropriate in view of the information at one's disposal.[53]

For the subjective theorists mentioned the probable, *qua* the belief-worthy is that which is deemed worthy, in appropriate conditions, to *act* upon.[54] To say in ordinary language that p is probable is, we think they would agree roughly with Toulmin, to present a guarded assertion as to the belief-worthiness and act-guiding-worthiness of p. (Whether ones own [subjective] assignment of Probability is *reasonable* depends on ones conformity to some of the criteria for reasonableness set in Chapter I.)

But they would add, if they chose Aristotelian language, that it is not such a commendation *simpliciter* (ἀπλῶς). It is rather such a commendation only relative to the existence of certain subjective utilities entertained by the decider. It is a guarded assertion that *p* is to be acted on as true, granted certain subjective Utility assignments. Because the Utility assignments to certain Outcomes (of belief, action chosen and truth as yet unknown) is subjective in that it is made by the agent does not entail that it is *irrational* or that, *pace* Hobbes, it is *selfish*. The *ways* in which the agent evaluates and assigns determine whether or not he is rational, considerate of others, etc. Toulmin is confused about what "subjective" means in the subjectivist theories which are most relevant to modern discussions of Probability.

To clarify this let us construct a very simple example.[55] I attend a race meeting not intending to bet, with only my bus fare home in my pocket. I have an extremely important appointment shortly after the meeting and must take the bus. A race comes up where the favourite appears all but certain to win. A successful bet would double my bus fare and allow me a most acceptable pint of bitter. What is the rational thing to do granted (a) the utilities that I personally place on making the appointment and on having a pint, (b) the degree of probability I assign to the horse's winning? The subjectivist or personalistic theorists mentioned have all addressed themselves to discussing criteria of rationality in view of the logical and mathematical techniques available.[56] Their approach has not been that of descriptive psychologists as Toulmin misleadingly[57] indicated but that of normative logicians. Their aim has not been to advance certain mental states as the designatum of Probability but to expound how one should act in relation to evidence and subjective utilities if one's behaviour is to count as rational.[58] (Relative frequency theories and other accounts have struck them as important but inadequate.) It might be that these subjectivists have not succeeded in explicating all of our relevant ordinary usage or in providing a wholly satisfactory interpretation for the 'probability concepts' of pure mathematics. It may or may well *not* be a legitimate complaint that they leave the assignment of probability and utility values to the individual in a philosophically scandalous manner.[59] (The selection of probabilities, utilities, options etc. can be *rationally made* by the person or subject – by some of the criteria for reasonableness in Chapter I – or irrationally by ignoring almost all of them. The nature

of the criteria used and not the number of selectors 'makes the difference'!)
But it is not the case that their theories are futile because they derive only
from a "Fido" – Fido fallacy concerning the real denotation of probability
judgments. It does seem to be the case that formal theories of subjective
probability are closely connected with ordinary sensible usage and
prudent ordinary concerns of men – the usage and concerns of making
decisions in the face of serious uncertainty. In fact the best introduction
to such theories would be those common pieces of usage where Toulmin's
analysis of probability judgments begins to break down – e.g. where
'probably p' is not a guarded assertion of p but an unguarded assertion
of the general though not overwhelming value of one's reasons for
believing p.

Summary: Here are some broad conclusions about Toulmin.

(1) Toulmin offers an analysis of probability judgments in terms of
guarded assertions invoking the 'early' Austin of 1946 on performative
uses of "I know". He never makes clear how much like 'purely' performatory expressions such guarded assertions are to be treated. The 'early'
Austin of 1946 introduced the term "performative" to contrast it with
"*declarative*", i.e., to separate certain types of indicative sentences from
true-or-false descriptive ones. Some sentences with "probably" might
seem to function like purely performatory expressions. ("Probably p"
might sometimes be used just to say "I back p fairly strongly".) It seems
natural to appraise as true or false a great many categorical indicative
sentences of the forms "Probably she'll come", "It's quite likely she'll
come", and so on.

(2) Toulmin also likens probability statements to gerundive expressions.
This, we saw, fits in well with etymological considerations. Since sentences including so-called gerundive expressions have many functions
in ordinary language, this would indicate, contrary to Toulmin's emphasis on the single performative function of guarded assertion, that
probability statements have many functions in ordinary language. And
even if present indicative statements like "It will probably rain" always
illustrated some 'gerundive' or 'pure performative' analysis of such
statements, this would not entail that what "probable" etc. 'really' meant
is revealed. Recall "Is it very probable?, "How probable?", "If it really
were probable that your son-in-law is broke, what would you do?"
A Searlean host of grammatical constructions must produce the same

meaning for a word, or *caution* is the best word for the philosopher.

(3) Toulmin's analysis forbids us to say "probable but false". If (i) this is at least in some cases a solecism but (ii) there are many counter-examples, then Toulmin's analysis would appear to be inadequate. Past tense uses do seem to supply some of the necessary counter-examples, unless one cleaves grimly to Toulminian dogmas.

(4) When one says and means "*p* is [present tense] probable" it need not to be the case, as Toulmin holds, that one does believe confidently that *p*. Sometimes it need only be the case that one has confidence in the *general* value of the sorts of reasons adducible for belief in *p*. In such cases "quite probably *p* but I don't really think so" would not be a solecism, even though the present tense is used.

(5) Even if "probable but false" were always a solecism, "probable but *possibly* false" and similar legitimate expressions need to be examined. The use and context of such expressions supply the basis of Subjective or Personalistic Theories of probability in the tradition of F. P. Ramsey. These theories are seriously misunderstood by Toulmin who accuses their sponsors of gross psychologism.

(6) None of these criticisms are meant to detract from Toulmin's *at times* wise if crude distinction between the force and the criteria of modal terms in their use. What is questionable is that all probability judgments have the same sort of force. We have only indicated very briefly some paths to follow in investigating the sorts of force to be found in ordinary usage. As Ramsey pointed out at once the varied sorts of force may give point to more than one theory of probability. (*The Foundations of Arithmetic*, London 1931, Chapter VII, see especially p. 158.)

III. RATIONAL COMMITMENT AND 'THE WILL TO BELIEVE'

Introduction. The believer in God who also toils seriously at philosophy may feel sunnily content like Saint Anselm to talk of his work in terms of *fides quaerens intellectum*. Many other philosophical believers, however, have at times found themselves feeling painfully torn between the ideals of Rationality and Commitment. Primary allegiance to the latter is urged by such illuminatingly religious theists as Pascal, Kierkegaard, Barth and Teilhard de Chardin. Amicable relations between both were encouraged by such illuminatingly philosophical theists as Socrates, Aquinas,

Descartes and Locke. If the believing philosopher is of a strongly empiricist bent the tension between Faith and Reason may seem all the greater
to him. How can one keep one's powers of reasoning open to the flux of
experience, yet truly *give* or commit oneself to God?

William James' essay 'The Will to Believe' is perhaps the most sug-
gestive of all attacks on this problem of philosophical theology. Yet we
have often found the very suggestiveness of this philosopher-psycholo-
gist, this partly mystical empiricist and pragmatist, quite bewildering in
'The Will to Believe'. A recent article by Robert W. Beard, '"The Will
to Believe" Revisited'[60] offers a valuable case that James' thought on
evidence and commitment deserves fresh, sympathetic study. Although
we disagree with Beard on several crucial points concerning James and
the philosophy of religion, we shall use his treatment as a helpful spring-
board.

Like Beard we do not wish to deny that there are undoubtedly nuggets
of obscurity, or that there may also be inconsistencies and serious errors
embedded in such a rhetorical specimen of James' prose. But we shall try
to suggest that Beard ends on too pessimistic a note about what James
has *begun* to offer concerning questions of rational commitment to ideals.
Our case will be based on what may seem glaringly large and charitable
assumptions about what James would now say if he were with us to
hear contemporary philosophical points and controversies. But these
assumptions are, we submit, fairly well encouraged by two reasonable
factors. First there are Beard's and that noted Pragmatist scholar Gail
Kennedy's[61] arguments for treating 'The Will to Believe'[62] more respectfully in view of other Jamesian positions made explicit in the corpus of
his numerous writings. Second there is the probability that James himself
would be only too eager to accept later philosophical insights from
modern thinkers in the empiricist tradition. How great is this probability?
Consider the *paradigmatically* reasonable and open-minded tone of the
penultimate paragraph in his essay. Consider his early recognition of
C. S. Peirce's genius and his eagerness to learn from him when others
were still writing Peirce off as a mere crank.

III.1. *Some Assumptions About James Redivivus*

(a) There is a distinction between doctrines in 'The Will to Believe' about
"the right to believe" and "the will to believe",[63] a distinction which

James was there careless about admitting and expounding, yet which should be reflected in reformulations of his basic themes.

(b) James does believe that there is *some* empirical evidence available to open-minded students of religion. This counts in favour of their *truth* as normal English speakers (and not as extreme "true if it works" pragmatists) would think of truth.[64]

(c) James may be confused in his *analysis* of probability but he does elsewhere recognize its pertinence. Like Pascal (if we interpret his Wager kindly), James would consider that in the face of radical uncertainty about a matter of high importance we should not only consider the possible *utilities* (including the *good of truth-gaining*) of alternative outcomes from deciding between interesting acts. We should also consider the probabilities of the possible events which are relevant to making such *decisions*.[65]

(d) Thus James would be brought to agree that some situations of perplexity about ideals where decisions must be made in the face of radical uncertainty, can be usefully mapped in a simple form of the modern Decision Theorist's representation, whence one can make a decision on the basis of *Maximizing Expected Utility*. On this formal basis the more reasonable choice can be computed from the individual's assignments of utility to outcomes and of probability to events. Take the folowing example based on one in L. J. Savage's pioneering work *The Foundations of Statistics*.[66] A cook has made a barely adequate omelette from eleven of the twelve eggs available but has some doubts as to the freshness of the last egg. In a situation of finely balanced doubt about the egg and widely different values for good and spoiled omelettes, he might represent the possibilities that interest him thus:

	Act 1 (Use last egg)	Act 2 (Don't use last egg)
Event A (Egg good)	Outcome 1–A Completely adequate omelette	Outcome 2–A Barely adequate omelette
Event B (Egg rotten)	Outcome 1–B Omelette ruined	Outcome 2–B Barely adequate omelette

Suppose Event A has probability 0.5 for the agent on a decimal scale between '0' for *impossibility* and '1' for *certainty*, and therefore Event B also has 0.5. Also suppose Outcome 1-A has a utility for him of 3, 1-B a utility of −25, 2-A and 2-B both have utilities of 1. Computation shows that for maximimizing expected utility Act 2 is rationally preferable, given these assignments. Only a minimum of multiplication by probabilities and addition of utilities and is required to show this. For one gets $\{[(3-25)\times .50]=\text{Minus } 11\}$ by looking at Act 1, whereas turning ones gaze to Act 2 yields a more soothing $\{[(3+3)\times 0.5]=\text{Plus } 3\}$.

(e) James would agree that the man moved by Pascal's Wager countenances only two couples of two alternatives: ('Event' A) a Catholic God exists and sends unbelievers to Hell and believers to Heaven; ('Event' B) no God exists, no after life will exist and no religion is worthwhile; ('Act' 1) live as a believing Catholic; ('Act' 2) live as one likes best. Hence, little is revealed about reasonable choice here simply by citing one single and purely formal rationality criterion of Maximizing Expected Utility. From Pascal's appeal to something like the principle of Maximizing Expected Utility the agent should thereby set about making himself a believer, unless he deems the probability of God's existence to be so fantastically low as to outweigh the apparently infinite utility of Heaven and infinite disutility of Hell. But this "should thereby" tends to confuse a valuable member of the Rationality-Family with *Reason* from Alpha to Omega.

(f) James, as an analyst of WTA-meanings, would only attribute a fully reasonable character to such an application of this formal criterion of rationality in faith's favour here *if* the person were himself already reasonable, relatively well informed in context about the breadth of ideological alternatives, etc., and had nonetheless come by truth-seeking deliberations to fix both upon just these pairs of Events and Acts and also upon something like the very probability and utility assignments which someone like Pascal would offer. Such a fully reasonable character would only be attributable to someone (formally – 'rationally') Maximizing Expected Utility after weeding out a set like $\{(1)$ adherence to James' intended range of possible wonder-worthy designata for 'eternal things', and (2) adherence to Clifford's extreme of epistemological chastity, and (3) adherence to diabolism and ... and ... and (n) adherence after reflection to all but unreflecting hedonism henceforth$\}$ *if* the person's fixing on this particular option n-tuple and on his particular related probability for Events, utility assignments for Outcomes, were the result of his having reasoned laudably well in relation to his intellectual and empirical opportunities. Even such a relatively reasonable fixing, James would insist, would remain reasonable only if the fixer respected others' intellectual freedom.[67]

(g) James would allow that assessments about appropriate option n-tuples, utilities and probabilities would often turn out to be different among reasonable men. But he would *also* allow that there remain honest criteria for concluding whether each different decider has made his assessments relatively reasonably and holds them in a rational, empiricist manner given his circumstances. Hences James' very subjective-sounding talk about "liveliness" of hypotheses [68] is not meant to encourage unfeeling and unreflecting *arbitrary* assessments – it largely reflects James' belief that, given the human situation, liberal empiricists of a reasonable temper are sometimes likely to reach differing conclusions about different faiths, systems and ideals. James would let these points of ours about tolerant empiricism reinforce Beard's point about the danger of formally trivialising [69] the force of forced options as mere contradictory pairs: hence forced options would normally lie between the several members of a rationally relevant n-tuple considered together.

(h) James would, in the face of advances in our understanding about the possible uses, Senses and References of psychological verbs, admit that there can be sometimes much more and sometimes much less to "believing p" (at t) than this formula "being measurably willing to act on p" (at t). Such a usefully simple criterion of belief for some experiments in behaviouristic psychology may also be *one* of the most useful criteria for common-sense. But the meaning (and/or legitimate scope for illocutionary use) of "believing p" is more complex and at least a small part of this complexity should be shown in reformulating James' 'The Will to Believe'. This would allow James to accept "inner", "outer", "occurrential", "dispositional", and other uses of psychological verbs like "believe", while quite possibly insisting like the earlier Peirce and the later Wittgenstein that the inner process stands in need of outward criteria.

III.2. *James' Crucial Section I*[70]

On his first page James introduces his work, directed principally against W. K. Clifford's [71] 'The Ethics of Belief', as "an essay in justification of faith, a defence of our right to adopt a believing attitude in religious matters, in spite of the fact that our merely logical attitude may not have been coerced". Clifford had advocated suspension of judgment whenever evidence was inconclusive. During Section I, pp. 2–4, James offers us in extremely elegant prose a loosely knit set of notions and observations, which are quite crucial to his arguments about rational commitment where evidence is relatively weak. This pervading Jamesian elegance, added to the brilliance and insight of individual remarks, lends a false air of clarity and systematic development to the whole. The following summary of what he offers in Section I is, we hope, both reasonably close to James and easier, though not ideally easy, to appraise as a developing system of ideas.

Df. 1 *To believe P=To be measurably willing to act on P.*
Df. 1.1 *To believe P up to degree n=to be measurably willing up to degree n to act on P.*
Df. 2 *Hypothesis=anything that may be proposed for our belief.*
Df. 3 *Live hypothesis=hypothesis which (a) appeals as real possibility to him to whom it is proposed for belief; (b) serves as strong stimulant to act as if it were true.*
Df. 3.1 *Maximally live hypothesis=one which (a) is at least as strong as any other belief stimulating the believer to act (strong both as belief and as stimulant to action); (b) is so strong that one is willing to act on it irrevocably.*
Df. 4 *Dead hypothesis=hypothesis which refuses to scintillate with any credibility at all.*

Observation I: A hypothesis, e.g., that the Mahdi has a profound religious authority and importance, will turn out to be live for certain Arabs but dead for almost all of James' expected readers. This typifies the status of numerous hypotheses held by varying people.
Observation II: Thus deadness and liveness in an hypothesis are not intrinsic properties, but relations to the individual thinkers.
Corollary to Dff. 1–4 *and to Observations* I *and* II: The liveness or deadness of an hypothesis for a person are measureable in terms of his willingness to act on it.

Df. 5 *Option=the decision between two hypotheses.*
Df. 6 *Living option=option in which both hypotheses are living ones.*
Df. 7 *Dead option=option in which neither hypothesis is alive.*
Df. 8 *Forced option=option whereby there is no standing place outside of the alternative.*

Observation III: Every dilemma based on a complete logical disjunction, with no possibility of not choosing, is of the forced kind.
Observation IV: If I say "Either accept this truth or go without it", I put you on a forced option.

Df. 9 *Avoidable option=option between two hypotheses towards both ofwh ich the agent remains indifferent.*
Df. 10 *Trivial option=option which satisfies one or more of these three conditions: (a) what is at stake is insignificant for the agent; (b) the opportunity for*

> *choosing between the alternative is not unique; (c) if the agent chooses between the alternatives now and later finds his decision unwise, he may then reverse it without likelihood of serious regret.*
>
> Df. 11 *Momentous option=option which satisfies none of the conditions for being a trivial one.*
>
> Df. 12 *Genuine option=option of the forced, living and momentous kind.*

III.3. *Beard's Pessimism About 'The Will to Believe'*

After doing a lot of good work to rescue James from misunderstandings and unfair criticisms, Beard reaches a very pessimistic conclusion about James' crucial concept of a genuine option:

> Now, if we summarize what seems defensible in James' notion of 'genuine option', we would have the following: A genuine option is one in which (i) there must be a significant degree of willingness to wager on the successful outcome of each of the alternatives; (ii) every alternative that we are willing to gamble on must be included in our survey; (iii) the alternatives must be mutually exclusive; and (iv) it must be unlikely that at least one of the important alternatives will become available to us again. This formulation may appear strikingly different from James' but the leading ideas are the same. If we examine the conditions rather carefully, I think the general difficulty with the right-to-believe doctrine is not that it allows too great a licence in belief, but rather that it imposes such stringent restrictions that one wonders whether even moral and religious hypotheses could satisfy the requirements.[72]

Such a conclusion about James' "genuine options" is disappointing enough after Beard's intitial suggestion that possibly this essay 'The Will to Believe' contains "an important philosophical thesis".[73] But *further* difficulties remain for Beard to which his final comments point.[74] How sure can we be when to apply a right-to-believe doctrine, and when to apply a will-to-believe doctrine? Are there many options, as James seems to suggest, or even any, when both sorts are simultaneously applicable? If we grant there are options which satisfy both doctrines at once, do we not thereby acknowledge a radical inconsistency in James? On the one hand, (a) there is his repeated insistence that all beliefs must be held as tentative. On the other hand, (b) he seems sometimes to be urging an idealistic or ideological *commitment* by the will which must exclude tentativeness; (c) he seems sometimes to be saying that the will-to-believe works so well upon what becomes known to be real that the intellect will lose its ground for being tentative. Both (b) and (c), if we interpret Beard rightly, jibe ill for him with (a). No less, too, does (d), James'unsupported expression of *full* confidence in his description of the "faith ladder" in his work *A Pluralistic Universe* that if we *decide* how things shall stand indeed they shall so stand.

Without endorsing (d) we interpose the suggestions that our Chapter I indicates how to align (a) and (b); that the treatment of WTA-meaning and "per se notum" in our Chapter IV tends to soften (c).

Beard concludes:

> The lingering dissatisfaction that many feel with James' discussions of belief can be attributed in part to the expectation that he is trying to justify the sort of conviction that we usually think of as religious faith, when in fact he is defending a relatively innocuous position."[75]

One is left with yet another uncomfortable question after reading these words. Even if the machinery of James' Section I can be deployed as a rational defence for commitment to a rather vague cosmic optimism about what James calls "the eternal things", of what use can it be for those propounding more specific, more substantial sets of ideals and commitments?

III.4. *Some Neo-Jamesian Tools to Clarify Rational Commitment*

It may be disappointing that Beard, after seeming to signal "Gold, here, now", leaves us still so puzzled about what 'The Will to Believe' has to offer of permanent importance, if anything at all. He did, however, present a relatively modest objective in his first paragraph:

> My main purpose in the subsequent remarks is to lay bare the logical essentials of James' argument, and to make some slight contribution towards an evaluation.[76]

With all respect to Beard on "logical essentials" we shall try in what follows to lay bare some of the logical *potentials* of James' argument. These potentials will sound quite plausibly Jamesian, we hope, given all or most of our assumptions in Part I about what James would say as a liberal empiricist in the 1960's and 1970's. At any rate, we put tentatively forward the following system of definitions after some years of real puzzlement about 'The Will to Believe'. Along with this puzzlement we have been goaded by the suspicion – perhaps still shared by Beard and Kennedy – that in Section I we can find in valuable raw material for shaping humanely just and insightful criteria by which to appraise the rationality of commitments of many kinds. Perhaps in what follows we have sometimes been too prolix or awkward, sometimes too niggardly or loose in drawing distinctions and lacing inter-relationships between these definitions. But we hope that we shall provoke others to improve on James *and* Beard *and* ourselves, and thus, perhaps, to improve on everyone's intuitions of rationality and reasonable choice concerning fundamental beliefs.

Postulates

There are *humans*: h_1, h_2, etc.
There are *propositions*: p_1, p_2, etc.
There are *contexts* (space-time slices): c_1, c_2, etc.
There are *options* (sets of propositions): o_1, o_2, etc.

Definitions

Df. 1: A proposition p_n is a *fully alive belief* for a person h_n during a context-set $(c_1, c_2, ..., c_n) \leftrightarrow$ (1) There are members of the context-set at which p_n is consciously thought of as true by h_n; *and* (2) There are no members of the set at which h_n thinks of p_n consciously with serious doubt or with disbelief; *and* (3) If ever there occurs to h_n as a member of this context-set an appropriate situation for thinking or speaking of p_n as true and/or manifesting this belief in fitting observable actions other than speaking, then h_n does so at that context.

N.B. 1: We do not believe that a complete set of necessary and sufficient conditions for *appropriateness* and *fittingness* here, satisfying all our intuitions and jarring with none concerning these evaluative terms, could be spelled out *a priori* in a definition to buttress Df. 1. Perhaps the Moorean term "Naturalistic Fallacy" would be somewhat too applicable to the dream of finding such an *a priori* set. But certainly one has a plenteous family of common-sense ideas about what would be appropriate contexts and fitting manifestations and what would not, depending on the sort of proposition to be believed and the sorts of circumstances the person encounters.

N.B. 2: Only the perfect believer would completely fulfill the conditions for holding p_n as a *fully alive belief* in a whole context set if it is very extensive. But keen believers among ordinary mortals could hold p_n as a relatively fully alive belief and could try to hold p_n as a fully alive belief.

Df. 2: A human h_n decides to *accept* p_n at $c_n \leftrightarrow h_n$ decides at c_n to try to hold p_n as a fully alive belief for the whole context-set of his present and future life, i.e. c_n, c_{n+1}, ..., etc.

Df. 3: A p_n is an *occurrential hypothesis* for h_n at $c_n \leftrightarrow p_n$ occurs to h_n's clear consciousness at c_n as a proposition which might from a logical point of view be worth his while to accept at c_n or later for some future context-set.

Df. 4: A p_n is an *occurrential live hypothesis* for h_n at $c_n \leftrightarrow (1)$ p_n fulfils Df. 3; AND (2) h_n consciously thinks at c_n that there are good reasons either only of (a) some relatively disinterested truth-and-wisdom-seeking sort, or of both sort (a) and (b) a more crudely practical sort, for trying to accept p_n at c_n; AND (3) h_n is conscious of an emotional inclination to accept p_n at c_n.

Df. 5: A p_n is an *occurrential dead hypothesis* for h_n at $c_n \leftrightarrow p_n$ fulfils Df. 3 but fails to fulfil conditions (2) and (3) for Df. 4.

Df. 6: A p_n is an *occurrential ailing hypothesis* for h_n at $c_n \leftrightarrow p_n$ fulfils Df. 3 and one but not both of conditions (2) and (3) for Df. 4.

Df.7: A p_n is a *dispositional live hypothesis* for h_n at $c_n \leftrightarrow$ should p_n occur to h_n at c_n, it would satisfy conditions (2) and (3) for Df. 4.

N.B. 3: By obvious similar means definitions can be constructed for *dispositional liveness over a context set*, for *dispositional deadness or ailingness*, for *mixed dispositions* of aliveness and/or deadness and/or ailingness, etc.

Df. 8: An option o_n is an *occurrential option n-tuple* ($= o.o.n$-*tuple*) for h_n at $c_n \leftrightarrow o_n$ is a set of at least two incompatible occurrential hypotheses for h_n at c_n all actually believed rightly to be incompatible by h_n at c_n.

Df. 9: An o_n is an *occurrential living option n-tuple* for h_n at $c_n \leftrightarrow (1) o_n$ is a set of hypothesis satisfying Df. 8 AND (2) o_n is such that all of its hypotheses are occurrentially live hypotheses for h_n at c_n.

N.B. 4: By obvious similar means one can define a *perfectly dead occurrential option* (an $o.o.n$-tuple with no occurrential living hypothesis); *a badly ailing occurrential option* (an $o.o.n$-tuple with only one occurrential hypotheses); an *ailing occurrential option* (an $o.o.n$-tuple with at least two occurrential live incompatible hypotheses but also with at least one occurrential dead, though still incompatible hypothesis) etc., etc. And so one could go on for definitions of *dispositional options* pure and mixed.

Df. 10: An o_n is an *occurrential forced option n-tuple* for h_n at $c_n \leftrightarrow o_n$ is such that h_n after reflection is aware of having now, by c_n, concluded on rational and emotional grounds, that all the hypotheses still worth considering on the relevant subject are contained within o_n.

Df. 11: An o_n is an *occurrential value-momentous option n-tuple* for h_n at $c_n \leftrightarrow (1) o_n$ is an occurrential live or occurrential ailing option for h_n at c_n; AND (2) h_n believes at c_n that the central matter about which the incompatible hypotheses of o_n differ is of paramount importance for the conduct of his own life and for his own pursuit of happiness, also of possibly small but still quite significant importance for the betterment of the universe as a whole (since at least each relatively sane person is capable of contributing something towards that betterment.)

Df. 12: An o_n is an *occurrential now-momentous option n-tuple* for h_n at $c_n \leftrightarrow (1)$ o_n is occurrentially living or occurrentially ailing for h_n at c_n; AND (2) h_n consciously believes at c_n that both his intellect and emotions provide impressively good reason for now immediately choosing to accept at least one and at most one of the hypotheses belonging to o_n.

Df. 13: An o_n is an *occurrential stay-momentous option n-tuple* for h_n at $c_n \leftrightarrow (1)$ o_n is occurrentially living and occurrentially ailing for h_n at c_n; AND (2) h_n consciously believes at c_n that both his intellect and his emotions provide good reasons for determining, should he once accept one and only one of the hypotheses, not to fail in loyalty to the hypothesis except in the face of quite unlikely and quite extraordinarily good arguments from sense experience, emotion and intellect.

Df. 14: An o_n is a *fully momentous occurrential option n-tuple* for h_n at $c_n \leftrightarrow o_n$ satisfies Dff. 11–13.

Df. 15: An o_n is a *trivial occurrential option n-tuple* for h_n at $c_n \leftrightarrow o_n$ satisfies Df. 8 but one of Dff. 11–13.

Df. 16: An o_n is a *genuine occurrential option n-tuple* for o_n at $c_n \leftrightarrow o_n$ satisfies Dff. 9 (living), 10 (exhaustive), and (14) (fully momentous.)

Df. 17: An o_n is an *occurrential truth-making option n-tuple* for h_n at $c_n \leftrightarrow o_n$ satisfies Df. 8; AND (2) h_n consciously believes at c_n that if he chooses to accept any one hypothesis p_j out of o_n then p_j probably or certainly will become true and that p_j probably or certainly would not otherwise become true.

Df. 18: An o_n is an *occurrential truth-seeking option n-tuple* for h_n at $c_n \leftrightarrow (1)$ o_n satisfies Df. 8; AND (2) h_n consciously believes at c_n that his intellect and emotions offer some fairly good reasons for believing (a) that a particular hypotheses p_j, a member of o_n, is true, (b) that if he accepts p_j at c_n or at some time in the future c_{n+m} he will receive every increasing confirmation of p_j; (c) that until he accepts p_j he will probably or certainly make no significant progress in adequately determining the truth-value of p_j and other members of o_n.

Df. 19: An o_n is a *super-genuine occurrentioal option n-tuple* for h_n at $c_n \leftrightarrow o_n$ satisfies Dff. 16 and 17, OR Dff. 16 and 18, OR Dff. 16–18.

Conclusion: We offer these definitions tentatively and in part prescriptively – not as formulas that lay entirely bare the CTA-meanings of of "Rationality", "Genuiness", "Momentous" and the like. They represent a set of trial formulations which might be of help to some of those who believe in human reason and who in believe in experiments with mixed CTA- and WTA-definitions as possible tools (and possible mirrors) for human reason. Why might these be useful because faith in human reason, when it is not *blind* faith, must accept what James urges us to accept in 'The Will to Believe': that many reasonable men can and do find paths to ideals between the extremes of scepticism and fanaticism. Again, they might indicate new dimensions of Rationality for the Arguments by appeal to Justifying Explanations of Chapter IV. We should, therefore, consider the range of rationally legitimate paths and thus the WTA-meanings of "rational" and "reasonable" in contexts of use concerning religious faith, questioning and commitment. In trying to sketch the range we must continue to take account of the fact that on questions of ideals many reasonable men may reach and stand by very *different* conclusions and remain reasonable for all that.[77]

NOTES

[1] *Philosophical Studies* (Eire) **16** (1967) 7–29.
[2] *Op. cit.* p. 29
[3] First published in German as *Logische–Philosophische Abhandlung* (1921). Father Dwyer wisely uses the *second* English translation. (D. F. Pears and B. F. McGuiness, London 1961.)
[4] Translated by G. E. M. Anscombe (Oxford 1953).
[5] *Tractatus* 3.3; Dwyer, *op. cit.*, p. 9, lines 8ff and 20, para. 3.
[6] Dwyer, *op. cit.*, pp. 14–16 and 27–29. Cf. F. C. Copleston's *Aquinas*, London 1955, pp. 263–64.
[7] *Op. cit.* pp. 19–20, Cf P. T. Geach's *Mental Acts*, London 1957, and A. G. N. Kenny's *Action, Emotion and the Will*, London 1963, for brilliant attempts to relate Thomist and Wittgensteinian insights in philosophical psychology.
[8] This is the opposite in P. F. Strawson, *Individuals*, London 1959, of "descriptive metaphysics". Strawson holds, as would Aquinas, that a descriptively inclined phi-

losopher must be prepared to *argue* with a revisionary metaphysician and take his reasons and arguments seriously. For an account of a viable (not necessarily desirable) but highly revisionary conceptual scheme see our 'Quantification Theory and Ontological Monism', *Zeitschrift für Allgemeine Wissenschaftstheorie* **4** (1972) 1–12.
[9] L. Wittgenstein, *Philosophical Investigations* (trans. G. E. M. Anscombe), Oxford 1953, Part I, pp. 98, 116, 119, 125. Presumably Dwyer's Thomist first principles about being and intelligibility (*op. cit.*, pp. 20–22) would be ruled out by Wittgenstein as '*theses*' Cf. *P.I.*, Part I, pp. 116–28.
[10] See Chapter IV, also John King–Farlow, 'Wittgenstein's Primitive Languages', *Philosophical Studies* (Eire) **18** (1969), 101–10; 'Two Dogmas of Linguistic Empiricism', *Dialogue* **12** (1972), 324–335.
[11] Cf. Norman Malcolm, *Knowledge and Certainty*, Englewood Cliffs, N.J. 1963, *passim*, and several of the more discipular contributions to G. Pitcher (ed.), *Wittgenstein: The Philosophical Investigations*, New York 1966.
[12] We suspect Aquinas also would gladly grant the intellectual importance and grandeur of both books even in mentioning points of disagreement – this seems a reasonable inference from his treatment of the earlier thinkers and contemporary medieval thinkers whom he so often cites.
[13] See Cyril Barrett (ed.), *Wittgenstein: Lectures and Conversations on Aesthetics, Psychology and Religious Belief*, Oxford 1966.
[14] First published in 1944–45; reprinted in A.G.N. Flew (ed.), *Logic and Language*, First Series, Oxford 1951, pp. 189–206.
[15] *Philosophical Investigations* II, p. 226.
[16] One of the cluster of "dark sayings" offered by Kai Nielsen as symptomatic of what he calls in the paper of his which we have repeatedly cited already, 'Wittgensteinian Fideism, *Philosophy* **62** (1967) 191–209, Nielsen adds in a footnote: "I do not necessarily lay all these aperçus at Wittgenstein's door, but all of them can clearly be found in one or another of his disciples" (193n). Nielsen's article offers a useful bibliography of Wittgensteinians whose objectivity, by Aquinas' and Dwyer's standards, apparently breaks down (*after* their recognizing Wittgenstein's shattering attack on scepticism) before the bogey of cultural relativism. A collection of essays where several philosophers express similar forms of relativism is D. Z. Phillip's recent anthology *Religion and Understanding*, Oxford 1967; see especially the papers by Peter Winch, Norman Malcolm, and Phillips himself.
[17] Cf. Phillips, *op. cit.*, p. 63. In C. Barrett (ed.), *Wittgenstein's Lectures on Religious Belief* Oxford 1966, p. 56, we read: "The point is that if there were evidence this would destroy the whole business." (In saying this Wittgenstein is *not condemning* faith; he seems to have admired the character and lives of friends whome he felt to be genuinely committed. Cf. Norman Malcolm's *Ludwig Wittgenstein, A Memoir*, Oxford 1966 (new edition), p. 72. Wittgenstein is condemning natural theology.)
[18] Copleston in *Aquinas* anticipates the point of Malcolm and others that "intellectual assent" to a metaphysical argument never afforded immediate participation in Christian faith and love (p. 114). But he does not go on to leave human reason out in the cold on many questions of natural theology. Compare our distinction between 'Gooper'- and 'Expo'-conclusions in Chapter II.
[19] So too, we expect, would our late and beloved tutor, Michael Foster of Christ Church, Oxford – though using a very different sort of *reductio ad absurdum*. See his '"We" in Modern Philosophy', in B. Mitchells (ed.), *Faith and Logic*, London 1957, pp. 192ff.

[20] We discuss the repugnance of such 'coercion' to John Hick and others in 'Cogency, Conviction and Coercion', *International Philosophical Quarterly* **8** (1968) 464–73. Compare D. F. Henze, 'Faith, Evidence and Coercion', *Philosophy* **42** (1967) 78–85.

[21] Cf. our earlier citations of J. N. Findlay, Norman Malcolm and J. J. C. Smart in Chapter IV.

[22] Cf. Dwyer's 'Proving God', *Philosophical Studies* (Eire) **14** (1965) 7–29; Copleston, *Aquinas*, pp. 127–28; I. M. Crombie on "the sense of contingency" in A. G. N. Flew and A. C. MacIntyre (eds.) *New Essays in Philosophical Theology*, London 1955, pp. 111–15.

[23] R. Carnap, 'Empiricism, Semantics and Ontology', *Revue Internationale de Philosophie* **11** (1950) 20–40. Cf. W. V. Quine's 'On What There Is', *Review of Metaphysics* **2** (1948) 21–48 to which Carnap is partially replying. These and related papers of great metaphysical interest are included in an outstanding anthology, P. Benacerraf and H. Putnam (eds.), *Philosophy of Mathematics*, Oxford 1964.

[24] S. E. Toulmin, 'Probability', *Proceedings of the Aristotelian Society*, Suppl. Vol. **24** (1950). This essay reappears in A. G. N. Flew (ed.), *Essays in Conceptual Analysis*, London 1956, pp. 157–91, and in Toulmin's *The Uses of Argument*, Cambridge 1958, Chapter III, pp. 69–97.

[25] J. L. Austin's 'Other Minds', *Proceedings of the Aristotelian Society*, Suppl. Vol. **20** (1946), reappears in A. G. N. Flew (ed.), *Logic and Language*, Second Series, Oxford 1953, pp. 123–58.

[27] See J. King-Farlow, 'Sea Fights Without Tears', *Analysis*, New Series **19** (1958) 36–42.

[28] *The Uses of Argument*, p. 70.

[29] Oxford 1962, pp. 94–131.

[30] Cf. J. R. Searle, *Speech Acts*, Cambridge 1969, p. 137, and 'Meaning and Specch Acts', reprinted from *Philosophical Review* **73** (1964), at W. D. Hudson (ed.), *The Is-Ought Question*, London 1969, pp. 120–34. Hudson offers many philosophers' replies.

[31] See J. L. Austin, *How to Do Things with Words*, Oxford 1962, pp. 93, 95, 97. On p. 100 he writes: "Admittedly we can use 'meaning' also with reference to illocutionary force – 'He meant it as an order', etc. But I want to distinguish *force* and *meaning* in the sense in which meaning is equivalent to sense and reference."

[32] J. L. Austin, *op. cit.*, pp. 109ff.

[33] Cf. Searle, *op. cit.*, and Paul Ziff's *Semantic Analysis*, Ithaca 1960, pp. 118, 223–27.

[34] Cf. J. J. Katz, 'Analyticity and Contradiction in a Natural Language'; J. A. Fodor and J. J. Katz, 'The Structure of a Semantic Theory'. Both appear in J. A. Fodor and J. J. Katz (eds.), *The Structure of Language*, Englewood Cliffs, N.J. 1964. See pp. 518–43 and 479–98.

[35] E.g. P. Ziff, *Semantic Analysis*, Ithaca 1960, pp. 118 and 227; also his partly Austinian sounding use of etymological considerations in Ch. VI. Cf. J. A. Fodor and J. J. Katz, *The Structure of Language*, previously cited, and J. J. Katz' *Philosophy of Language*, New York 1966, pp. 79–88.

[36] W. P. Alston, *The Philosophy of Language*, Englewood Cliffs, N.J. 1964, pp. 38–39. L. J. Cohen's *The Diversity of Meaning*, 2nd edition, Oxford 1966, casts valuable light on positions in philosophy of language because of his wide range of sympathies with formal and informal linguistic analysis.

[37] *The Uses of Argument*, p. 97.

[38] See Urmson for similar points on 'validity' in 'Some Questions Concerning Validity', in A. G. N. Flew (ed.), *Essays in Conceptual Analysis*, London 1956, pp. 120–33.

[39] See J. King-Farlow, 'Seafights Without Tears', in *Analysis*, New Series **19** (1958) 36–42. Cf. J. R. Searle, *Speech Acts*, Cambridge 1969, pp. 66–67 and 122.

[40] See our previous reference to W. P. Alston's *The Philosophy of Language*, pp. 38–39. "A meaning of W_1 is $W_2 = $ df. In most sentences in which W_2 occurs, W_1 can be substituted for it without changing the illocutionary act potential of the sentence."

[41] See A. M. Quinton's 'The Problem of Perception' (1955), reprinted in R. J. Swartz (ed.), *Perceiving, Sensing and Knowing*, New York 1965, pp. 497–526; W. S. Sellars, 'Empiricism and the Problem of Mind' (1956), reprinted in his *Science, Perception and Reality*, London 1963, pp. 127–96.

[42] 'Probability' in A. G. N. Flew's *Essays in Conceptual Analysis*, p. 191.

[43] *The Uses of Argument*, p. 65.

[44] *Op. cit.*, p. 68. Cf. S. E. Toulmin's *The Philosophy of Science*, London 1953, pp. 112–13.

[45] We do not wish to suggest that common-sense intuitions about sense-distinctions leave no philosophical problems in their wake. Cf. W. V. Quine's *From a Logical Point of View*, Cambridge 1954, Ch. II, and *Word and Object*, New York 1959, Ch. I; our 'Senses and Sensibilia', *Analysis*, New Series **23** (1962) 37–40; Alston's *The Philosophy of Language*, Ch. II.

[46] Oxford 1933, Vol. II, pp. 1588–89: "1. The quality of being probable; likelihood. 2. A probable event, circumstance, belief, etc; something which judged by present evidence is likely to happen. 3. *Math.* As a measurable quantity: The amount of antecedent likelihood of a particular event, as measured by the relative frequency of occurence of events of the same kind in the whole course of experience."

[47] S. E. Toulmin's 'Probability', in A. G. N. Flew's *Essays in Conceptual Analysis*, London 1956, pp. 157–91.

[48] Cf. S. E. Toulmin's *The Uses of Arguments*, p. 83: "'probable' ... is closely linked with the idea of evidential support, but is distinct from that idea ...."

[49] *Op. cit.*, p. 52: "What an utterance actually states is one thing. What it implies is another." Cf. Wittgenstein, *Philosophical Investigations*, Part I, p. 593: "A main cause of philosophical disease – a one-sided diet: one nourishes one's thinking with only one kind of example."

[50] This NEVER injuction is given by Toulmin at 'Probability' in A. G. N. Flew's *Essays in Conceptual Analysis*.

[51] See S. E. Toulmin, *The Uses of Argument*, p. 37.

[52] F. P. Ramsey, *The Foundations of Mathematics*, London 1931. (See especially Chapter VII.) L. J. Savage, *The Foundations of Statistics*, New York 1954. A list and archive of Patrick Suppes' steadily increasing and already vast line of publications on this subject are obtainable at The Applied Mathematics and Statistics Laboratory, Stanford, Calif.

[53] See S. E. Toulmin, *The Uses of Argument*, p. 37.

[54] F. P. Ramsey, *The Foundations of Mathematics*, London 1931, pp. 169–71; L. J. Savage, *The Foundations of Statistics*, New York 1951, p. 60.

[55] Cf. F. P. Ramsey, *op. cit.*, p. 174; L. J. Savage, *op. cit.*, pp. 17ff.

[56] See F. P. Ramsey, *op. cit.*, pp. 173ff; L. J. Savage, *op. cit.*, pp. 13–14 for more complex examples.

[57] S. E. Toulmin, *The Uses of Argument*, p. 64.

[58] Cf. F. P. Ramsey, *op. cit.*, p. 193; L. J. Savage, *op. cit.*, p. 20.

[59] Cf. L. J. Savage, *op. cit.*, p. 2 (relation to mathematical theory of probability); p. 27 (relation to ordinary language).

[60] *Ratio* **8** (1966) 169–79.

[61] 'Pragmatism, Pragmaticism, and the Will to Believe – A Reconsideration', *Journal of Philosophy* **55** (1958) 578–88. Beard cites Kennedy and rightly emphasizes the value of his exegesis.

[62] 'The Will to Believe' was first published in the journal *New World* during June 1896. We shall refer to the Dover edition of 1956: *The Will to Believe, Human Immortality, and Other Essays on Popular Philosophy*, New York 1956, pp. 1–31. Henceforth we shall refer to this collection of essays as simply *The Will to Believe*.

[63] See Kennedy, *op. cit.*, especially pp. 580–82; Beard, *op. cit.*, especially pp. 170–73. Some readers of W. I. Matson's rather glib section on James and pragmatism in *The Existence of God*, Ithaca 1965, pp. 202–15, may have serious after-thoughts, if they subsequently read Beard and Kennedy.

[64] See Beard, *op. cit.*, pp. 171–73. Cf. Kennedy, *op. cit.*, pp. 581–82.

[65] See Beard, *op. cit.*, pp. 175–76 and his reference to James on probability at 'Faith and the Right to Believe', in James' *Some Problems of Philosophy*, New York 1916.

[66] New York, 1954. Cf. Chapter VII of F. P. Ramsey's *The Foundations of Mathematics*. For less formal discussions see Anatol Rapoport's 'Escape from Paradox', *Scientific American* **217** (1967) 50ff;

[67] Cf. James at *The Will to Believe*, p. 30.

[68] Cf. *The Will to Believe*, p. 2.

[69] Beard, *op. cit.*, p. 176.

[70] *Op. cit.*, pp. 2–4.

[71] 'The Ethics of Belief' was published from *The Contemporary Review* of 1876 in W. K. Clifford's *Lectures and Essays*, London 1879, pp. 1ff. See pp. 8, 10, 18ff.

[72] Beard, *op. cit.* p. 178.

[73] P. 169.

[74] Pp. 178–79.

[75] P. 179.

[76] P. 169.

CHAPTER VII

GAMBLING ON OTHER MINDS – HUMAN
AND DIVINE

I. "EVIL", "OUGHT" AND "CAN" AS SPRINGBOARDS FOR THE WILL TO BELIEVE

Our examination of "Probability" in the last chapter brought out the central importance for understanding central uses of that term of *value judgments* like "There is *good (truth-seeking) reason* to believe *P*", "Thanks to our familiarity with *Q* we have *good (truth-seeking) reasons* to believe *P*", "If we could establish *a strong (truth-seeking) case* for accepting *S*, then we could have an even *stronger (truth-seeking) case* for accepting *P*". The notion of there being *good (truth-seeking) reasons to believe P*, like the notion of ones having *a strong (truth-seeking) case for accepting the truth of P*, is one of the most crucial notions, perhaps conceptually "primitive notions", relevant to understanding why thought is not merely a flow of consciousness and language is not merely the rather predictable occurrence of scratches and sounds. At the risk of seeming tiresome we have repeated the insertion "(*truth-seeking*)" in order to distinguish the sort of good reasons and strong cases relevant to *Probability as such* from the complex sort (involving reference to the former) relevant to Maximizing Expected Utility. Let us say that 'paradigmatically' good, truth-seeking reasons form a family from which beliefs arrived at by application of the Principle of Maximizing Expected Utility are excluded. When the Justifying Explanation Argument for belief in God is used by a sincere, reasonable person, the use should in the initial steps work only from what the user takes to be 'paradigmatically' good, truth-seeking reasons. But the Justifying Explanation Argument CAN so be used as to culminate in what the user takes to be a strong case for making a commitment from the standpoint of Maximizing Expected Utility. But if it is used properly (in a way closer to James' approach to harmonize in this life with 'eternal things' than to Pascal's Wager), then the envisioned utilities should include ones like living now in accordance with the most important truths, like realization of one's human best now, like growth now in wisdom and in a spontaneous moral sense of fraternity, like enjoying innocent happiness now in a way that makes others happy now. Utilities like eternal closeness to truth in a possible afterlife, eternal growth in spontaneous goodness and innocent happiness in a possible afterlife can be organically included as natural correlates of the first ones. Given the right utilities, the quest for Maximizing Expected Utility can as strongly affirm the sovereignty of The True and The Good as the quest for Probability about what counts. But as emerged from our clarification of James' 'The Will to Believe' (in the final section of Chapter V), *discovering more truth* and *coming closer to certainty* can be perfectly respectable utilities for one to try to maximise in making commitments in accordance with the Principle.

Reason and Religion can find mutual expression in certain appeals to Probability and to the Principle of Maximizing Expected Utility – when the latter is taken as a principle for rationally seeking to attain those goods that are most worthy of a rational person's dignity or affections and concern. But as we emphasized in Chapters IV and V, both reasons and religion are together called quite rationally into question by certain current waves of scepticism, deeply reflected in Western man's intellectual history at least since the Sophists and other early cultural relativists. These are the waves of scepticism about the *objectivity*, *cognitivity*, Reference and even Sense of moral and related other judgments. This kind of scepticism has become firmly rooted not only in technical work among influential philosophers, but in popular intellectual traditions and ideologies. Teachers of philosophy sometimes compare notes about radical brands of relativism which a fair number of modern students beginning work in their Introductory classes unquestionably accept. Such students would often accuse 'neo-positivists', 'existentialists' and others of dragging their feet in the war on old-fashioned objectivism: claims about TRUTH, let alone claims about morals or related values merely express some individual's present feelings or passing preferences. Any proposition *P*, their relativism leads them so say, openly and cheerfully, can be just as true for you as it is false for the next man, and each is right, insofar as anyone can be subjectively right, about the truth value of *P*: the truth-condition of *P* is a set of feelings that someone has about *P*. What is more, some beginning students will just as gaily add, the soundness of their subjectivist position on Truth, Goodness etc. has been proven *objectively true* by comparative anthropologists and sociologists like Margaret Mead and Dr. Kinsey – and any realistic, properly up-to-date and tolerant person who doesn't want to manipulate, exploit or dictate to others clearly *ought* to get in step with the modern outlook. And so one takes up the work Socrates began against Sophists' implicit contradictions with some of one's freshmen in philosophy at the beginning of many an academic term.

Convincing freshmen of non-cognitivism's incoherence may require repeated examples. The same, and more of it, is required with mistrained philosophers. We shall offer in this opening section one further example of this incoherence because it links so beautifully together our earlier concerns with theodicy in Chapter V and our present concerns with rational employment of the Will to Believe in relation to the Principle of Maximizing Expected Utility. This example may throw fresh light on the rationality of moving in a full inferential circle from "GOD" to "IS" to "OUGHT" to "CAN" to "GOD".

I.1. *Madhare Back on the March*

Much of the two valuably challenging atheist papers on theodicy by Edward Madden and Peter Hare that we discussed in Chapter V have been incorporated with ideas from other articles and with fresh arguments into their important book *Evil and the Concept of God* (Springfield, Ill. 1968 – henceforth referred to as *ECG*). In this work they are now at pains to shift atheist treatment of "God" and "Evil" from traditional stress on *logical inconsistency* to a weaker but allegedly more shattering charge of radical implausibility. As they had already written for publication in a journal before *ECG* appeared:

> The riddle of God and Evil, we believe, is not one of formal inconsistency as King-Farlow and Pike would have us believe. We do *not* believe that the following statements constitute an inconsistent set: God is almighty, God is all-knowing, God is infinitely good, and Evil, created by this Being, exists in the finite world. To state the problem in this way misses the crucial point at issue, namely, whether or not the evil which is plainly evident is gratuitous or serves some purpose. ('Why Hare must Hound the Gods', *Philosophy and Phenomenological Research* 29 (1969) 456.)

Thus at the start of *ECG*'s enterprise we read:

> While the problem of evil as we formulate it is not a question of formal inconsistency, the theist is sometimes straightforwardly inconsistent, we shall see, in trying to meet it. This problem arises when the logically possible reasons for the existence of an evil are incompatible with the moral principles which the theist has previously claimed were sanctioned by God (or with the moral principles built into the very concept of God).

As soon as one formulates the problem of evil the question inevitably asked is: "How do you define evil?" To ask for a definition or analysis of *evil* seems like a promising move at first, but in fact turns out not to be. The point is this: Defining the notion of evil is irrelevant to the problem of evil we have posed because the problem remains unchanged for whatever definition is accepted. Supposed, for example, one accepts St. Augustine's definition of *evil* as "the privation of good". Evil has no being itself but is simply the absence of good. Being itself is always good, and evil occurs only as the corruption of a substance. The problem of evil still remains, however, because now one has the problem of explaining why, in the present world, there is so much *prima facie* gratuitous absence of good, so much apparently needless privation. Since the problem of evil will arise on a non-question-begging definition of *evil*, we shall not embark upon our own analysis of this term.

While a definition of *evil* is irrelevant to our problem, the specification of what is to count as evil is very relevant indeed. The problem is to specify examples of evil in a way that does not prejudice the question of gratuity. The safest way to achieve this goal, and the one frequently followed, is to draw only from the ordinary and common-sensical extension of evil, thereby avoiding the philosophical criteria of evil which have caused so much confusion in the past (*ECG*, pp. 4–5).

At first, this proclaimed freedom from useless hairsplitting sounds welcome. How hardheaded it will be, we want to say with Madhare, to junk that rock of Sisyphus, that unfulfilled task of satisfying everyone's intuitions with an uncontroversial yet substantial *definition* of "Evil" or of "Good". And, it might be added, the task of *analyzing* the intension or Sense of such a term, brought in by tiresome modern practitioners of meta-ethics, sometimes partly convinced by Moore that no definition of "Good" or "Evil" would really do, is in fact just another futile stone to give Sisyphus variety at asymptotically roly-poly labour on a Neo-Positivist Sabbath. The intension of "Evil" can be set aside and the extension skimmed easily "from that whole set of undesirable experiences and deeds which all of us, minus our philosophical views, would prefer to avoid" (*ECG*, p. 5).

But no, there seem to be things diabolically wrong here. First, it is odd to be asked by Madhare to take the question of God's existence or non-existence with philosophical seriousness, to be asked to query the extension of "God" through dwelling on arguments from Evil, even though we may happen to come from a large religious but nevertheless linguistic community where no one seriously questions the ordinary, commonsensical extension of "God" and all dwell piously only on the word's intension – except when doing philosophy. Why is this odd? It is odd because Madhare would seem to feel entitled not to question seriously as philosophers the ordinary, commonsensical extension of "Evil"; they feel entitled to use arguments which simply presuppose that "Evil" must have non-null extension in order that we may come with worldly 'Naturalist' piety by the end of their book to swallow their vague but emotive 'Naturalist' intension of "Good" and "Evil". They never clarify quite what Naturalism is, but assure us that it is the only rational foundation for taking morality seriously. (Cf. *ECG*, pp. 17–18, 131–132.)

A second thing that seems to be diabolically wrong is this. We do understand at least one thing about the intension of "Naturalism" from Madhare, that, because of this intension, it is at best a fruitless ploy for any pantheists and panentheists to take the extension of "God" to be the extension of what the right kind of Naturalist or Humanist takes to be the extension of "Nature" (see *ECG*, p. 36). Insofar as pantheists, and Death of God theologians stick completely and consistently to that extensional identity Madhare would claim to have "no quarrel" with them, only (one infers) a great deal of philosophical contempt.

Now this "No Quarrel – BUT ..." tactic here is surely bad philosophy. For if a good part of the intension or sense of "God" or "Divine Being" is "something worthy of worship, awe, complete reverence and praise, loving self-sacrifice, dedication, etc.", and if two good parts of the intension of "Nature" are, e.g, (1) "Totality of physical entities and forces", and (2) "everything completely governed by scientific laws", then the rational philosopher wants to *debate* very seriously certain questions pertaining here to explosive combinations of relevant extensions and intensions. He wants to ask among other things: (a) Is every physical entity and force felicitously and wisely taken to be completely *governed* by scientific laws? (b) Must something felicitously said to be completely governed by scientific laws be felicitously and wisely taken by Naturalists like Madhare to be worthy of complete reverence and praise, awe, loving self-sacrifice and dedication, etc. ? (c) Even if we can felicitously and wisely talk of a totality of physical entities and forces, is there the slightest good reason for someone keen on Truth and Knowledge to have a reverential and loving 'Naturalist' attitude towards such a totality, especially if, like Madhare, he considers many things *within* that totality to warrant horror, sadness, active hostility and the like?

A third problem is this. Many modern philosophers who began by trying to analyse the meaning of *terms* like "good" and "evil" moved on to trying to analyse the meaning and semantic status of whole *claims* that we seriously try to make about what is good or evil. Suppose one accepts one from among several certain kinds of *Really Deflationary Non-Cognitivist Analyses* of the intension or Sense of attempted claims about what is good or evil, involving indicative, categorical sentences in which the terms "good" or "evil" occur. What we call a Really Deflationary Non-Cognitivist Analysis commits one to saying that after analysing the term and the attempted claim involving such a sentence, the apparent claim reduces simply to an emotive exclamation, a spot of emoting and persuading, a command, a resolution, etc. Suppose we overlook earlier problems and accept Madhare's injunction to be as generous as anyone might like about the intension, meaning and analysis of "Evil", as long as we take the extension of "Evil" to be of the sort that philosophically unbiassed people sometimes CALL "Evil". Then we escape initial controversy about "Evil" at the price of being in a way allowed, and in a way obliged, to fall in with conclusions about "Evil" that would not permit us as a matter of sheer semantics to argue as Madhare would want us to argue. Madhare would want us to argue that because there are so many things in the world that philosophically unbiased people *call* "Evil", there is very good reason not to believe in any being with a good number of the attributes which various and much-varied types of theists have associated with the intension of "God": vast power, vast knowledge, ability to create things out of nothing, love for each man that will bring about a tremendous preponderance of positive entries for each man's personal rating in a ledger of Felicific Calculus, etc.

Really Deflationary Non-Cognitivist Analyses will, if properly understood, bring all philosophically serious reasoning to a grinding halt – including, mercifully enough, all philosophically serious reasoning in favour of Really Deflationary Non-Cognitivist Analyses. Non-Arbitrary uses of vital tools of reasoning like Modus Ponens (outside certain arbitrarily adopted forms of work with uninterpreted calculi) have no serious justification, philosophical and or more mundanely rational. We can choose to use tools like Modus ponens because we can choose to call them *"useful"* for pursuing goals that we can choose to call *"worth pursuing for their own sake"* or choose to call *"worth pursuing for use in reaching still further goals worth pursuing for their own sake"*.

Consider again the passage just cited from Madhare:

"The riddle of God and Evil, we believe, is not one of formal inconsistency, as King-Farlow and Pike would have us believe. We do *not* believe that the following statements constitute an inconsistent set: God is almighty, God is all-knowing, God is infinitely good, and Evil, created by this Being, exists in the finite world. To state the problem in this way misses the crucial point at issue, namely whether or not the evil which is plainly evident is gratuitous or serves some purpose. (Cf. *ECG*, pp. 3–4.)

It is plain from the paper containing this passage, from *ECG* and other Madharean writings that there is a *right* way to state the problem; or that there *is* a point which we *should* treat as *crucial*; that we will, if *wise* and *rational*, accept as decisively *good* reason from a *logical* and a *moral* point of view for rejecting theism as being *unreasonable* and perhaps as close to being *immoral* in crucial respects.

I.2. *Madhare's Premises and Bare Presuppositions*

One way that a 'crucial' Madhare argument could be stated is like this:

(1) It is undesirable from a logical and moral point of view to believe in a Divine Creator Who is worthy of worship, unless we actually find after an appropriate but limited amount of searching at least a very good (truth-seeking) reason to believe that apparently gratuitous Evil is justified.

(2) It is logically and morally sound only to look for a limited period for such a good reason.

(3) Since that limited period is now clearly long over and no good (truth-seeking) reason is available, the question of finding such a reason will only be worth raising again if someone later comes up with a quite new argument that clearly warrants attention from the standpoint of both logic and morality.

(4) Therefore, it is quite undesirable from a logical and moral point of view for any philosophically aware and knowledgeable person to believe in any form of theism given present circumstances.

One might try to formulate this argument still more rigorously so that we have an unquestionably valid deductive argument. But without cognitivist presuppositions about the intensions of "Evil", etc., how could such a revised argument be any better than the following piece of 'reasoning'? Says a *sophist* : Let us first assume that one could succeed, according to some interpretation of 'deductively valid' in one's natural language, in constructing a bit of *deduction* that one feels one finds highly acceptable. Let us then assume that one *feels* one finds the premises highly plausible. Let us further suppose that one *feels* the negation of the conclusion to be the thing one wants to believe. Finally let us suppose that one *feels* one finds the negation of the conclusion a good thing to believe, not from any desire for truth or wisdom or honesty, whatever we might *feel* them to be, but from a desire to believe something that one thinks makes it much easier for oneself to feel good about kicking others around, pleasing oneself as much as possible at the cost of suffering for as many others as possible, etc. Therefore, we should believe the negation of the conclusion!! Why can we see at least as well as we see the *sense* of Moore's "Here is a hand", that Madhare's sort of argument is at least somewhat better than this 'sophistry'? Because we *can* and do *SEE* it is – as clearly as we see anything as fallible beings to be true. Because we almost certainly fall into a futilitarian abyss by denying it. Logic, rationality, morality and meta-ethical cognitivism hang together. Without meta-ethical cognitivism Madden and Hare's Atheist Argument from Evil – either as a deductive argument or as a Good Reasons argument cannot operate. It cuts no ice. And if anyone reading these words would like to try to tell us why any substantial argument involving a claim about what we ought to conclude does not presuppose cognitivism about moral and many related value judgments, we should like to see by what rational means he could conceivably try to make such a telling stick. It is not that we need to be able to use *rules of inference* or perhaps even odder things called *inference tickets* to operate with a Natural Language's analogues of axioms, well-formed formulas, definitions, and the like (cf. Lewis Carroll on Achilles and the tortoise). It is that we need to know why it is good and wise to follow such axioms, rules of inference or perhaps even odder things called *inference tickets*, and the like in the particular case.

Moral values are inextricably bound up with the rest of the vast, complex web of reasonable values that a rational agent needs for operating in a host of contexts. These contexts will sometimes seem to be paradigmatically moral ones, sometimes seem to be paradigmatically non-moral ones. But generally the contexts will be a mixture seeming both to fit and to miss innumerable paradigms and categories of context. *Wise, rational, healthy, sick, true, prudent, relevant, responsible, reasonable, appropriate, right, wrong, logical, valid, cogent, honest, bad, clearheaded, hypocritical, human, good* and *evil* are terms of appraisal which stand or fall together. There seem to be three interesting possibilities: (a) All their meta-analyses are accepted as rightfully cognitivist. Or (b) a few of them can be treated non-cognitively at the price of increasing the work and scope of those at the price of increasing the work and scope of those that are still treated cognitively. Or (c) one gives up talking seriously at all; one drops any claim to be able to communicate fallibly but fairly rationally with other fallible but fairly rational persons; one ceases to offer arguments with even the semi-seriousness of Diogenes masturbating in his tub in a *public* marketplace; one thinks and thinks of oneself merely as bombinating in a vacuum until one can lose the trick of thinking coherently at all.

I.3. *Possible Consequences from a 'Normatively Logical Point of View'*

Suppose that we were to agree with Madhare that "Evil" has an obvious (and philosophically interesting) extension for reasonable people. Let us allow Madhare to conclude (though disdaining analysis of "Evil's" intension) that we should opt for the second of the following fragments of intensional analysis as correct:

I.   If something is evil, then it ought not to exist at all.

II.   If something is evil, then it ought only to exist as long as it is clearly conducive to much greater developments of good things.

We must now ask Madhare to face the point that arguments from Evil have been used by some cognitivists like Kant to argue just as enthusiastically and seriously for God's existence. Crucial to much thinking on these lines are the beliefs: that Evil is wrong and all wrong should ultimately be overcome, that a proper analysis of "Evil's" intension reveals that "Evil ought to be overcome", and that a proper cognitive analysis of "Ought"'s intension reveals that here a relevant "Ought" entails a relevant "Can".

Let us consider some alternative partial analyses of "This is Evil and (*ergo*) ought to be overcome".

(Alpha) "This is evil and really ought to be overcome" simply entails "This is evil and the totality of things would be better if this were overcome, but whether it can or can't be overcome is an open question". Madhare might argue that if (Alpha) is a correct description of any state of affairs, then it follows that *either* the extension of "this" can and should be overcome by beings like men who are limited in power, *or*, if "this" stands for something too powerful for men to overcome and be improved by in overcoming, then its existence would not be allowed by traditional theims's omnipotent, benevolent God were He to exist. But, Madhare would add, there just are too many powerfully evil things that ought to be overcome by an omnipotent, benevolent God were He to exist – hence there is no such Being.

A somewhat Kantian theist believing in disembodied survival and/or resurrection, or a Platonic theist believing in Transmigration might simply retort that if there is such a just God, then such an extension of "This" WILL be *overcome* or *put right*; that if Madhare find no evidence of certain sorts of evils which cause *people* to suffer greatly being overcome or put right, and if there is such a God, then He must *ex hypothesi* grant an after-life in which it is put right since He is omnipotent, benevolent to each person. Moreover, *ex hypothesi*, since such a God, if existent, would be so benevolent, He must have a perfectly good reason for not overcoming or putting right certain evils here and now.

Thus, given analysis (Alpha) of "This is evil and ought to be overcome" there may be no overwhelming moral argument *for* God's existence, but a Madhareish moral argument from (Alpha) would beg far too many questions also. And so analysis (Alpha) produces a stand-off.

(Beta) It is rational to say "this is evil and really ought to be overcome" if and only if (i) this is evil and (ii) any man afflicted by it can overcome it in his life *or* (iia) the group within mankind to which the man contemporarily belongs can overcome it in his life, (iib) mankind collectively can and will eventually succeed in overcoming it during the course of human history.

Analysis (Beta) helps neither Kantian arguments for God's existence nor Madharean arguments against God's existence.

(Gamma) "This is evil and really ought to be overcome" entails "This is evil and *can* be overcome or put right in a purely logical sense of 'can'" – thus there is nothing self-contradictory about supposing it will be overcome. Such an attempt at analysis leads to practically the same sort of stand-off as we indicated in connection with (Alpha).

(Delta) "This is evil and ought to be overcome" entails "This is so appalling that a rational being should believe in (i) working towards overcoming it at least partly himself; (ii) encouraging others to join him in fighting it; (iii) *either* (iiia) accepting a particular (and otherwise attractive) ideology, metaphysic or religion which postulates its being overcome or put right and which gives some idea of *how* such a good thing will be brought about *or* (iiib) accepting that there is *some* such ideology, metaphysic or religion which is correct (though he knows not which)."

Notice that (Delta) is compatible with many metaphysical visions as well as many forms of religions that teach survival of physical death in which some forms of evil suffered by people are completely overcome. Orphism, Hinduism and some schools of Buddhism may turn out to qualify as well as certain Judaeo-Christian faiths. But if one cannot accept the idea that personal survival is plausible or even conceptually intelligible, *and* if one can accept a relatively 'Organic' or 'Collective' attitude towards Humanity and Man's continuing history, *and* if one believes that many harshly real things ought to be overcome according to analysis (Delta), then some form of Socialist Humanism may well appeal. Marx, for example, seems to have accepted at least tacitly a rather Humanistic version of Kant's arguments for God (a perfect arranger) and survival (a paradise without revolution) in the *Critique of Practical Reason*. And Marx was both a socially perceptive, morally sensitive person and a far from totally irrational metaphysician.

Some conclude from this variety of possible uses that moral arguments cut no metaphysical ice – how can arguments from Evil, for example, be of value if they seem to aid so many and varied metaphysical positions? But such a negative conclusion about moral arguments generically, or arguments from Evil more specifically, is not warranted. We have held in Chapter VI and for brevity's sake will simply reaffirm here that the doctrines of William James' 'The Will to Believe', can be felicitously combined with elementary tools of modern Decision Theory to make some moral arguments serve reasonable metaphysics. We do not say that moral arguments about God, Evil or Future Bliss and Evil are rational *per se*. We say rather: Moral arguments for metaphysical commitments can be largely rational if that rationality is relativised to an *individual's* high degree of reasonableness in selecting relevant Events and Acts, also in assigning probabilities to Events and utilities to Outcomes. If one has reasonably arrived at certain 'live options', *n*-tuples of relevant events, between which one reasonably feels bound to decide, if one has reasonably assigned *probabilities* (values of worth as truth-seeking reasons) to those Events and *utilities* (values of worth as goals) to the outcomes of commitment if one is correct, then one can as an individual make a rational choice by trying to Maximize Expected Utility. If the realization of certain moral values counts for an agent in many, many contexts as an obvious thing to be counted in assigning such utilities, that agent can surely be rational. For a rational agent, as we argued earlier, must either live in a moral world or, for consistency's sake, withdraw to a private, infantile world of buzzing, blooming confusion.

II. 'THEODICY AND RATIONAL COMMITMENT' OR 'ÜBER FORMAL ENTSCHEIDBARE SÄTZENKONJUNKTIONEN DER "PRINCIPIA THEOLOGICA" UND VERWANDTER SYSTEME'

It seems, as discussed in Chapter VI, that Nelson Pike showed decisively in 'Hume on Evil'[1] that certain key propositions held by theists about a perfect God's existence and the reality of Evil in the world are not logically – "formally" – inconsistent. In other words it seems decidable with appropriate clarity that no manipulation of the obviously relevant semantic and logical rules will produce a contradiction between these theologically respectable propositions. Madden and Hare, as just noted, have argued now that the real problems about God and Evil are not ones of formal inconsistency at all, but ones of reasonableness or rationality in the face of hard and bitter facts. Notions like those of plausibility and probability deserve vastly more notice, they believe, than that of formal contradiction.

We shall try to show that, not surprisingly, the Madden-Hare strategy soon falls back, as analytical reasoning usually must, on a crucial stroke of deduction – hence on a central concern for avoiding contradictions. Then, we shall argue, Madden and Hare are badly confused about the appropriate "rationality criteria" for judging many reasonable beliefs and decisions. We would like to suggest also that Pike in his unnecessary eagerness to rescue natural theology from ALL *a posteriori* teleological reasoning has encouraged this very sort of confusion during a crucial passage of his generally valuable 'Hume on Evil'.

To illuminate the compressed argument which follows, we end these prolegomena with quotations from Madden and Hare and then from Pike:

(I) The very possibility of stating the problem of evil as a formal contradiction depends upon claiming that 'there is no morally sufficient reason for an almightly God to allow any instances of evil' is necessarily true ... such a claim would be absurd .... [The theist] would not have to show even that there is a reasonable or probably explanation of evil ... only that there is some possible explanation (Madden and Hare, *ECG*, p. 4).

No one denies that success always remains a logical possibility for the religious cosmologist, the question is rather what likelihood is there, in view of the present state of evidence, that success will occur (*ECG*, p. 14).

(II) When claiming that evil in the world supports a hypothesis which is counter to the one offered by Cleanthes, I think Philo simply means to be calling attention to the fact that evil in the world provides evidence against Cleanthes' theological position ... [Cleanthes is like an unreasonably stubborn astronomer] .... A decision to retain the planet hypothesis (in the face of my failure to observe the planet and in the absence of an explicit explanation which "squares" this failure with the planet hypothesis) is made correctly only when the evidence for the planet hypothesis is such as to render its negation less plausible than would be the assumption of an (as yet unknown) circumstance which explains the observation failure (Pike, G. and E., pp. 100–01).

We now try to show that the formally decidable consistency of various important sets of theological propositions throws far more light on problems about God and Evil than Madden and Hare, or even Pike realise. Suppose that a fellow named Fairman strikes one generally as a very reasonable, fair-minded person: he is not given to holding inconsistent or uncritical beliefs; he is glad to hear and evaluate others' arguments and criticism carefully; he offers what he takes to be good reasons for his own views; he appears to be tolerant, open to possible change in basic views, undogmatic, etc. In spite of all this, however, Fairman is a theist and believes that there is something impressive about various forms of *a posteriori* teleological arguments. To oblige Madden and Hare he makes some such opening statement:

The following propositions are not formally contradictory, even though granting the truth of (4) and (5) may be granting far more to atheists than is necessary anyway:

(1) Evil exists.
(2) A perfect (that is, completely good and omniponent and omniscient) Creator exists.
(3) A perfect Creator would only allow Evil to exist if He had a morally sufficient reason (such that all Evil served a good purpose in the best way).
(4) Appallingly much evil is '*prima facie* gratuitous' – that is, appears to us to serve no good end whatsoever.
(5) There must, therefore, be a morally sufficient reason for Evil's existence, but in many, many cases the reason remains utterly mysterious to us.

A Madden-Hareite, one Madhatter, jumps up and cries: "Set $\{(1)–(5)\}$ is indeed consistent! But it is not therefore *rational* to believe (2) and (5)!! Fairman counts this credibility jump rational because (a) it is rational to believe (1) and (3) and (4), and because (b) his (2) and (5) are formally consistent with these first three rational beliefs of his. But actually it would be rational for Fairman to believe (2) and (5) IF AND ONLY IF two further conditions (c) and (d) were actually met as well. Condition (c) is that there should be independently good reasons for believing (2) to be true (such strongly good, reasonable grounds in appropriate contexts as to support (5) rationally also). Condition (d) is that the truth of {(1), (3), (4)} should not represent far better reason for rejecting (2) and (5) as too improbable. Now (c) is at best only moderately well satisfied by agreeable and *prima facie* teleological features of the world. And thus, with Evil so immoderately pressing, (d) is not satisfied in the least. Therefore, one may deduce that it is not rational to believe (2) and (5) after all."

At this stage, Fairman is entitled to retort to Madhatter that the rationality of someone's decision whether or not to believe a proposition, simple or compound, is often a function not just of his following evidence and probability but also of his weighing the utilities of correct and incorrect belief. Were Pascal or William James with us and Decision-Theoretically moved, they would say with Fairman that there are situations of perplexity about ideals where decisions must be made in the face of radical uncertainty. These can often be usefully mapped in a simple form of the modern Decision Theorist's representation, whereby one makes a rational decision on the basis of *Maximizing Expected Utility*. On this formal basis the more reasonable choice can be computed from the decision-maker's assignments of utility to outcomes and or probability to events. Consider again the example in L. J. Savage's pioneering work *The Foundations of Statistics*.[2] A cook has made a barely adequate omelette from eleven of the twelve eggs available, but has some reasonable doubt as to the freshness of the last egg. In a situation of finely balanced doubt about the egg and widely different values for good and spoiled omelettes, he might represent the possibilities which count for him so:

	Act 1 (Use last egg)	Act 2 (Don't use last egg)
Event A (Egg good)	Outcome 1-A Completely adequate dish	Outcome 2-A Barely adequate dish
Event B (Egg rotten)	Outcome 1-B Omelette ruined	Outcome 2-B Barely adequate dish

Suppose Event A has a probability of 0.5 for the agent, and therefore Event B also has one of 0.5. Also suppose Outcome 1-A has a utility for him of 3, Outcome 1-B a utility of -25, while 2-A and 2-B both have utilities of 1. Computation shows that for maximizing expected utility Act 2 is rationally much the preferable one, given these assignments. For only a minimum of multiplication by the Events' probabilities and addition of the Outcomes' utilities is required to show this.

We now suppose that Fairman is like the William James of 'The Will to Believe' in that first he engages in serious and respectably open-minded reflection on many relevant questions and alternatives. He is next like a Decision-Theoretically 'with it' James in that he eventually believes that the utility of believing his proposition (2) and being right about the "eternal things" is staggeringly great. Now Madhatter, as a Madden-Hareite, will grant that "teleologically" pleasant features of the world do offer Fairman some evidence for (2). Hence this vast utility can be multiplied by the probability of (2), though the latter is perhaps much less than staggering, to deliver a far higher product than the results of multiplying utilities and probabilities for most interesting beliefs which strictly rule (2) out. Once he can gain this product, then for Fairman the rationality of strong commitment to (2) speaks very strongly indeed for the rationality of commitment to (5). And Fairman is likely to be reasonable in letting his thoughts proceed thus, despite commitment to (3) and (4), *provided that* he is reasonably assured that {(1)–(5)} or an associated series of beliefs decidably constitute a formally consistent set.

It would appear that for Fairman condition (c) and so condition (d) can indeed be reasonably satisfied when there is respect for formal consistency and when the utility as well as the probability component of "good reasons", "rationality", etc., can be taken into account. And so it will not only be consistent for Fairman to stick with {(1)–(5)} as a whole. It might be in an important way inconsistent for him not to hold onto (2) even if he finds (1), (3) and (4) quite glaringly acceptable. For if he did not hold onto (2) while maintaining the same utilities for Outcomes, he could not be consistently relating his probability and utility assignments for all five propositions.

The formal decidability of what is consistent in the way of conjoined beliefs is very relevant to Madhatter's conditions (c) and (d) for rationality in the matter of decisions to believe in (2) and (5). Madden and Hare are misguided to pooh-pooh Pike and supporters for the extent of their lusts after formal consistency in *Principia Theologica*. But something more important should now be more evident. Pike's beautiful clarification of the theist's consistency can indicate to those who sympathize with William James on Faith that a whole host of thinkers, including Madden and Hare, are not at all obviously warranted in querying all theists' rationality about God and Evil.[3]

III. GAMBLING ON DEITY AND FRATERNITY

Consider the most controversial words of Alvin Plantinga's brilliantly controversial book *God and Other Minds*:

... the analogical argument finally succumbs to a malady exactly resembling the one afflicting the teleological argument. I conclude that belief in other minds and belief in God are in the same epistemological boat; hence if either is rational, so is the other. But obviously the former *is* rational; so, therefore, is the latter. (*God and Other Minds*, Ithaca, N.Y. 1967, p. viii. Compare the last two sentences of his book at p. 271.)

Plantinga's conclusion is unsatisfactory largely because he tends to consider the two major philosophical questions of his book only as 'theoretical' or 'speculative' questions, and never as questions vitally related to men's need to choose, act and live in the face of radical uncertainty. As a result, his sole criterion of rationality appears to be: Belief is reasonable if and only if it is adopted just on the 'pure' (truth-seeking) basis of near certainty or high probability. Drawing on what we have been explaining and arguing we suggest that problems about God and Other Minds need not be always so epistemologically abstract. Hence beliefs about *Other Minds*, as well as about God, can be at least as relevantly judged rational by appeal to the Principle of Maximizing Expected Utility. Suppose one takes one sound criterion of Rational Belief – at least about what a reasonable agent holds to be pressing and profoundly challenging human questions in the face of radical uncertainty – to involve sensibly weighing then logically relating considerations of *both probability and utility*. We argue that if one accepts such an approach one can much more plausibly get something like the sameness of logical boatability which Plantinga wants. But then it can also be illuminating to have God and Other Minds logically boated in order reversed from Plantinga's embarkation plan. "Take a rational agent for whom a θ-God and Other μ-Minds are at a similarly disappointing but not too desperate epistemological distance. Let this agent reasonably arrive at the conclusion that the assertions and denials of 'A θ-God exists' and of 'Other μ-Minds exist' are the crucial possibilities to concentrate on. Let this agent then reasonably attach fairly similar and extremely high utilities to the outcome of believing in a θ-God and believing in Other μ-Minds WHEN THE BELIEF IS RIGHT. Let him also attach some slight negative (or some slight positive) utilities to the outcome of belief in each and BEING WRONG about each. Let him reasonably attach some positive measure of probability to the assertions. We can then see that active commitment to belief in a θ-God is rational in his case. So therefore is active commitment to belief in Other μ-Minds rational in his case." (We tag "God" and "minds" with "θ" and "μ" respectively to show that we want the agent to be reasonably specific about what he takes the putative reference of "Gods" and "minds" to be.)

We have already held that, given certain requirements of formal consistency and personal reasonableness, the formal principle of Maximizing Expected Utility can yield an excellent argument for the possibility of rational belief in God. Should this be sound or mainly sound, it would surely be quite remarkable if similar considerations did not apply at least as easily to vindicating the reasonableness of belief in other minds. For one thing the putative reference of "minds" as used in a good deal of ordinary English seems rather less problematical than that of "God".

A number of objections have already been raised about Plantinga's approach to sameness of logical boatability, and many other objections will sooner or later be raised. We now try to overcome a few that would bear on our approach.

Objection 1: If Pascal is to be believed, the reasonable wagerer on the event of God's existence can assign a really overpowering utility to the outcome of that successful belief because he assumes that the outcome involves eternal happiness after death. However, no such correspondingly massive posthumous utility can attach simply to the outcome of successful belief in Other Minds. But just such a massively strong utility assignment is needed if our multiplication with a not too strong probability is to deliver a really sound prudential basis for commitment to a metaphysical hypothesis.

Reply: As one sees in William James, "The Will to Believe" a reasonable person can attach a massive utility to such a God-outcome, setting aside the chance of posthumous benefits, because he wishes HERE AND NOW to live and act in harmony with 'eternal things' and the truth about them. So, like Socrates and James, he can want urgently to live now as one should live. Well, suppose that a reasonable agent, Prodoxasticus, is in such a situation that he is actually *torn* between (a) "I am the only conscious being in a world of many human-like but non-conscious machines", and (b) "I am a conscious being and so are all, or almost all, the other human-like beings that I meet". Suppose poor Prodoxasticus' long and careful study of philosophy leads him to assign a not over-whelming but still distinctly uncomfortable degree of probability to (a), and an uncomfortably middling degree to (b). Why is it impossible for him reasonably to conclude that the utility of the outcome of success-ful belief in (b), enabling him to live in better harmony with other per-sons here and now, would be quite strong enough to make up in mul-tiplication for the low, though positive probability of (b)? Similarly, why it is not possible for Prodoxasticus reasonably to conclude that the utility of the outcome of unsuccessful belief in (b) could be almost similar-ly high? Finally, why could he not reasonably conclude that the utility of the outcome of both successful and unsuccessful belief in (a) would be negative or positively feeble? Might not many an agent reasonably as-sume that a life lived in the belief, true or false, that one was a person among other persons is much more likely to be valuable because warm-hearted, happy, creative, etc., than a life lived in the belief, true or false, that one was the sole person 'cast up' in high existential tragedy among lowly automata? If someone reasonably assumes this, and also reason-ably holds these contraries to be *the* two relevant alternatives, then he reasonably assumes that by believing in Other Minds and acting accord-ingly he is delightfully well set to come out ahead. (Compare James' tactics in 'The Dilemma of Determinism'.)

Objection 2: It can be argued that the sceptic's alleged problem of other minds has been exposed by Wittgenstein, Malcolm, Shoemaker, and others, (whom Plantinga tries to attack in his book), to be a pseudo-problem. Plantinga's resort to the analogical argument is a philosophical error because there can be no real problem about there being other per-sons than myself – of course there are and there must be.

Reply: Our proposed strategy allows for the fact that very reasonable people can disagree about whether there is any livable Angst-making 'existential' problem or at least there *is* some genuine, but abstract 'epis-temological' problem about Other Minds. And the kind of powerfully reasoned, carefully qualified, apparently open-minded and cautious in-quiry pursued by Plantinga in *God and Other Minds* gives one excellent reason to suppose that Plantinga is a paradigm case of not only a reason-able man but also a man to whom there seem to be at least epistemologi-cally genuine problems about both God and Other Minds. We only wish to suggest that those who have already become reasonably convinced that there *are* problems and that there can be '*existential*' problems about both and, furthermore, who reasonably go on to conclude that each such 'existential' question may call for *rational commitment* and should give some serious thought to using our strategy.

Objection 3: It might be argued that the offer of our symmetrical strategy is worthless because Plantinga's original conclusion about belief in God belonging with belief in Other Minds in sharing the same logical boat is silly. Some recent critics have already passed just such a judgment on Plantinga's conclusion:

(i) Hence, as a tentative response to Plantinga's tentative conclusion, I suggest *a* reason why evidence must be provided for rational belief in God but need not be provided for rational belief in Other Minds, is that while it is not at issue whether we know with certainty that there are Other Minds, it surely is at issue whether anyone knows with certainty that the God of traditional theism exists. (William L. Rowe, *Nous* **3** (1969) 270.)

(ii) Hence my tentative conclusion (in response to Plantinga's): if belief in God is basic (and hence justified) for the theist, so is belief in the nonexistence of God basic (and hence justified) for the atheist .... But we are not one bit closer to the far more interesting question: Which of the two beliefs is true? (J. E. Tomberlin, *Journal of Philosophy* **67** (1970) 38.)

(iii) Wouldn't it have been wiser of Plantinga to have assumed that since it is reasonable to believe in other minds, and since such belief must be supportive if it is reasonable, there must be a sound argument for other minds...? And it is also not more reasonable to assume that such an argument will be found ... than that any argument could be devised to justify belief in God? After all, for us humans, the existence of God entails the existence of another mind, but not vice-versa. (Michael A. Slote, *Journal of Philosophy* **67** (1970) 45.)

Reply: We reply that an overzealous supporter of Plantinga may err in thinking (even tentatively!) that *every* reasonable person properly familiar with his book will want to put God and Other Minds in the same logical boat. We also reply that Plantinga's critics certainly do err in thinking – even tentatively – that *no* reasonable person who properly follows the drift of their attacks will want to do this. (We add that the critics err as much as Plantinga in assuming that problems about God and Other Minds can only be exercises for very abstract epistemologists.) For, as James would say, very reasonable people, as well as rather unreasonable people, can disagree, after work on hard, probing arguments, about which propositions do and which do not present *Live Options* that demand reasoned decision and action. Descartes, for example, may have often been mistaken. But time and again Descartes' work offers us *models of reasonable enquiry* by a human being. Thus Descartes was hardly unreasonable, to argue, *pace* Slote, that he really needed to be absolutely certain of the truth of "A perfect God exists" to be at all sure that *ANY* mind other than Descartes' existed. Moreover, a conscientious, gifted and careful neo-Popperian like W.W. Bartley in *The Retreat to Commitment* (New York 1962) might be mistaken, but he would hardly be unreasonable to argue, *pace* Rowe, that it should be at issue whether we know *with absolute certainty* the truth of any substantive claims like "Other minds exist". Bartley might reasonably prefer just to assert very confidently (while accepting the possibility of needing to defend himself against worthwhile criticism) the unacceptability of a claim like "Now at time *t* I am the only conscious being in the universe and all other person-like beings are robots". Finally, a theist who admires James and Kierkegaard might reply to Tomberlin: "My belief in God is basic in the sense that I am *committed* most centrally to his existence in fashioning my way of life. This does not mean that it is epistemologically basic – I seem to know plenty of things so well that I don't need to *will* to believe them! You may claim that Plantinga, James, Kierkegaard, Christensen and King-Farlow talk a lot about theism and atheism but bring us not one bit closer to the ... question: Which of the two beliefs is true? Well, what concerns me as an individualist (and that is the best thing to be on philosophical and religious matters) is *Which belief is it more reasonable for ME to take to be true?* This question about which is more reasonable arises for ME as a person and rational being in pursuit of truth and wisdom, as an agent with a life to live."

IV. GAMBLING ON REFERENCE AND SENSE

Ours is not a popular stance among philosophers of religion. (a) It is bad enough in certain quarters even to affirm belief in the temporally eternal, incorporeal, perfectly loving and all-justifying personal God of the Biblical tradition. One is viewed as an obscurantist by the Naturalist, as a man without a nose for nonsense by the Neo-Positivist, as a fuddy-duddy Fundamentalist by 'Death of God' demythologizers and 'secularizing' interpreters who think they have a symbolic monopoly on Being Itself, Ultimate Concern and the Needs of Modern Man. (b) It is worse still in no few circles to profess admiration for the Thomist tradition. Theists and atheists often recoil with equal scorn from the intellectualist belief that there is a Natural Light of Reason in man which transcends the rationality criteria of particular Circles or Ways of Life. Theists and atheists can recoil with similar scorn from the intellectualist belief that reasonable men can use the Natural Light to find good (truth-seeking) reasons for believing in the need for a Justifying Explanation and the existence of a transcendent God Who is the Justifying Explanation of the world. The 'Internal' approach of Norman Malcolm, Peter Winch, D. Z. Phillips and other neo-Wittgensteinians, the '*Blik* and no bloody hypotheses' approach of R. M. Hare, and the 'Choose your own *seeing as*' approach of John Hick [4], the fideist 'Leap of Faith' attributed as a blind leap to Kierkegaard, and other such alternatives to the Natural Light of Reason seem far more palatable to varied believers and unbelievers alike. (c) But worst of all is the resentment one faces if one not only 'errs' according to signs (a) and (b) of folly, *but also* (c_1) concedes to the Sceptic the wisdom of talking in terms of hypotheses and probability rather than complete certainty in matters of faith, *and also* (c_2) concedes some measure of insight to Pascal for focussing on utilities, *and also* (c_3) tries to link through the Principle of Maximizing Expected Utility the intellectualist wisdom of a Catholic like Aquinas with the feeling for human passion and agency shown by a Protestant like William James in "The Will to Believe" and the "Dilemma of Determinism".

One very common reaction to the bringing in of the Principle of Maximizing Expected Utility (henceforth *Primaxeput*) is the self-righteous muddiness of reactions to James which has left "The Will to Believe" bespattered with confused critics' mud: "Oh, No! I'm sorry, but I'm a *philosopher*!! I'm not interested in mere utility, only in TRUTH!!!" The notion that making progress with regard to Truth and living in accordance with the most important truths might be among a fellow-philosopher's highest 'utilities' (i.e., *values*) seems to be a notion beyond such self-righteous people's grasp once Primaxeput is mentioned. We have already indicated in Section I of this chapter why *Truth* and *Utility* can have Venn Diagrams importantly like those of *Even Numbers* and *Numbers* and importantly unlike those of *Even Numbers* and *Odd Numbers*. If prejudice absolutely determines some people to reject the obvious, then perhaps it will be no utility for them or us in our labouring the obvious. "Happily, even Rip

Van Winkle woke up in time": that, *pace* Boethius, perhaps must be our present consolation of philosophy when this issue is discussed.

There are some objections, however, to the use of Primaxeput in the philosophy of religion which it now seems timely to consider. The first objection is culled from various writings by Kai Nielsen[5] and in many contexts it is a very sensible objection. The other objections that we shall consider, objections directed in recent print against ourselves as well as Primaxeputic Theism, may serve to illustrate how easily any attempt at blending riches of faith with the conceptual wealth of the broad "Reason" family will tend to be misunderstood.

First objection: If "God exists" lacks Sense, then either the probability of the so-called *Event* which it purports to state must be counted as zero or "God exists" must simply be dismissed *a priori* as a non-starter *qua* Event-stater. Infinity times zero is still zero. No amount of utility attached to the outcome of a nonsensical sentence's being true warrants rational backing of its truth by reference to Primaxeput. The First Objection shows much good sense, and reflects how right Leibniz was to query a Cartesian Ontological Argument. Leibniz rightly pointed out that one must not beg the question about the *possibility* that a perfect God exists. Just so, a proper counter to Pascal's Wager can be not only Santayana's point that the Events and relevant Act-options, outcomes and utilities have been very narrow-mindedly drawn up, but a Nielsenish point that, unless the Sceptic can be somewhat assured of the Sense of "God exists", he would be mad to gamble away his life or life-style on the Reference's being what Frege called *The TRUE*. Or we may use Nielsen's own words:

If a concept is incoherent, one ought not, even as an article of faith, to take it on trust that the concept in question has application (see note 5).

Thus we sympathise with Nielsen against Tertullian and his "*Credo quia absurdum*", or against any 'dialectical' fideists among Trinitarians who wish there were four of Them so they could contradict themselves more abjectly about more of Them. If someone is *quite convinced* by Nielsen, Ayer, Carnap or anyone else – in spite of all we have said about a God for reasonable men – that 'God-talk' is radically incoherent or plain nonsensical, then linguistic therapy and not Primaxeput is the right thing for theists to prescribe at present.

Unfortunately for Nielsen, however, we found strong reason to believe in Chapter Five that it is his brand of new Wittgensteinian fideism about the dogma that talk of *disembodied persons* must be senseless which makes him on one score an unwitting enemy of Reason. And unfortunately again for Nielsen, Primaxeput has much to offer those theists who are far from *convinced* by attacks on 'God-talk', yet feel somewhat *discouraged* that such learned and likeable atheists as Nielsen *are* convinced. There is an important degree of analogy here with the problem of Evil.

Let Mr. X believe, like Fairman, that he has found impressively good (truth-seeking) reasons for *believing in* and *acting on* the truth of "God exists". Let Mr. X also feel somewhat rattled by those who argue from Evil about the truth of "God exists". Primaxeput, as we saw, may be the best means of restoring harmony between Faith and Reason for Mr. X. Let a reasonable Mr. Y believe, like Fairman and Mr. X, that he has found impressively good (truth-seeking) reasons for accepting "God exists". Let Mr. Y also feel somewhat rattled by those *a priori* linguists who carry on so confidently about the incoherence of 'God-talk'. If this reasonable Mr. Y believes that he has some good (truth-seeking) reasons for denying that 'God-talk' is senseless, and similar good reasons for agreeing that if 'God-talk' is about a Supreme Being it should indeed often cause *some considerable* bewilderment for humans, then given certain reasonably assigned *n*-types of Acts and Events and values of Probability to Events and of Utility to Outcomes, Primaxeput may extricate a Mr. Y almost as handily as it did a Mr. X. Someone may protest that one cannot assign probabilities to the *metalinguistic n*-type {"'God exists' is true", "'God exists' makes no sense and is neither true nor false", "'God exists' makes sense but no man can know whether it is true nor false", "'God exists' is false" etc.}. But if probability assignments are numerical expressions of what one reasonably takes to be the *goodness* of the *(truth-seeking) reasons* or *strength* of the *(truth-seeking) case* for assenting to such propositions, there is no cause for wringing of hands about the Event-staters' metalinguistic status, meta-metalinguistic status or whatever. It is when the primitive and generic notion of a *good* (truth-seeking) *reason* becomes identified with a single more specific and subordinate notion (or pseudo-notion) like *relative frequency* or *logical degree of inductive confirmation within a scientific theory* or *gut-feeling about Empirical Reality* that puzzles tend to arise about assigning probability to a rich variety of Events.[6]

Some objections from Joel Rudinow: Rudinow's paper 'Gambling on Other Minds and God' (*Sophia* **10.2** (1971) 27–29) attacks our use of

Primaxeput primarily on the ground that "Sceptical problems are generated whenever the type of certainty desired in certain situations is found
to be or thought to be logically unattainable" (p. 28). Rudinow allows
that it may be rational simply as a "prudential alternative" to believe in
God. But a philosophical problem about Other Minds, he insists, must
always be "the" purely "epistemological" problem. Primaxeput, he further
insists, can only show us "what are the most useful, desirable, or felicitous beliefs to hold" (p. 28) – it cannot help us with epistemological quests
for greater certainty. Rudinow seems neither to understand James' 'The
Will to Believe' nor our own writings. Some philosophical problems about
Other Minds may be tackled as purely intellectual exercises in epistemology where epistemology is explicitly construed as some intellectual game or
rule-governed activity in which Primaxeput is not an admissible strategy.
Rudinow does not explain, nor *could* anyone explain *a priori*, it would
seem, why a reasonable person *could not* be placed in an unhappy enough
situation for an 'existential' problem about Other Minds to arise for him
where he as the agent wishes more to act in harmony with the truth about
Other Minds and adopt the most moral policy towards reality, rather
than to know the truth about Other Minds with certainty. Rudinow neither tries to explain his dogmatic stand on what he calls *the* problem of
Other Minds, nor does he even note that we specifically excepted our approach from eligibility IF problems about Other Minds or God or whatever are to be approached only as Plantinga does in pursuing his epistemological interests. Rudinow also ignores the point in James' writings and
ours that utilities sought by Primaxeput certainly need not be purely
"prudential" ones or the mere harmonization of actual belief with what
we most *desire* to believe. (How often has poor James himself been accused
by myopics of preaching a mere Will to Wishful Thinking!) The utilities
sought in a Primaxeput exercise of the Will to Believe may be greater
harmony with important truths or *greater understanding* of and *insight
into* the 'eternal' things. Acquiring certainty about *P* or, better, coming
closer to certainty about *P* CAN be a relevant utility! (See the final section
of Chapter VI.) Rudinow's 'Gambling on Other Minds and God' seems
to reflect a Will to Fail to Understand which besets critics of ideas in 'The
Will to Believe'.

Lawrence Resnick's objections: Resnick has attacked us rather bitterly
in 'Evidence, Utility and God' (*Analysis* **31** (1971) 87–90). He thinks we

are not willing to make "attempts to explain the legitimacy of theism which take account of it as a religious doctrine" (p. 90). This mainly indicates his unwillingness to look at other work of ours explicity referred to *(Reason and Religion)* in material he criticizes. At any rate, we hope that Chapters I and II of *this* book make it quite evident that our Primaxeput defence of theism against arguments from evil is relatable and related (a) to theism conceived as a *religious* doctrine and (b) to accounting for the legitimacy of theism. There are suggestions on p. 88 of Resnick's article, however, which indicate an eagerness to associate theism as a *religious* doctrine with a fideist Voluntarism proclaiming:

I *see* the contradiction – or at any rate the logical side of me sees it – but ... I must believe in God. Some demands are more powerful than a commitment to consistency (p. 88, lines 12–17).

This sort of proclamation, he assures us, is only in a "narrow sense non-rational" and is inappropriately called "irrational" (p. 88). Paragraphs two and three of p. 88 and paragraph one of p. 89, as well as his final paragraph of p. 90, take issue with any serious connection between theism as a *hypothesis* or *explanatory hypothesis.* Thus it seems that we are asked to embrace contradictions, forswear evaluations and THEN "explain the legitimacy of theism" (p. 90). But outside dialectical circles, unsettling for sanity, this seems to be asking too much.

Resnick's sympathy for religion as the resting place for 'legitimate' contradictions may help to explain what is otherwise quite baffling to us. His first page and his last page offer examples of consistent but clearly *irrationally* held sets of beliefs accompanied by irrationally assigned utilities. The first set is held by an obvious "paranoid" whose firmest belief is "(6) Every person I meet is single-mindedly engaged in a plot to destroy me" (p. 87). The second set is held by "a nervous man given to timidity" feeling an "intense premonition of disaster" (p. 90). These alleged analogies are meant to parallel in some shattering way the case of Fairman who *ex hypothesi* appeared clearly to entertain his beliefs and assign his utilities in a reasonable manner. But, we repeat, the alleged analogies are not analogous since Resnick has paid no attention to our requirement that Fairman *qua* rational Primaxeputter should seem to hold his beliefs in a reasonable way, etc. Of course, Resnick's reasoning (otherwise mysterious) may have gone: my alleged analogies are no good, but the subject is religion and religion as I prefer it requires at least one contradiction, there-fore they *are* good.

Another claim of Resnick's is that Fairman cannot consistently count teleologically pleasant features of the universe as evidence for a perfect Creator if he is already aware of other ugly feature of the universe (pp. 88–89). For because,

Those data are clearly incompatible with the hypothesis of a perfect Creator, it makes no sense to speak of the pleasant features of the world as independent evidence for a perfect Creator(p. 89).

It is curious that Madden and Hare as atheists do allow teleogically pleasant features of the world to count as *some* evidence for the existence of a perfect God, though insisting that other facts count much more heavi-ly against His existence. Resnick as ally of 'dialectical fideists' considers that this makes no sense and makes great play of the epithet "independent" in connection with "evidence". And Madden, a noted historian and phi-losopher of science, is surely right. We may have as strong grounds for belief as one can normally get for believing P ("Wong stole the car") and believe tentatively P as a hypothesis, but very firmly indeed. Yet we may still reasonably grant that Q ("Wong had a strict Chinese upbringing of a kind that makes adolescent thieving very rare") is even better confirmed than P and Q does offer some small degree of good (truth-seeking) reason for believing *Not-P*. And Resnick simply begs the question that what counts strongly against a hypothesis must "be clearly incompatible with" it – in the sense of clearly making the hypothesis a non-starter. Darwin found that scientifically very respectable hypotheses about the earth's age and cooling counted heavily against his own evolutionary hypotheses: he neither despaired of the latter nor spurned the former as unscientific. Nor did Darwin revel in the contradiction. Had Darwin been Resnick, biology might be less advanced, perhaps, and more of a consolation to fideists. But a rational theist might find the inferential strategy of our 'Evil and Other Worlds' in Chapter V to be interestingly like Darwin's hunch that an explanation would become available which would uphold his hypothe-sis, yet would show good reason for there appearing even among eminent-ly reputable, reasonable scientists to be such strong evidence against it.

The kinds of utilities discussed by Resnick – keeping alive despite enemies (p. 88) and avoiding a fight with nasty relatives (p. 90) – suggests that he IDENTIFIES all *utilities* with hedonic joy units of crude *utilitaria-*

nism. Like Rudinow he is better at being upset by his free associations with words he reads than at reading James' words or ours with understanding.

Here the Case for the Defense had better rest. Primaxeput has much useful and much dangerous employment in the modern world with its penchant for Cost-Benefit Analyses in business, armies and governments. Many philosophers would do better to distinguish wise uses from foolish ones, rather than ignore it – let alone ignore it in the name of *Truth* or Religion.

NOTES

[1] Reprinted from *Philosophical Review* (1963) in Nelson Pike (ed.) *God and Evil,* Englewood Cliffs, N.J. 1964, pp. 85–102 (henceforth *G & E*). Madden and Hare's attack on Pike occurs in Chapter 1 of their *Evil and the Concept of God*, Springfield, Ill., 1968, and is repeated in 'Why Hare Must Hound the Gods', *Philosophy and Phenomenological Research* (1969). We refer to their book as *ECG*.

[2] New York, 1954. Cf. Chapter VII of F. P. Ramsey's *The Foundations of Mathematics*, London, 1931. The example was discussed in the final section of Chapter VI.

[3] Other strategies to counter the "Theodicy's consistent but utterly implausible and improbable" sort of move are to be found in Alvin Plantinga's *God and Other Minds*, Ithaca, N.Y. 1968, pp. 128–30, and in J. King-Farlow, *Reason and Religion*, London 1969, Chapter V, Section III, pp. 81–83.

[4] Cf. John Hick, *Faith and Knowledge*, 2nd ed., London 1966. Chapter I attacks 'The Thomist-Catholic View of Faith', pp. 11–31; Chapter VI, 'Faith and Freedom', pp. 120–48 proclaims the preciousness of our freedom for "total interpretation" a freedom supposedly endangered by the Thomist or intellectualist approach. See D. F. Henze, 'Faith, Evidence and Coercion', *Philosophy* 42 (1967) 78–85 and J. King-Farlow, 'Cogency, Conviction and Coercion', *International Philosophical Quarterly* 8 (1968) 464–73.

[5] See Kai Nielsen *Contemporary Critiques of Religion*, Toronto 1971, p. 115: "If a concept is incoherent, one ought not, even as an article of faith, to take it on trust that the concept in question has application." Cf. Kai Nielsen, 'On Talk about God', *Journal of Philosophy* 55 (1958) 888–90; 'Can Faith Validate God-Talk?', *Theology Today* 20 (1963) 158–73; 'On Fixing the Reference Range of God', *Religious Studies* 2 (1966) 13–36.

[6] It is a pity that Brian Skyrms' generally very useful text-book on Inductive Logic, *Choice and Change* (Belmont, Cal., 1966), culminates in a final 5th chapter (pp. 149–61) 'Interpretations of the Probability Calculus', which ignores this basic philosophical point. It is significant that Skyrms ignores Toulmin – Toulmin's insights as well as his mistakes. We discuss further aspects of The Gamble on Sense in our recent 'Metaphysics, Probability, Meaning and Justification', *Philosophical Studies of Eire* 20 (1972) 203–209.

CHAPTER VIII

RATIONAL ACTION, AQUINAS AND WAR

What is it to be a reasonable person? Can a reasonable person still feel respect for any answers about the nature of rational agency which the main contributors to the Judaeo-Christian tradition have had to offer? From the very start of this work we have sought to explicate a cluster of sound criteria for being a person who is reasonable about *any* systematic ideals, about *any* all-encompassing religion, metaphysic, or ideology. The Judaeo-Christian tradition is one in which, quite possibly, there has been less stress on *contemplation* than is found in that of the Buddhists or the Hindus. It is a tradition in which quite clearly, there is less stress on prompt and very likely violent *action* than is espoused by many exponents of Marxism or Immediate Republicanism or Anarchism or Militant Nationalism. But the Judaeo-Christian tradition, despite its diversity and despite obvious disparities in the credibility or wisdom of its rather mixed spokesmen, has persistently stressed the importance of both contemplation and action. Contemplation, for example, has been encouraged not only by mystics and monastic orders, but by the influence of Platonic, Aristotelian, and Neo-Platonic ideals (such as *theoria*) upon Judaism, Christianity and Islam. On the other hand, the Pentateuch, the Prophets, the Gospels and the Koran rightly emphasized the importance of acting and reflecting on how to improve one's actions. Humanists have often found inspiration in such Scriptures for acting reasonably and wisely, much as Humanists have deplored – sometimes very justly deplored – the results of religious institutions' attempts to spell out and enforce what they deem reasonable, just and wise through spidery excesses of legalism and casuistry, sometimes accompanied by mastodontic attempts at brainwashing and repression.

The most important question today about future human actions is widely taken to be: "How should men act so as to avoid destroying all life on Earth with modern warfare?" In Chapter I we held that men desperately need to cultivate further an ideal of reasonableness which will place open-minded commitment to the discovery of truth and the doing of good above the fixed precepts of The Plain Truth and The Final Good taught by particular ideologists – including Judaeo-Christian ideologists. Whether enough men with enough influence *will* succeed in cultivating such open-ness in time to prevent a Third World War is impossible for us to answer. We do say that man *can* succeed in this (and as Christians we add that we believe God will offer Grace to all ideologists who sincerely try). We also say that philosophy, including philosophical analysis with its emphasis on clarity and consistency, can be *used* to contribute to this success. It can also be misused to perpetuate indifference to so much of the world of action, or even to support worse fanaticisms about that world.

It is too fashionable, at any rate, to conclude that the Christian tradition can only be used to promote three of the many possible stands which men may take on questions of action, violence and war. *Either* it is assumed, a few Gospel passages can be carefully chosen and isolated to promote Pacifism: we should *only* turn the other cheek, and *only* turn it in *any* context. *Or*, it is assumed, some such isolated passages are good for making us such Pacifist Uncle Toms that we favour even the rejection of *Non-Violent* Resistance to tyranny! We should render unto Caesar what is Caesar's; if Caesar's troops want us to carry conventional ammunition on our backs for them for one mile we should offer to carry the latest in Biological Warfare's bacterial containers on our heads as well and to push mobile gas ovens for an extra eight-fifths of a kilometre after that. *Or*, finally it is assumed that the Christian tradition must be so fatuously Establishmentarian that it can serve only to enforce obedience to the bellicose ambitions of any Power Elite.

The latter assumption has been publicized very widely indeed in the last few years. In this final chapter we shall seek to show how Aquinas, one of the greatest spokesmen for reasonable Christianity, *did* offer very valuable guidance for our times concerning action, violence, revolution and warfare, but has been atrociously misconstrued by many foes and probably some sincere friends in high places.

Recently no few analytical philosophers, especially in North America, have been subjected to almost hysterical pressures from within and without to make their work 'more relevant'. Instead of being invited to cope merely with strings of printed wisecracks from Russell and Gellner, then with ensuing letters in the London Times, participants at some recent meetings of the American Philosophical Association[1] have been dis-

turbed by noisy confrontations over 'relevance'. Analytical admirers of
genuinely systematic thinkers like Aquinas, Artistotle, Hegel, Hume, Kant,
Locke, Marx, Plato, Sartre and Spinoza have in many cases been moving
over the years towards broadening the application of the tools of modern
analysis.[2] Among them some would say that such disturbances are not
necessarily bad. Perhaps more analysts should be moving more quickly
in this direction towards a broader view of their field.[3] But no progress is
made when a journal noted for strong analytical contributors simply bows
to the demand for 'relevance', when it prints a polemical paper that dis-
torts and wildly castigates the history and 'relevance' of Christian thought
in order to further a dubious political thesis. When such a paper is then
rapidly placed in an anthology which will command much wider attention,
it is suitable for Christian philosophers in particular, but also for any
philosopher concerned with standards of historical exposition and critical
thinking, to examine the paper and strike back.

The essay that we are discussing, Professor Donald Wells' 'How Much
Can the "Just War" Justify?', appeared first in an issue of *The Journal of
Philosophy* during December, 1969[4] and was shortly afterwards antholo-
gized by A. K. Bierman and J. A. Gould in *Philosophy for a New Generation* (New York 1970). Some of its numerous errors will repay careful examination by Christian philosophers of many kinds, especially for two
reasons. First, it seems to reflect a good deal of popular or easily popu-
larisable confusions about ethics and war. There are monsters of muddle
in moralist dress that Christian philosophers can really perform a 'relevant' service by unmasking. Second, the dissection of these errors affords
a pleasing chance to show how the allegedly sterile tools of analysis can be
used together with concrete (sometimes elementary) political and historical
points[5] to very good advantage. The main analytical tool we shall use,
and use often, is the old and much maligned one of drawing 'relevant' distinctions. And so we must apologize in advance for a profusion of distinguishing numbers and letters in brackets.

I. AN INTRODUCTION TO SOME CONFUSED MODERN
THINKING ABOUT WAR

Throughout 'How Much Can the "Just War" Justify?', Professor Wells
alternates to emotive advantage between two largely incompatible views of

war as if they were the same. The view (V_1) holds that war, violence and taking of life are intrinsically wrong always:

In addition, however, there is an implicit contradiction which discussants of war and justice ordinarily recognize. Since the havoc of war is normally classed with immoral actions and evil consequences, what the notion of 'the just war' attempts to do is to show that under some circumstances it would be 'just' to perform immoral acts and to contribute to evil consequences. Some justifications of war aim to show that actions deemed normally forbidden by moral mandates are now permissible when performed under the aegis of war.

Since the history of ethical speculation has virtually no other instance of the defense of immoral acts under the extenuating circumstances of prudential risk, the 'just war' concept needs special attention. It constitutes an anomalous instance in moral discourse, namely, a glaring exception to an otherwise accepted prohibition of acts of human brutality (pp. 819–20).

The other view (V_2) maintains that war may have once been justifiable in the Middle Ages and before, but is no longer so in the 20th Century's world of armaments that indiscriminately kill huge numbers of civilians.

The medieval hub of this argument was the doctrine of the 'double effect'. A just belligerent intended only as much deaths as would be proportional to the threat or the offense, and he would intend to kill only combatants. It was presumed that we ought not to kill non-combatants. In the middle ages the weapons made such concern practical. Although the archer might shoot his arrow into the air and not be too clear about where it landed, he was not in doubt about whether he was shooting it at combatant enemies. He might miss a small barn, but he hit the right city. Modern weapons make such sensitivity about the recipients of our missiles inoperable and unfeasible (p. 826).

The discussion of 'intention' in the 13th century, when the weapons were relatively limited in scope so that a king could implement his wish not to harm non-combatants and could practice some kind of proportionality, is something that modern men can no longer carry out (p. 827).

Since the notion of the 'just war' has been revived after nearly two centuries of silence on the issue, it seems appropriate to look again at the medieval claims to see whether, if they had a defense then, they have any rationale now (p. 820).

Note that V_2 itself leaves Wells' position ambiguous. Is he saying (V_{2a}) that all wars and violent uprising must be unjustifiable *even if* they occur in militarily backward nations and *even if* 'total' civilians there who are genuine non-combatants are most unlikely to be affected? If so, then what is so arithmetically *magic* about the 20th century itself? Or does he really mean (if he reflects harder) to say only (V_{2b}) that wars *at any time* which threaten mass destruction (by atom or by spear) of genuine non-combatants *must be* unjustifiable, but that wars *at any time* which involve death and suffering only for the soldiers of both sides (and only a small number of soldiers at that) *may be* justifiable? If he opts for V_{2b} he must get clearer still and clarify his position about revolutionary civil wars so that 'soldiers' will cover more than the official and uniformed troops of the government against whom the revolt takes place. Also he must revise his formulations very carefully to cover cases like the Vietnamese war where the distinctions between civilians and combatants, women-with-children and combatants, the unarmed and combatants, etc., frequently break down.

Note that if view V_{2a} is meant by Wells, then he goes so far as to (Ban – I) ban small scale revolutionary civil wars that in certain countries even to-day could result in the overthrow of rigorously authoritarian ('tyrannical') regimes. And he also then bans from consideration (Ban – II) the possibility that small states on the borders of another small state like Duvalier's Haiti could conceivably be justified in invading that dictator's country, even if it could overthrow a highly oppressive regime with very little bloodshed. Moreover, if V_{2a} is meant by Wells, then he must further reject as a possibility (Ban – III) that a major power could conceivably be justified in supplying smallscale conventional weapons like rifles and grenades to Haiti's more democratic revolutionaries. Similarly, if Wells is committed to V_{2a}, he would be precluded from saying that had 20th Century Britain refused in the 1920's to relinquish the colonial area which became the Irish Free Republic, then because of the arithmetically magic number of the 20th Century the I.R.A. would have been wrong to take more drastic, though still relatively limited, means on behalf of an oppressed majority in that area. Nor could he allow that other nations could have justifiably supplied the I.R.A. with arms. Nor could he allow that England and France should have tried force to stop Hitler from remilitarizing the Rhineland or from seizing Poland. If Wells really means V_{2a} and is willing to defy both Marxists and Thomists on the question of the possible justifiability of at least *some among* the wars of liberation today, then so much the better we say, as admirers of St. Thomas, for both Marxists and Thomists.

II. 'A JUST WAR IS ONE DECLARED BY THE DULY CONSTITUTED AUTHORITY'[6].

Wells attacks the medieval Christian tradition, notably its debts to the ideas of St. Thomas, because he thinks that it made all but impossible the growth of a brotherly, united world.

Incidentally, the concept functioned as a defense of national sovereignty and of the 'right' of nations to defend themselves in a basically lawless world. It made national survival feasible, while making international organization unlikely (p. 820).

But this attack derives, as we shall soon try to show, from a confusion (Conf – A) of what is (Confd – i)[7] superficially explicit in St. Thomas' major doctrines about an 'authoritative sovereign' (and only transitorily relevant to Christian feudalism) with what is (Confd – ii) profoundly implicit in St. Thomas major doctrines and vitally relevant to a century where many (not *all!*) forms of increasing internationalism are both possible and very often desirable.

In order to clarify the value of this distinction let us now note the main strategy of Wells' paper and digress briefly on three further confusions in that strategy. He first mentions three conditions of justification in Aquinas:

In order for a war to be just, three conditions had to be met: (1) an authoritative sovereign must declare the war; (2) there must be a just cause; and (3) the men who wage the war must have just intentions, so that good actually results from the war (p. 820).

He next cites seven conditions recently put forward by a Catholic thinker, Joseph McKenna, building on St. Thomas:

More recently, Joseph McKenna has revised the 'just war' doctrine with an expanded list of seven conditions. They are: (1) the war must be declared by the duly constituted authority; (2) the seriousness of the injury inflicted on the enemy must be proportional to the damage suffered by the virtuous; (3) the injury to the agressor must be real and immediate; (4) there must be a reasonable change of winning the war; (5) the use of war must be a last resort; (6) the participants must have right intentions; and (7) the means used must be moral (p. 821).

He then concentrates mainly on attacking McKenna's conditions (1), (2), (5) and (6).[8] He is content to imply that this 'attack' is a sufficient answer to St. Thomas after explicitly tossing the Angelic Doctor these two lean bones of criticism regarding his three conditions:

In application of these criteria, the criticisms that did emerge of particular wars were so few as to suggest that princes were basically moral men or that the criteria were too vague to be useful. In addition, the critics were commonly persons not officially in government, so that their protests were a kind of baying at the moon (pp. 820–21).

This pair of objections notably involves a confusion (Conf – B) of (Confd –iii) questions about the wisdom and relevance of Aquinas' ideas with (Confd – iv) questions, whether, if Aquinas' ideas were wise and relevant, politicians claiming to be Christians thought carefully about their proper application and made good use of them. But a far worse pair of confusions seem to bedevil Wells' 'attack' at McKenna's conditions (1), (2), (5) and (6). The first of these confusions is (Confd – C): to treat (Confd – v) what is put forward as ONE necessary condition of justification among several necessary conditions that only TOGETHER, (as a SET), could constitute a sufficient condition *as if it were (Confd – vi) a sufficient condition by itself.* Thus on pp. 821–22 he dismisses McKenna's first condition ("A just war is one declared by the duly constituted authority") as being *of no relevance at all* to modern war because so many modern leaders of States and Churches seem to him immoral or amoral. Even if this 'argument' showed that the condition looked unpromising when taken *alone*, it would not show that it could not *combine* usefully with *other* necessary conditions to help with appraisals of justification! The second of these confusions is (Conf – D): to think of (Confd – vii) a proof, however sound, that something is not *always a necessary condition of justification* as (Confd – viii) a proof that this something cannot *often* be a *relevant INDICATOR* of *justifiability*.

To clarify Wells' confusion (Conf – D) consider simple, 'relevant' examples. Many relatively unconfused Christians would agree that the expressions 'authoritative sovereign' and 'duly constituted authority' should not be applied to a revolutionary leader like George Washington in the 1770's who instituted a guerilla organization and declared war on a tyrannical regime and/or colonial oppressor. (They would mean 'should not' on pain of semantic, political and philosophical confusion.) But they would not argue that therefore revolutionary leaders like George Washington, Thomas Lord D'Arcy and Eamon De Valera caused unjustifiable wars. Thus, for such Christians, declaration of war by someone naturally and unconfusingly called an 'authoritative sovereign' or 'duly constituted authority' need not always be a necessary condition for justifying a war. But they would not therefore deny that very often an *excellent indication* that a war is not justified or at least not fully justified is the fact that generals or war-lords have pre-empted their central government's duly constituted powers and responsibilities for starting a war. And some relatively unconfused Christians in the United States hold that one of the reasons they should query American involvement in Viet-Nam is that the heavy degree of involvement was due to President Johnson's Gulf of Tonkin declaration and not to an act of Congress, the American Constitution's 'duly constituted authority' for making decisions on so great a degree of martial involvement. Such Christians, at least some of whom largely approve and some of whom strongly disapprove of considerable American involvement in South East Asia, would say that under certain CONCEIVABLE[9] circumstances Johnson's plunge into 'escalated war' without a formal Congressional declaration of war, (A) could have been fully justified – IF special time factors and the national interest of both America and Viet-Nam had truly made his immediately acting without Congressional assent imperative – but (B) could not be justified under the actual circumstances in 1964.[10] Thus Wells' confusions (Conf – C) and (Conf – D) seriously distort our understanding of how relatively clearheaded and morally concerned people do think about war – as well as obscuring points relevant for any explanation of how they ought to think.

At any rate, the time has now come to look more closely at what an English-speaking St. Thomas would mean by 'an authoritative sovereign' or a 'duly constituted authority' in cases where he would be using such terms *technically* in the course of doing Thomist political *philosophy* rather than Wells' kind of semi-philosophical, polemical journalism. The *conventional* use of such a term by journalists and arm-chair politicians, and also the *legal* use of such terms by a state's conventionally certified lawyers or judges and its power-wielding politicians, need not coincide for St. Thomas with their *philosophically proper* use at all. Failure to explore this point results in Wells' feeling able (a) to dismiss Aquinas with the comment that many historical sovereigns – people to whom these terms could apply conventionally or legally according to their state's particular laws – have not been "very reliable or sensitive" by Christian or humanist standards (p. 821). The same failure results in Wells' feeling able, as was briefly mentioned before, (b) to ignore those *implications* of Aquinas' political philosophy that are vitally relevant to peace and international co-operation today. (Some of the most crucial of these implications we shall shortly try to make clear.) For Wells seems completely unable to grasp what Aquinas would call in modern English "the technical, philosophical distinction between *genuine* authority and a leader or governing group only *said* to have sovereignty by those who follow misleading conventions or bad laws; the technical distinction between genuinely authoritative sovereignty and the pseudosovereignty of a *tyrannical* power".

According to St. Thomas, at least two conditions must be met by a ruler or ruling body if it is to have any authoritative sovereignty at all. First, it must in its basic approach respect the Natural Law, the body of moral truths which God gives all sane men of all remotely sane societities the power to grasp, at least dimly, by the Natural Light of Reason. Pointless killing and cruelty, for example, are obviously to be deplored by sane members of remotely sane societies. (Compare Saint Paul on 'Gentile' and 'Conscience' at Romans 2 : 14–15.) Second, it must try in creating its particular *Positive Laws* – conventionally instituted statutes regularizing a feasible form of community life at a historical period for certain humans (who like all other men have a *natural need* for organized society) – both to enhance respect for the Natural Law and to promote the citizens' Common Welfare (*bonum commune*). St. Thomas did not, despite the repeatedly scathing remarks of Wells about modern Catholic and Protestant thinkers with any regard for the Thomist tradition [11], preach a doctrine of supporting the Establishment policies on war and economics for the Establishment's sake. Indeed, St. Thomas explicitly laid down criteria for assessing the justifiability of violent revolutions against tyrannical regimes. The revolutionary criteria would include (RC – i) the persistent failure of the government to respect the Natural Law and/or the Common Welfare; (RC – ii) its failure to grant citizens effective means of peacefully gaining redress against such tyrannical abuses of power; (RC – iii) the strong likelihood that such a revolt would succeed in toppling the government and not merely result in a tyrannical bloodbath; (RC – iv) the serious chance that toppling those in power would lead to a much better government, not to mere anarchy or to another form of outright tyranny. [12]

There are some modern meta-moralists who would now dismiss St. Thomas' appeals to Natural Law and the Common Welfare as utterly unhelpful. They would argue that the diversity of societies with their varying moral codes and fundamental beliefs, makes his appeals to something like universal intuitions of morality and fairness a piece of antiquated junk. [13] There may well be other meta-moralists who would simply dismiss Aquinas' appeals to our ethical knowledge about matters of social and sexual morality, fairness, etc. as examples of the fallacious belief that ethical principles have a *cognitive status*. And it may be legitimate or rational for them to do so, at least until they can be convinced otherwise by reading or hearing better meta-moralists. [14] But it is not open to Wells himself to disagree with Aquinas' view that some fundamental moral truths are universally graspable, that some value judgments are true and correct, others false and incorrect. This course is not open, upon pain of radical inconsistency, to a man who proclaims as all but too obviously true and readily knowable views:

There may be a credible case for claiming that the medieval discussions of the just war added to man's moral *insights* ... (p. 828)[15]; If the just war ever had *moral significance* in the past, it is *clear* today that it *justifies* too much (p. 828)[15]; we would still need to *show* that the last resort ought, in this case, to be taken (p. 825) etc.[15]

Wells, in effect appeals to a broad range of readers on the assumption that, as sane and informed persons, they can already share in many of his moral insights rather clearly and can be brought with his help to clarify others as matters of moral knowledge.

If the Natural Law forbids us to cause pointless death and pain, if the Natural Law urges us to have a brotherly concern for *all* men everywhere according to the Golden Rule, and if every society's Common-Welfare in-the-20th-Century is now rather clearly linked with avoiding a nuclear holocaust, then any modern government that St. Thomas would consider authoritatively sovereign would be bound today to be greatly concerned with the protection of world peace and with international co-operation. It is now, of course, vastly easier than in the Thirteenth Century for a good leader or good government to communicate quickly with foreign powers over great distances. It is obviously far clearer to governments that failure to improve international relations may well lead to enormous amounts of pointless (hence morally intolerable) human suffering or death; that such failure might lead to the extinction of their own societies with all citizens. An authoritative sovereign concerned both with the Natural Law and with his society's Common Welfare must surely find today that St. Thomas' concept of authoritative sovereignty points far away from narrow forms of nationalism.

Some might then complain (as we suspect Wells would in reply) that St. Thomas, if he was politically wise at all, should have been in his politics (Pol – 1) a far more explicit and outspoken advocate of international co-operation; (Pol – 2) an open supporter of a strong centralized World Government. Such complaints deserve the following replies among others. (Pol – 1): To admire St. Thomas' political philosophy and count it very relevant today is not to attribute omniscience to him, or wisdom only to him and to no one else. St. Thomas, like all human thinkers, was seriously limited in various philosophical and political respects by the times and traditions in which he worked. Nor was political philosophy his most central concern in his research and reflection. Perhaps, like most other good philosophers, he could have helped mankind more by devoting further time and effort to the area and to questioning harder the political assumptions of his day. (Pol – 2): It is questionable whether even now a strong centralized World Government would be feasible for present nations with such divergent interests and forms of life. It is tempting to say that, because of nuclear armaments' threat to mankind such a World Government must quickly be made feasible and imposed upon mankind. Even if this could be done, however, might not the consequence of imposing it be an intolerably bloody succession of nationalist revolutions as well as an intolerably inhuman suppression of person liberty and communal aspirations? The appalling possibilities that might result from the attempted impositionof *one ideology* on the whole world through a self-perpetuating contest between one or more rival World Governments have been brilliantly, perhaps very prophetically, explored by George Orwell in *1984*. In spite of the nuclear threat, or perhaps because of it, the forming of a genuinely healthy type of strong World Government may only be feasible if and when what Montesquieu called the Spirit of the Nations will have changed greatly through some of the possibly more beneficial effects of modern technology and 'ideological dialogue' later on. Possibly the common primary concern of all genuinely philosophical and genuinely systematic philosophers with carefully investigating what is true and what is right can gradually help through widening ordinary men's education in serious philosophy to change the Spirit of the Nations. Careless polemics would seem rather less promising.

III. 'A JUST WAR USES MEANS PROPORTIONAL TO THE ENDS'

It never becomes clear exactly what Wells thinks he is 'attacking' when he lashes out at "proportionality" as a Thomistically inspired criterion. Perhaps the fault lies as much with a long tradition of ambiguous "proportionality"-talk as it does with him. At some places in the verbal fog we suspect that he is again committing confusions (Conf – C) and (Conf – D), confusing (Confd – v) alleged necessary conditions with (Confd – vi) non-alleged sufficient conditions, confusing (Confd – vii) alleged necessary

conditions with (Confd – viii) assumed indications, etc. What he means by
"proportionality" and what he has to say against it must largely be gleaned
from the following two vitriolic passages (the least emotional parts of this
section). He begins the section by writing:

Franciscus de Victoria had observed ... that if to retake a piece of territory would
expose a people to "intolerable ills and heavy woes" then it would not be just retake it.
We must be sure, he continued, that the evils we commit in war do not exceed the evils
we claim to be averting. Now how do we measure the relative ills? This is the problem
of the hedonic calculus on which Mill's system foundered. Since Victoria granted
princes the right to despoil innocent children if military necessity required it, it ceased to
be clear what proportionality meant or whether any limit at all was being proposed.
    In a recent paper on this issue Father John A. Connery stated that the morality of
the violence depends on the proportionality to the aggression. What is required is
some calculus to make this measurement. The latitude with which conscientious persons
have interpreted this suggests (what was clear enough to Mill) that we possess neither
the quantitative nor the qualitative yardstick for this decision. Pope Pius XII thought
the annihilation of vast numbers of persons would be impermissible. John Courtney
Murray thought this prohibition was too restrictive (pp. 822–23).

And shortly afterwards we read:

Not only do Christian prelates seem a fairly callous lot, but the notion of proportionality
has lost sense.
    Where should we draw the line? Pope Pius XII decided that Communism was such a
cosmic threat that atomic, chemical, and biological bombs could all be justifiably used.
But where then is the proportion? (p. 823).

The idea of proportionality in Christian thinking derives partly from the
Pentateuch, but also very considerably from Aristotle's discussions of proportional justice at *Nichomachean Ethics*, V, 113061–1134a15. Rather than
hasten to discuss whether Wells and the numerous people he denounces
here have been true to the Pentateuch, or to Jesus' revisions of its moral
approach, or to Aristotle and Aquinas, let us first note that Wells rightly
links medieval problems about justifiable violence in war with medieval
problems about justifiable violence in punishment.[17]
    We shall next try to isolate what is wisest in the long tradition of talk
about proportionality and violence by distinguishing two vastly different
'proportional' approaches to violence. Here we shall be making some use
of A. M. Quinton's classic analytical paper 'On Punishment'[18], not necessarily a use that he would entirely approve of. At the risk of making this
chapter read like a philosophical horror comic, we shall baptize these approaches (Ap – 1) or 'The Retributive-Deontological-Isomorphic-Pro-

portionality Approach', and (Ap – 2), or 'The Teleological-Estimative Reasoning-Sense of Proportion Approach'.

Approach (Ap–1) states that *if X commits a wrongful violent act of form F and gravity G against Y, then Y and/or his lawful legates (such as his fellow citizens or his widow and orphaned children) may-just-because-he (or his legates)-just-may impose upon Y a violent penalty which is as closely as is humanly achievable of Form F_n and gravity G_n.* The variables X and Y can have individuals, families, tribes, or other groups within nations, as well as entire nations for their values. The variables F_n and G_n can range over the forms and gravities of thefts, rapes, tortures, maimings, murders, destructions of peoperty, civil insurrections, invasions by other nations, etc.

Approach (Ap – 2) states that *if X commits a wrongful violent act of form F_n and gravity G_n against Y, and if such defeasible conditions as X's act being deliberate, X's being sane and adequately knowledgeable are met, then X should be punished (civilly, martially, etc.) but only if (i) some appropriate and important good end(s) will thereby be served and (ii) and no greater evil consequence will result and (iii) the form and gravity of the punishment to be prescribed is properly judged by an agent or body with a wise 'SENSE OF PROPORTION' regarding the gravity of X's act, the importance and further beneficial effects of the good end(s) served and the possible harmful by-products of the punishment.* Here the variables can range roughly over the same things as in (Ap – 1), but the wiser the approach to the the Approach the more carefully the range will be reflected on and controlled. Approach (Ap – 2) retains an important retributive element from Approach (Ap – 1). It does not prescribe 'tellishment'. It does not license pseudo-punishments. It does not encourage pseudo-retributive violence against innocent but irritating persons and groups merely on the grounds that a greater balance of good ends will be served in the long run. As Quinton would put it: punishment must be *for guilt* – personal or governmental guilt.

Insofar as Wells seems to be addressing himself to proportionality *qua* Approach (Ap – 1), he is addressing himself to something which Jesus himself often seemed very eager to eject from monotheist morality. (See the Gospels' versions of the Sermon on the Mount, especially Matthew 5.) But Wells might rightly reply that sometimes Christian leaders, philosophers and laymen have lapsed back in their thinking into some such 'isomorphic' forms of really barbaric, irrational, infantile retributivism.

This may be especially true of certain sadomasochistic and crudely pictorial interpretations by Catholics and Protestants of 'estrangement from God' in the Afterlife.[19] And lapses back into such infantile forms of irate isomorphism also characterize the darker side of humanity, whatever its creed, when men, even very good men, think about the justifications of violence in war and in civil and family punishment. At any rate, insofar as Wells is addressing himself to Approach (Ap – 1) or something like it, he is himself lapsing into barbarism by the kind of 'arguments' he apparently uses against it. The rational aswer to (Ap – 1) is not to suggest first that "What is required is some calculus to make this measurement", (p. 823), and then to claim that we can no longer make such measurements, that perhaps one could in feudal times when an army's retributive volleys would not hurt civilians, but not now, and so on.

Nor is it a rational argument to suggest that ideally such a deontologically-minded and isomorphic-retribution-minded measurement of proportion might be made to good purpose by genuine saints, then to add that actual prelates and rulers do not measure up in their mental and moral powers to the standards of such saintly measurers. Surely *one* rational reply that Christians, Jews and other religious folk, as well as secular humanists should make is this. "Approach (Ap – 1) is infantile, barbaric, inhuman, immoral, irrational. It is contrary to the Natural Law and the Golden Rule and the Rule of Love and the Categorical Imperative, if you believe in any of these. In secular talk, it is contrary to certain basic human intuitions of decency and respect for all persons, which are sound intuitions and count as moral knowledge even though they often need to be socially nurtured. To try to attack Approach (Ap – 1) philosophically *after* accepting its insane terms of mensural reference is itself a form of philosophical insanity. This might be called a dogmatic reply, not an argument. But sane arguments, as St. Thomas saw – and as very varied philosophers like Plato and Aristotle, Marcel, Marx and Moore have seen – must start with the acknowledgement of certain hard truths grasped in human experience, including moral truths."

Insofar as Wells seems to be addressing himself to proportionality *qua* Approach (AP – 2) or something like it, he seems to *presuppose* the wisdom of using (Ap – 2) today in order to show that it is unwise today. For his main 'argument' seems to be that the arrival of nuclear armaments makes it impossible for us nowadays to advocate rationally *any* form of martial violence on *any* scale. Why ? Because (Premise a) no one with a sane Sense of Proportion' about ends and means can advocate an *all*-out *nuclear* war in which vast numbers of non-combatants will be killed. Because (Premise b) many of the political and religious leaders to whom we once tried looking for improving our 'Sense of Proportion' about war obviously disagree widely with one another and obviously diverge greatly in view from what we ordinary mortals know that someone with a sane 'Sense of Proportion' would have to believe and have to reject on such matters. These two must be among his real premises. But how can such a general conclusion about all future warfare in any form conceivably be delivered by such premises about nuclear warfare and the limitations of some leaders ? A hidden assumption seems to be (Premise c) that because we ordinary mortals, unlike so many leaders, can and do retain a 'Sense of Proportion'[20] about means, ends and violence, we can see (or be philosophically brought by Wells to see) that in a nuclear age no one does or can retain a 'Sense of Proportion' about means, ends and violence of any kind! This self-contradictory assumption goes perhaps together with another hidden and conflicting assumption (Premise d) that we the powerless still have enough 'Sense of Proportion' to see that if any individual obtains political or martial power in a so-called Military-Industrial-Complex it corrupts his 'Sense of Proportion' absolutely. Such assumptions would seem to be needed as premises to explain why Wells arrives at his moralisms so confidently. This wild assortment of conflicting premises may help to explain the tangle of Wellsian confusions that we discussed in Section I. This tangle in turn may help to explain the conflicting premises.

IV. FAREWELL TO ANTI-MARTIAL MUDDLES?

Wells goes on to pour scorn on two of McKenna's other neo-Thomist conditions for justifying wars. These are (5) that the use of war must be a last resort (pp. 824–26); then finally (6), that the participants must have right intentions (pp. 826–29). But these discussions involve essentially the same kinds of confusion we have already tried to diagnose: muddles about necessary conditions, sufficient conditions and useful (usefully relevant) indicators; muddles about sorts of 'proportional' retaliation, etc. He makes, in effect, the useful point that those with a 'Sense of Proportion'[20] should seek to study far more alternatives to a further arms race than the nuclear powers encourage their citizens to study. But this very point is largely made by utilising assumptions shared by Christians about moral knowledge, about a 'Sense of Proportion' arising from man's Natural Light of Reason, about our remaining ability at least dimly to distinguish justifiable from unjustifiable violence in the pursuit of various *modern* ends. Wells seems unaware that he may well have been helped to grasp some of his wiser, more 'relevant' assumptions by being born into a culture with a considerable Christian tradition, a culture shot through with Aristotelian and Thomist ideas derived through Hooker and Locke, and then the authors of the American Constitution. Wells appears quite bizarrely unaware of such a possibility – especially because he has so little but evil to say of Christian thinkers' 'relevance' to the modern world.

At this late stage we had better confess again to a sociological prejudice. We have not attacked Donald Wells' essay on the 'Just War' as a purist exercise in analysis. We have attacked him because we suspect that he is very much a man of our period, that his confusions about war and justification may be widely shared and shared at times by ourselves as men of the same period. But part of the task of a *philosophia perennis* which Christian analysts can endorse should be to dredge up such confusions about matters so crucial to human politics and morality. Then the confusions can be criticised in the light of several analytical traditions: classical, medieval, rationalist, empiricist, pragmatist, and modern. All the traditions are relevant to man and to his most important questions about his existence.

NOTES

[1] For example, those in New York, December, 1969, and Berkeley, March 1970.
[2] See especially writings by Iris Murdoch, Thomas Nagel, Wilfrid Sellars, Kai Nielsen and Joel Feinberg.
[3] We welcome the institution in 1971 of a journal designed to speed this movement: *Philosophy and Public Affairs* (ed. by Marshall Cohen), Princeton University Press.
[4] **66** (1969) 819–29.
[5] Cf. John King-Farlow, 'The Concept of *Mine*', *Inquiry* 7 (1964) 268–76.
[6] Wells, *op. cit.* pp. 821–22.
[7] For (Confd – i) read "the first thing confused", for (Conf –A), read "the first confusion", etc.
[8] The entire remainder of Wells' paper (pp. 821–29) is written under four headings which state these four conditions.
[9] For us to speak of the CONCEIVABLE here is to imply nothing about the justifiability of what is currently 'actual'.

[10] St. Thomas, if he were with us, might well say, in answer to a universal parliamentary fanatics' complaint that he had failed to advocate parliamentary democracy everywhere in the Middle Ages, that such a critic had shown no understanding of human needs and tendencies in Europe at that period. He might similarly comment that those who today seek to impose a regime with the trappings of parliamentary democracy on all men everywhere *or* a Soviet or Maoist style regime on all countries everywhere are grossly insensitive to the actual, historical circumstances in which different nations' needs for different forms of society arise. Marx himself, who believed that different societies evolve at strikingly different rates, might well show a considerable measure of agreement Wells himself would seem at p. 824, paragraph 2, also largely to agree!

[11] See his footnotes on pp. 821–23, 826–27.

[12] St. Thomas Aquinas, *De Regimine Principum*, Book 1, Ch. 6 (ed. by Matis), Turin, 1924.

[13] Cf. the excellent discussion of meta-ethics, social relativism and ethical relativism in E. Sprague and P. W. Taylor's *Knowledge and Value* (2nd ed., New York 1967), pp. 502–06. Aquinas himself was clearly aware of this diversity of human societies' beliefs – see for example his reply to Anselm's ontological argument and its definition of 'God' in the *Summa Contra Gentiles*. Like Aristotle, Aquinas did not differ radically from the social relativist in the matter of anthropological knowledge, but rather in the manner of interpreting such knowledge philosophically.

[14] For example P. T. Geach, 'Good and Evil', *Analysis* **17** (1956) 33–42; Gabriel Marcel, *Homo Viator*, especially pp. 125–65 (New York 1962); G. E. Moore, *Principia Ethica* (Cambridge 1903); Peter Glassen, 'The Cognitivity of Moral Judgments: A Rejoinder to Miss Schuster', *Mind* **72** (1963) 137–40. Cf. our Chapters IV and V.

[15] Our italics emphasize these 'epistemologically loaded' words that commit Wells to moral cognitivism.

[16] See Wells, *op. cit.*, pp. 822–26.

[17] Cf. p. 820, para. 4.

[18] *Analysis* **14** (1954) 512–17. Reprinted in *Contemporary Ethical Theory* (ed. by Joseph Margolis), New York 1966, pp. 474–84.

[19] Wells, in making such a reply as this, could turn to the Nietzsche of *On The Genealogy of Morals* to support his contention.

[20] This extremely valuable term in ordinary language 'A Sense of Proportion' (which is not a literalistic mensural term) is, unfortunately, not used and discussed in Wells' essay.

A SHORT BIBLIOGRAPHY

Adams, E. M., *Ethical Naturalism and the Modern World View*, Chapel Hill, N.C., 1960.
Ahern, M. B., 'God and Evil', *Sophia* 3 (1967).
Alston, W. P., *The Philosophy of Language*, Englewood Cliffs, N.J., 1964.
Alston, W. P., 'Dispositions and Occurrences', *Canadian Journal of Philosophy* 1 (1971).
Anscombe, G. E. M., *Intention*, Oxford, 1958; Ithaca, 1957.
Anscombe, G. E. M. and Geach, P. T., *Three Philosophers*, Oxford, 1967; Ithaca, 1961.
Anselm, *Opuscula Anselmi, I*, esp. 'Proslogion', Oxford, 1964.
Aquinas, St. Thomas, *Basic Writings* (ed. by A. C. Pegis), New York, 1945.
Austin, J. L., *How to do Things with Words*, Oxford, 1962.
Austin, J. L., 'Other Minds', *Proceedings of the Aristotelian Society*, Suppl. Vol. **20**.
Ayer, A. J., *Logical Positivism*, New York, 1959.
Babbage, C., *The Ninth Bridgewater Treatise*, London, 1837; reprinted by Frank Cass
    Ltd. Intl. School. Book Serv. in 1967.
Bartley, W. W. III, *The Retreat to Commitment*, London, 1964.
Beard, R. W., 'Pragmatism, Pragmaticism, and the Will to Believe – a Reconsideration',
    Journal of Philosophy **55** (1958).
Beard, R. W., '"The Will to Believe" Revisited', *Ratio* **8** (1966).
Benecerraf, P. and Putnam, H. (eds.), *Philosophy of Mathematics*, Oxford, 1969.
Bergmann, G., *The Metaphysics of Logical Positivism*, London, 1954.
Boas, G., *The Inquiring Mind*, Illinois, 1959.
Boethius, *The Consolation of Philosophy* or *De Consolatione Philosophia*, Oxford, 1868;
    'Library of Liberal Arts', New York, 1965.
Bourke, V. J., *Will in Western Thought*, New York, 1964.
Broadbeck, M. and Feigl, H., *Philosophy of Science*, New York, 1953.
Brown, T. P., 'Religious Morality', *Mind*, New Series **77** (1963).
Butler, R. J. (ed.), *Analytical Philosophy*, Oxford, 1962.
Camus, A., *The Plague*, Paris, 1947; London, 1948.
Carnap, R., 'Empiricism, Semantics and Ontology', *Revue Internationale de Philosophie*
    11 (1950).
Carnap, R., *Meaning and Necessity*, Chicago, 1956.
Carter, J. C., 'The Recognition of Miracles', *Theological Studies* **20** (1959).
Clifford, W. K., 'The Ethics of Belief', *Lectures and Essays* (London, 1879), published
    from *The Contemporary Review* of 1876.
Coburn, R. C., 'Professor Malcolm on God', *Australasian Journal of Theology* **41** (1963).
Cohen, L. J., *The Diversity of Meaning*, Oxford, 1966.
Cohen, M. (ed.), *Philosophy and Public Affairs*, Princeton University Press.
Copleston, F. C., *Aquinas*, London, 1955.
Crombie, I. M., 'The Sense of Contingency' in *New Essays in Philosophical Theology*
    (ed. by A. G. N. Flew and A. D. MacIntyre), London, 1955.
Davidson, D., 'Actions, Reason and Causes', *Journal of Philosophy* **60** (1963).
Descartes, R., *Philosophical Works of Descartes*, 2 vols. (ed. by E. L. Haldane and

G. R. Ross), Cambridge, 1967. There are many other translations and collections of Descartes' work.

John Duns Scotus, 'De Divisione Naturae', *Philosophical Writings* in 'Library of Liberal Arts' (New York, 1964).

Dwyer, P., 'Proving God', *Philosophical Studies* (Eire) **14** (1965).

Dwyer, P., 'Thomistic First Principles and Wittgenstein's Philosophy of Language', *Philosophical Studies* (Eire) **16** (1967).

Edwards, P., 'Why', *Encyclopedia of Philosophy*, Vol. 8 (New York and London, 1967).

Elton, W. (ed.), *Aesthetics and Language*, Oxford, 1953.

Feigl, H. and Broadbeck, M., *Philosophy of Science* (New York, 1953).

Fitch, F. B., 'The Perfection of Perfection', *The Monist* **47** (1963).

Flew, A., 'Theology and Falsification' in *New Essays in Philosophical Theology* (co-edited with A. C. MacIntyre), London, 1955.

Flew, A. (ed.), *Logic and Language*, 1st and 2nd series, Oxford, 1951, 1953.

Flew, A. (ed.), *Essays in Conceptual Analysis*, London, 1956.

Fodor, J. A. and Katz, J. J. (eds.), *The Structure of Language*, Englewood Cliffs, N.J., 1964.

Foster, M. B., *Mystery and Philosophy*, London, 1957.

Geach, P. T., *God and the Soul*, London, 1969.

Geach, P. T., *Mental Acts*, London, 1957.

Geach, P. T., 'Good and Evil', *Analysis* **17** (1956).

Geach, P. T. and Anscombe, G. E. M., *Three Philosophers*, Oxford, 1967; Ithaca, 1957.

Glassen, P., 'The Cognitivity of Moral Judgments', *Mind* **68** (1959).

Glassen, P., 'The Cognitivity of Moral Judgments, A Rejoinder to Miss Schuster', *Mind* **72** (1963).

Hardan, J., 'The Concept of Miracle from Saint Augustine to Modern Apologetics', *Theological Studies* **15** (1954).

Hare, P. and Madden, E., 'On the Difficulty of Evading the Problem of Evil', *Philosophy and Phenomenological Research* **28** (1967).

Hare, P. and Madden, E., *Evil and the Concept of God*, Springfield, Ill., 1968.

Hare, P. and Madden, E., 'Why Hare Must Hound the Gods', *Philosophy and Phenomenological Research* **29** (1969).

Hare, R. M., *The Language of Morals*, Oxford, 1952.

Hare, R M., 'Theology and Falsification' in *New Essay on Philosophical Theology* (ed. by A. G. N. Flew and A. C. MacIntyre), London, 1955.

Harrison, C. R., 'The Ontological Argument in Modal Logic', *The Monist* **54** (1970).

Hartshorne, C., *The Logic of Perfection*, La Salle, Ill., 1962.

Heimbeck, R. S., *Theology and Meaning*, London, 1969.

Henze, D. F., 'Faith, Evidence and Coercion', *Philosophy* **42** (1967).

Hick, J. (ed.), *Faith and the Philosophers*, New York, 1966.

High, D. M., *New Essays in Religious Language*, Oxford and New York, 1969.

Holland, R. F., 'The Miraculous', *American Philosophical Quarterly* **2** (1965).

Hudson, W. D., 'The Alleged Objectivity of Moral Judgments', *Mind* **71** (1962).

Hudson, W. D., *The Is/Ought Question*, London, 1969.

Hume, D., *An Enquiry Concerning Human Understanding* (2nd edition by L. A. Selby-Bigge), Oxford, 1902.

Husserl, E., *Ideas* (trans. W. R. Boyce Gibson), London, 1931.

James, W., 'Faith and the Right to Believe', *Some Problems of Philosophy*, New York, 1916.

James, W., *The Will to Believe, Human Immortality, and Other Essays on Popular Philosophy*, New York, 1956.

Katz, J. J., *Philosophy of Language*, New York, 1966.

Katz, J. J. and Fodor, J. A. (eds.), *The Structure of Language*, Englewood Cliffs, N.J., 1964.

Kenny, A. G. N., *Action, Emotion and the Will*, London, 1963.

Kierkegaard, Søren, *The Concept of Dread*, Princeton, 1944.

King-Farlow, J., 'Sea Fights without Tears', *Analysis* New Series **19** (1958).

King-Farlow, J., 'Myths of the Given and the "Cogito" Proof', *Philosophical Studies (U.S.)* **12** (1961).

King-Farlow, J., 'The Concept of Mine', *Inquiry* **7** (1964).

King-Farlow, J., 'Religion, Reality and Language', *Pacific Philosophy Forum* **5** (1967).

King-Farlow, J., 'Wittgenstein's Primitive Languages', *Philosophical Studies (Eire)* **18** (1969).

King-Farlow, J., 'Quantification Theory and Ontological Monism', *Zeitschrift für Allgemeine Wissenschaftstheorie* **3** (1972).

King-Farlow, J. and Espinaco-Virseda, J., 'Matter, Form and Logic', *Rassegna Internazionale di Logica* **3** (1971).

King-Farlow, J. and Rothstein, J., 'Dialogue Concerning Natural Metaphysics', *Southern Journal of Philosophy* **6** (1968).

Kitely, M. J., 'Existence and the Ontological Argument', *Philosophy and Phenomenological Research* **19** (1958).

Madden, E., *Structures of Scientific Thought*, Seattle, 1960.

Madden, E., 'Evil and the Concept of a Limited God', *Philosophical Studies (U.S.)* **18** (1967).

Madden, E. and Hare, P., 'On the Difficulty of Evading the Problem of Evil', *Philosophy and Phenomenological Research* **28** (1967).

Madden, E. and Hare, P., *Evil and the Concept of God*, Springfield, Ill., 1968.

Madden, E. and Hare, P., 'Why Hare Must Hound the Gods', *Philosophy and Phenomenological Research* **29** (1969).

Maimonides, Moses, *Guide for the Perplexed* (trans. Shlomo Pines), Chicago, 1963.

Malcolm, N., 'Anselm's Ontological Arguments', *The Philosophical Review* **69, 70** (1960, 1961).

Malcolm, N., *Knowledge and Certainty*, Englewood Cliffs, N.J., 1963.

Marcel, Gabriel, *Homo Viator*, New York, 1962.

Marcel, Gabriel, *The Philosophy of Existentialism*, New York, 1963.

Martin, C. B., 'The Perfect Good', in *New Essays in Philosophical Theology* (ed. by A. G. N. Flew and A. C. MacIntyre), London, 1955.

Martin, J. R., 'Another Look at the Doctrine of Verstehen', *British Journal for Philosophy of Science* **20** (1969).

Martin, J. R., *Explaining, Understanding and Teaching*, New York, 1970.

Mascell, E. L., *Existence and Analogy*, London, 1949.

Matson, W. I., *The Existence of God*, Ithaca, 1965.

Mellor, D. H., 'God and Probability', *Religious Studies* **6** (1969).

Mitchell, B., *Faith and Logic*, London, 1957.

Moore, G. E., *Principia Ethica*, Cambridge, 1903.

Nahnikian, G. and Salmon, W. C., '"Exists" as Predicate', *Philosophical Review* **66** (1957).

Nielsen, K., 'On Talk about God', *Journal of Philosophy* **55** (1958).

Nielsen, K., 'Can Faith Validate God-Talk?', *Theology Today* **20** (1963).
Nielsen, K., 'On Fixing the Reference Range of God', *Religious Studies* **2** (1966).
Nielsen, K., 'Wittgensteinian Fideism', *Philosophy* **43** (1967).
Nielsen, K., *Contemporary Critiques of Religion*, Toronto, 1971.
Olson, R. G., *An Introduction to Existentialism*, New York, 1962.
Otto, R., *The Idea of the Holy*, Oxford, 1923.
Penelhum, T., 'Divine Necessity' in *The Cosmological Arguments*, pp. 143–61, (ed. by D. R. Burill), New York, 1967.
Penelhum, T., *Religion and Rationality*, New York, 1971.
Phillips, D. Z. (ed.), *The Concept of Prayer*, London, 1965.
Phillips, D. Z. (ed.), *Religion and Understanding*, Oxford, 1967.
Phillips, D. Z. (ed.), *Faith and Philosophy*, New York, 1971.
Pico della Mirandola, 'Oration on the Dignity of Man' in *The Renaissance Philosophy of Man* (ed. by E. Cassirer, P. O. Kristeller and J. M. Randall Jr.), Chicago, 1948.
Pike, N., 'Hume on Evil', *Philosophical Review* **72** (1963).
Pike, N., 'The Freewill Defence', *Philosophy in America* (ed. by Max Black), New York, 1964.
Pike, N., *God and Evil*, Englewood Cliffs, N.J., 1964.
Pike, N., *God and Timelessness*, London, 1970.
Pitcher, G. (ed.), *Wittgenstein: The Philosophical Investigations*, New York, 1966.
Plantinga, A., *God and Other Minds*, Ithaca, 1967.
Plato, *Collected Dialogues of Plato* (ed. by E. Hamilton and H. Huntington Cairns), Princeton, 1961.
Popkin, R. H., *Philosophy Made Simple*, New York, 1956.
Prior, A. N., *Time and Morality*, Oxford, 1956.
Quine, W. V. O., *From a Logical Point of View*, Boston, 1953.
Quine, W. V. O., *Word and Object*, New York, 1959.
Quine, W. V. O., 'Senses and Sensibilia', *Analysis*, New Series **23** (1962).
Quine, W. V. O. and Ullian, J. S., *The Web of Belief*, New York, 1971.
Quinton, A. M., 'On Punishment' in *Analysis* **14** (1954) and reprinted in *Contemporary Ethical Theory* (ed. by J. Margolis), New York, 1966.
Quinton, A. M., 'The Problem of Perception' in *Perceiving, Sensing, Knowing* (ed. by R. J. Swartz), New York, 1965.
Ramsey, F. P., *The Foundations of Mathematics*, London, 1931.
Ramsey, I. T., *Religious Language*, London, 1957.
Ramsey, I. T., *Prospect for Metaphysics*, London, 1961.
Rapoport, A., 'Escape from Paradox', *Scientific American* **217** (1967).
Reeder, J. P., 'Patterson Brown on God's Will as the Criterion of Morality', *Religious Studies* **5** (1969).
Resnick, L., 'Evidence, Utility and God', *Analysis* **31** (1971).
Ross, J. F., 'Analogy as a Rule of Meaning for Religious Language', *International Philosophical Quarterly* **1** (1961).
Rudinow, J., 'Gambling on Other Minds and God', *Sophia* **10** (1971).
Russell, B., 'On Denoting', *Mind*, New Series **14** (1905).
Ryle, Gilbert, *The Concept of Mind*, London, 1949.
Sartre, J. P., *Existentialism is a Humanism* (trans. P. Mairet), London, 1948.
Sartre, J. P., *What is Literature?* (trans. B. Frechtman), New York, 1949.
Sartre, J. P., *The Flies* (trans. S. Gilbert), London, 1946.
Sartre, J. P., *Being and Nothingness* (trans. H. Barnes), New York, 1956.

Savage, L. J., *The Foundations of Statistics*, New York, 1951.

Schuster, C., 'Glassen on the Cognitivity of Moral Judgments', *Mind* 70 (1961).

Searle, J. R., 'Meaning and Speech Acts', *Philosophical Review* 73 (1964).

Searle, J. R., *Speech Acts*, Cambridge, 1969.

Sellars, W. S., 'Empiricism and the Problem of Mind', reprinted in *Science, Perception and Reality*, London, 1963.

Skyrms, B., 'Interpretations on the Probability Calculus', in *Choice and Chance*, Belmont, Calif., 1966.

Smart, N., *Reasons and Faiths*, New York, 1959.

Stiernotte, A. P., *Mysticism and the Modern Mind*, New York, 1959.

Strawson, P. F., 'On Referring', *Mind*, New Series 70 (1950).

Strawson, P. F., *Individuals*, London, 1959.

Strong, A. H., *Systematic Theology*, Philadelphia, 1907; reprinted in London by Pickering and Inglis, 1956.

Stroud, B., 'Transcendental Arguments', *Journal of Philosophy* 65 (1968).

Suppes, P., *Introduction to Logic*, New Jersey, 1957.

Swinburne, R., *The Concept of Miracle*, London and New York, 1970.

Taylor, R., 'The Problem of Future Contingencies', *Philosophical Review* 66 (1957).

Tillich, P., *Biblical Religion and the Search for Ultimate Reality*, Chicago, 1955.

Tillich, P., *Systematic Theology*, 2 vols., Chicago, 1951.

Toulmin, S. E., 'Probability', *Proceedings of the Aristotelian Society*, Suppl. Vol. 24.

Toulmin, S. E., *The Philosophy of Science*, London, 1953.

Toulmin, S. E., *The Uses of Argument*, Cambridge, 1958.

Toulmin, S. E., *Foresight and Understanding*, New York, 1963.

Urmson, J. O., *Philosophical Analysis: Its Development Between the Two World Wars*, Oxford, 1956.

Vendler, Z., *Linguistics in Philosophy*, Ithaca, 1967.

Vignaux, P., *Philosophy in the Middle Ages*, London, 1959.

Waismann, F., *How I See Philosophy*, New York and London, 1968.

White, M., *Towards Reunion in Philosophy*, Cambridge, 1956.

Wisdom, J. O., 'Gods', in *Logic and Language*, First Series, (ed. by A. G. N. Flew), Oxford, 1951.

Wisdom, J. O., *Philosophy and Psychoanalysis*, Oxford, 1953.

Wittgenstein, L., *Philosophical Investigations* (trans. G. E. M. Anscombe), Oxford, 1953.

Wittgenstein, L., *Wittgenstein: Lectures and Conversations on Aesthetics, Psychology, and Religious Belief* (ed. by C. Barrett) Oxford, 1966.

Ziff, P., *Semantic Analysis*, Ithaca, 1960.

INDEX